*Second Edition*

# CASES IN CONSUMER BEHAVIOR

**Hale N. Tongren**
*George Mason University*

PRENTICE HALL, Englewood Cliffs, N.J. 07632

*Library of Congress Cataloging-in-Publication Data*
TONGREN, HALE N, [date]
   Cases in consumer behavior / HALE N. TONGREN.—2nd ed.
     p.  cm.
   ISBN 0-13-116344-2
    1. Consumer behavior—Case studies.   2. Consumers—United States
Case studies.   I. Title.
HF5415.32.T66    1992
658.8′342—dc20       91-31026


Acquisitions editor: *Tim Kent*
Editorial/production supervision: *Edie Riker*
Cover design: *electric pencil studio, inc.*
Prepress Buyer: *Trudy Pisciotti*
Manufacturing buyer: *Robert Anderson*

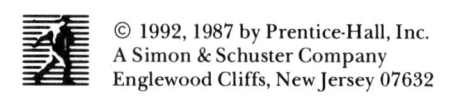

© 1992, 1987 by Prentice-Hall, Inc.
A Simon & Schuster Company
Englewood Cliffs, New Jersey 07632

All rights reserved. No part of this book may be
reproduced, in any form or by any means,
without permission in writing from the publisher.

Printed in the United States of America

10  9  8  7  6  5  4  3  2  1


ISBN    0-13-116344-2


Prentice-Hall International (UK) Limited, *London*
Prentice-Hall of Australia Pty. Limited, *Sydney*
Prentice-Hall Canada Inc., *Toronto*
Prentice-Hall Hispanoamericana, S.A., *Mexico*
Prentice-Hall of India Private Limited, *New Delhi*
Prentice-Hall of Japan, Inc., *Tokyo*
Simon & Schuster Asia Pte. Ltd., *Singapore*
Editora Prentice-Hall do Brasil, Ltda., *Rio de Janeiro*

# CONTENTS

|  | CASE TOPICS | *vi* |
|---|---|---|
|  | PREFACE | *ix* |
| Case One | THE RESTAURANT EXPRESS | *1* |
| Case Two | THE OLDE ODEON THEATER | *15* |
| Case Three | NIKE, INC. | *26* |
| Case Four | SOURCE PERRIER II— THE SEQUEL | *41* |
| Case Five | THE NEW FRAGRANCE INDUSTRY | *55* |
| Case Six | JACK DANIEL'S OLD TIME DISTILLERY | *72* |

| | | |
|---|---|---|
| Case Seven | THE NEW L. L. BEAN | 82 |
| Case Eight | NEPTUNE KITCHEN AND BATH REMODELERS, INC. | 92 |
| Case Nine | THE HOME SHOPPING NETWORK | 105 |
| Case Ten | THE SPORT OF KINGS | 113 |
| Case Eleven | PROCTER & GAMBLE— THE SIGN AND THE SYMBOL | 120 |
| Case Twelve | MARY KAY COSMETICS | 129 |
| Case Thirteen | THE PEARL TRAVEL SERVICE | 143 |
| Case Fourteen | THE PALACE WARSAW | 150 |
| Case Fifteen | THE WHEELS AND BOARDS OF FORTUNE | 158 |
| Case Sixteen | THE OLD SPAGHETTI MILL | 167 |
| Case Seventeen | RIVERSIDE SAVINGS BANK | 178 |
| Case Eighteen | HATTON AND MAYER GENTLEMEN'S WEAR | 186 |
| Case Nineteen | TOYS R US | 199 |
| Case Twenty | THE POLAROID CORPORATION | 209 |
| Case Twenty-One | RADLEY DEVELOPMENT CO., INC. | 219 |

| Case Twenty-Two | FROM INNOVATIVE TO TRADITIONAL: CAMPBELL'S SOUP | *231* |
|---|---|---|
| Case Twenty-Three | THE DISTILLED LIQUOR INDUSTRY | *245* |

# CASE TOPICS

| | RESTAURANT EXPRESS | OLDE ODEON THEATER | NIKE INC. | SOURCE PERRIER II—THE SEQUEL | THE NEW FRAGRANCE INDUSTRY | JACK DANIEL'S OLD TIME DISTILLERY | THE NEW L. L. BEAN | NEPTUNE KITCHEN & BATH REMODELERS | THE HOME SHOPPING NETWORK | THE SPORT OF KINGS |
|---|---|---|---|---|---|---|---|---|---|---|
| Attitudes | | | | | x | | x | | | x |
| Attitude Change | | | | x | | | | | | |
| Consumer Research | ✓ | | | | ✓ | | ✓ | x | | x |
| Culture | | ✓ | ✓ | | x | x | | | | |
| Consumer Decisions | ✓ | | ✓ | | | | | x | x | |
| Diffusion of Innovation | x | | x | | x | | | | | |
| Family Decisions | x | | | | ✓ | | | x | ✓ | |
| Involvement | | | | ✓ | | x | x | | | ✓ |
| Learning | | | | x | | | | | | |
| Marketer Communications | ✓ | x | x | x | x | x | x | | x | |
| Motivation | ✓ | | | | ✓ | | | ✓ | x | |
| Perception | | | x | x | ✓ | x | x | | | |
| Personal Communications | | ✓ | ✓ | | | ✓ | ✓ | x | | |
| Psychographics | x | ✓ | | ✓ | | | ✓ | | | x |
| Reference Groups | | | x | x | | | | x | | |
| Segmentation | x | x | ✓ | ✓ | x | | ✓ | x | ✓ | ✓ |
| Social Class | | x | | ✓ | | | | | ✓ | |
| Sub/cross Culture | | | | | | | | | | |

x = Primary Topic
✓ = Secondary Topic

|  | PROCTER & GAMBLE | MARY KAY COSMETICS | PEARL TRAVEL SERVICE | THE PALACE WARSAW | WHEELS & BOARDS OF FORTUNE | OLD SPAGHETTI MILL | RIVERSIDE SAVINGS BANK | HATTON & MAYER GENTLEMEN'S WEAR | TOYS R US | POLAROID CORP. | RADLEY DEVELOPMENT CO., INC. | INNOVATIVE TO TRADITIONAL: CAMPBELL'S SOUP | DISTILLED LIQUOR INDUSTRY |
|---|---|---|---|---|---|---|---|---|---|---|---|---|---|
| | x | x | | | | | | ✓ | x | | | x | ✓ |
| | | | | ✓ | | | | | | | | x | x |
| | | | | | ✓ | x | | | | | | | |
| | | ✓ | | x | | | | | x | x | | | x |
| | | ✓ | | | | x | ✓ | | | | | x | |
| | | | | | | x | | | | x | ✓ | x | |
| | | | | | | x | | | ✓ | | ✓ | | |
| | ✓ | | | | x | | | | | | | | |
| | | | | x | | | | | | | | ✓ | |
| | x | | x | | | | x | x | ✓ | ✓ | x | x | x |
| | | | | | x | ✓ | | | | | | x | |
| | x | | | ✓ | ✓ | | ✓ | | x | | | x | |
| | | x | ✓ | | | x | | | | ✓ | ✓ | | |
| | | x | ✓ | | ✓ | ✓ | | ✓ | | | | ✓ | |
| | ✓ | ✓ | | | | | ✓ | ✓ | | | | | x |
| | | | x | | ✓ | ✓ | x | x | | | ✓ | | ✓ |
| | ✓ | | ✓ | | x | | | | | | x | | ✓ |
| | x | | | x | | | | x | ✓ | | | | |

# PREFACE

Cases in this book provide a wide spectrum of consumer behavior situations and problems, from the mighty Procter & Gamble to a small, rural motion picture theater. They also include both for-profit and non-profit organizations as well as service firms. An effort has been made to vary both the style and presentation of the cases and to suggest different approaches to their analysis and solution. Generally, all data and information needed for the analysis is given in the cases and exhibits, supplemented, of course, by class lectures and discussions of the pertinent concepts.

The second edition of *Cases In Consumer Behavior* contains eight completely new cases in a wide variety of situations such as the Polish Warsaw Palace Hotel; Wheels and Boards, about consumers in the gambling industry; Neptune a kitchen-bath remodeling business; and the Home Video Shopping channels. There are also six completely revised and updated cases such as Nike's market battle with Reebok; The search for "behavior-altering" Scents; Campbell Soup's new consumer strategy; and the Perrier benzene disaster. The most popular cases from the previous edition have been continued in this one. There is also an expanded matrix of cases to consumer behavior concepts that will enable users to expand the scope of the case analyses.

American consumers are different from those in most other parts of the world! We tend to be more spontaneous, more interested in the shopping process, and more *committed* shoppers. We choose from an almost endless array of products, brands, and services, yet producers constantly search for more types and varieties of older products as well as new ones to fill expanding needs. Our malls are social centers, entertainment arenas, and exercise areas, as well as purveyors of merchandise.

For these and many other reasons, the study of consumer behavior is the most fascinating aspect of marketing. In most of our college courses, we learn facts, terminology, concepts, and theories. Then, we repeat these on examinations, often through true-false or multiple-choice instruments. This method works reasonably well in the more "exact" fields such as the hard sciences, finance, accounting, and statistics. But it is less appropriate in those fields where boundaries are defined less rigidly. In marketing, particularly in consumer behavior, there may not be a "right" or "wrong" way of doing something. One of several methods may work equally well in a given situation, while others may be entirely or partially inappropriate.

Understanding consumers and why they behave as they do is a complex task. In the process of analyzing cases in this book, the important things are understanding concepts and techniques from your Consumer Behavior course, knowing which ones are most appropriate, and using them to recommend solutions. When you eventually go to work in a marketing organization, your manager is not likely to ask you to describe "types of consumer conditioning." But you will surely be expected to apply consumer conditioning knowledge in problems involving product trial and re-buying.

In case analysis, *you* are responsible for analyzing problems and forming solutions, using information provided for you. Evading this responsibility by asking for more data or further research is not usually an acceptable conclusion. Only through practice in analyzing real case problems can you develop an expertise that will set you apart from others in the business world.

A challenging aspect of case analysis is defining the central problem of the case. For example, the failure of consumers to re-buy a new product after the initial trial is more likely to be a *symptom* of a problem rather than the problem itself. Once the "real" problem is identified, analysis can begin. But you must read the cases carefully because important factors may be presented in off-hand remarks by people in the situation. For example, a prospective home-buyer, after talking with families who are living in a new development, may observe, "These people are just like us." This might normally be considered a pleasant, ordinary remark. But if the prospective buyer is upwardly mobile, it may be construed to mean, "We don't want to live here. We are looking for an area where people are ahead of us in social class, and we can move up."

A common pitfall in case analysis occurs when students, having decided upon the central "problem," immediately decide upon its solution. Then, they search for and accumulate only information in the case to support that conclusion, often ignoring significant information or other indications that do not support it. It is embarrassing when other students bring up the negative points in oral case discussions. A good analysis includes both the pros and cons of the situation, and suggests how the cons may be overcome, or why they are not important. If a case has been carefully analyzed and presented, the reader should be able to predict the solution or recommendations before they are actually presented.

Another common problem occurs when the data are ignored or are analyzed only superficially. A good analyst is able to use quantitative information to develop qualitative relationships. For example, a few heavy users of a product may purchase and consume more than many light users, suggesting perhaps, that a narrower target market might be considered.

Of those who were most helpful in the preparation of this book and the previous edition, I want to express my appreciation to three reviewers: Wayne B. Hoyer from the University of Texas at Austin; Bruce Stern, Portland State University; and Peter B. Turk, University of Oklahoma; as well as several anonymous reviewers who have offered suggestions and comments on the new and revised cases in this edition.

Hale N. Tongren

# CASE ONE

# THE RESTAURANT EXPRESS

Jeff Baker drove into his garage, turned off the engine, and sat for a minute in the dark. With a huge sigh, he picked up his bulging brief case and went into the house, noticing that his wife's car was not there. As he walked in, he glanced at the kitchen clock, 7:30. "Over an hour and a half to get home," he muttered as he dropped the brief case in the hall and hung up his coat. He went back into the kitchen just as Terri Baker, his wife, came in. "I'm bushed and I'm starved!" she said, "I thought I would never get out of there tonight."

Jeff was a CPA with a large accounting firm in the downtown area of Brainerd, a city of about two million in the southeast United States. Terri was a partner in a beauty salon in a medium-sized shopping area of the affluent suburb of Pine Valley, where they lived.

This was the third evening in a row they had both arrived home late, tired, and with leftover work to do that evening. Monday, they had a Domino's pizza delivered. Tuesday, Terri brought home a take-out dinner from a restaurant near her shop. Now, they stood in the kitchen, each waiting for the other to suggest what to do about dinner. Finally, Terri sighed, "I just can't face cooking tonight. Do we have time to go out?" "I've got a lot of work to do," said Jeff. "Maybe I can just make a couple of sandwiches and some soup."

## A NEW IDEA

They sat in front of the television set eating their makeshift dinner. Jeff was unusually silent. Finally, he began to think out loud. "Wouldn't it be great if we could phone a real restaurant and order a full dinner to be delivered, just like hotel room service," he said. "I'll bet there are a lot of others in our situation wishing for the same thing."

"It might work for a while," Terri replied, "but you would get tired of the menu before long."

"There wouldn't be only one restaurant," Jeff replied. He was excited. "A whole group of them could be served by a delivery service. You would phone your order to a restaurant. The delivery service would pick it up when it was ready and rush it to your home."

## THINKING IT THROUGH

Jeff was quite busy at the office for several weeks after he and Terri had talked about the delivery service. But he thought about it a lot while driving to and from work, and waiting in the traffic. He mentally organized a "transfer center" where customers would place their phone orders, and he decided just how the orders would be recorded and transmitted to restaurants. By timing his progress, and making notes, he was able to estimate how long it would take for deliveries at that time of day. He was also able to decide how wide an area a delivery service would be able to cover.

After a quick lunch one day several weeks later, Jeff stopped at the Brainerd main library to gather some data on restaurant take-out services—the demographics of people who use them and how frequently they order. While he was there, he bought a copy of an annual book of county population and other statistics. Back at the office, he borrowed a set of zip code data for Brainerd and its suburbs that an auditor had used for a recent case.

## ANALYZING THE BASIC INFORMATION

At home that evening, he and Terri examined his information. They determined that a group of seven townships and districts adjacent to Pine Valley had been a rural farm area 20 years ago. The population of this group had more than doubled from about 40,000 in 1970 to 88,000 in 1980, increased again to 140,000 by 1990, and was expected to reach 175,000 by the end of the century. Brainerd itself is a center for education, technical, and information-processing industries. The city has two major universities and a number of research, consulting, and engineering firms, many of which are located within the seven-district territory Jeff and Terri had chosen. The rapid expansion of the population came about through inward migration of highly educated individuals, most of whom possessed the skills needed by the "knowledge" industries.

Jeff and Terri set the boundaries of the tentative territory of seven adjacent districts on a local map, shown as Exhibit 1-1. They then superimposed zip codes on these areas and found that five zips covered them, with only a relatively minor overlap. Using the zip demographics, they were able to prepare a set of characteristics that described a "typical" resident of the area. These are listed in Exhibit 1-2.

## A GAME OR REALITY

Until this evening, the speculation about a food delivery service, the data collection, and analysis had been a "game" for the Bakers as a relief from the routine problems of their jobs. Now, however, they came to realize they were caught up in the challenge of putting the "puzzle" together. Here were the beginnings of a basic plan that might actually become a reality, and a profitable one at that.

Neither Terri nor Jeff actually said so, but suddenly they were approaching the problem in earnest. They began to arrange more of the population data from zip codes into meaningful sets, such as the number of different types of dwelling units in each area, the household size in each of them, and area median incomes. These are shown in Exhibits 1-3, 1-4, and 1-5. County demographic data also revealed that the overall population of the seven areas was composed of the following groups:

| | |
|---|---|
| Dual Income Families, no kids (often referred to as "DINKs") | 22% |
| Empty Nesters (older couples whose children have left the home) | 19% |
| Small Nuclear Families (three-person families) | 16% |
| Medium Nuclear Families (four-person families) | 24% |
| Large Nuclear Families (five or more person families) | 13% |
| Single Persons | 6% |

Since the mid-1970s, the percentage of husband-wife–headed households in the seven areas has dropped from 86.5 percent to 65.3 percent in 1991. Although married-couple families remain the dominant type, they have been decreasing steadily while nontraditional living arrangements have increased. These include primarily single parents, persons living alone, and persons living within a household with nonrelated individuals.

Unemployment has been relatively low in the entire Brainerd area with a rate of only 2.8 percent in 1990. Nearly three-quarters of the work force is concentrated in white collar occupations, as follows:

| | |
|---|---|
| Managerial/Professional | 40.9% |
| Administrative Support | 25.7% |
| Technical/Services/Sales | 10.4% |
| Other | 23.0% |

## A PROMISING POTENTIAL

Later that evening the Bakers looked over the data they had assembled. "From all the demographics, it looks as though this kind of service has a lot of potential," said Terri. "Do you think we could actually start something like it?" Jeff shook his head and said, "We're both over our heads in work now, and more has piled up in the last couple of weeks while we've been working on this. And we still need more information about the business. If prospects still look promising after we get that, then we have to think about our jobs and if one or both of us can give all our time to starting up the service."

"Won't we need a good deal of capital to start?" asked Terri. "It will probably take most of our savings as a base for a bank loan. Do you think we can take in one or two partners who would invest and work in the business too?"

They also realized they needed more information about the food delivery industry if they were to project sales and expenses for the area they selected. These and other projections were needed to prepare pro forma balance sheets and income statements for the bank and prospective partners. Since it was getting late, they decided to "sleep on the problem" and come to some decision the next evening.

## TO PROCEED OR NOT

They met after work at a local restaurant and during dinner discussed the merits of flinging themselves headlong into the project, approaching it more cautiously, or forgetting it altogether. Oddly, they had both decided on the middle course as they mulled over the matter that day. Although this course may simply have been a device to delay a final decision, it seemed to be a prudent one and involved two additional steps:

1. Hire a consultant to obtain information and data on prepared food delivery operations already in existence, including procedures, operating systems, customer characteristics, restaurant relationships, financial break-even considerations, and any other pertinent items.
2. Both Terri and Jeff would "talk-up" the proposal to friends and business acquaintances who might be contacted later as prospective investors or partners.

## TWO SPECIFIC RESEARCH PROJECTS

The next morning, Jeff called Bob Weinberg, a former client who headed a large business consulting firm. After listening to Jeff's problem, Bob exclaimed "You couldn't have called at a better time. One of our restaurant group is making his final presentation today on a job, and the next client doesn't need him for two weeks. I can give you a nice break on the hourly billings." Over lunch, Jeff and Bob came to an agreement, that the researcher, Bob Larsen, would begin work the next day.

The following weekend, Jeff and Terri mentioned the idea to several people they knew at a party given by the senior partner of Jeff's firm. They were careful, however, not to elaborate but to give hints about the potential profitability. Terri also brought the subject up at the shop, describing the service briefly to customers whenever the occasion arose. She also asked them if they thought it was a good idea and if they would use it. The grapevine had begun, and before long, friends began asking about the venture and when it would start.

After several days of questions-and-answers at the beauty shop, Terri began to wonder if some type of general survey in the area might not sharpen their focus on the market and give a better indication of how the service might be received. She knew that the restaurant research would include some information about consumers of delivered food nationally, but local data would be more useful in specific planning. The research was going to cost over $2,000, even with the discount, so the survey would have to be inexpensive.

She and Jeff discussed how it might be done. Jeff recalled reading about a survey that business school students at the nearby university conducted for the Chamber of Commerce and wondered if it would be possible to hire them at a reasonable rate. He phoned Professor Fred Holmes from the Marketing Department, whom he had met at a business luncheon, to see if such an arrangement was possible. "Certainly," the professor replied after Jeff gave the details, "I can hire several students to do personal interviews at five locations in the area and help with the questionnaire for about $1,700. But you will have to do the tabulating and cross-referencing yourself. Keep in mind, though, that this will be a rather quick-and-dirty operation at that price, but it should give you a reasonable feel for the market and its potential." They met a few days later, worked out the questionnaire, decided on the interview locations, and set a date for the survey the following week.

## RESEARCH RESULTS

Meanwhile, Bob Larsen had been conducting his secondary research and promised a report the following Friday, right on schedule. Excerpts from the report are shown in Exhibit 1–6.

About ten days later, Fred Holmes delivered a stack of 350 completed surveys. "There are roughly 50 from each of your seven areas," he said. "Not too reliable a sample, but they are not all that different, so the information should be helpful. You can make a straight tabulation on your computer, but you will need more sophisticated software for cross tabulations. Why don't you see if the tabulation gives you what you need and if not, perhaps I can find some help for you. Good luck!"

Jeff and Terri, together with Terri's partner in the shop and her friend worked on the surveys the next Saturday evening. They first tabulated the results by individual area, then decided that the most useful groupings for market segmentation could be made primarily on the number of persons in the household, and secondarily on age. They arrived at four of these segments and were able to write short descriptions of each of them, relating to their potential use of the delivery service, and the extent to which they might use it. The descriptive segments are shown in Exhibit 1–7.

## THE FINAL DECISION

When the others left, the Bakers looked at the mass of information they had collected over the past several weeks. "Let's go over it all tomorrow," Jeff suggested, "to see if the numbers and other information show that the service will really be a big moneymaker, and worth the big change it will make in our lives.

## CASE ANALYSIS QUESTIONS

1. How did the Bakers go about making their decision as to the segment of consumers and geographical area they planned to target? Was this a reasonable way to do it?
2. What other segment does the case data indicate they might have considered? What additional information would help in evaluating this segment?
3. How are consumer "expectations" involved directly in the success or failure of this venture?
4. If you were the Bakers, would you go ahead with the venture on the basis of information they now have? Why or why not?

## REFERENCES

"Middleman Delivery Systems Put Your Meals on Wheels," *Restaurant Management Today,* Jan. 16, 1989, p. 1; "Takeout Taxi: Life in the Fast Food Lane," *Washington (DC) Business Journal,* Jan. 20, 1989, p. 1; "In Herndon, Va., Growth Elicits Some Mixed Feelings," *Wall Street Journal,* Mar. 28, 1989; "Restaurant Deliveries: Beyond Pizza," *New York Times,* Apr. 18, 1989, p. 34; "The Culinary Cadillacs of Delivery," *Restaurant Hospitality,* April, 1989, p. 1; "Top Credit Card Companies Explore Fast Food Tie Ins," *New York Times,* May 1, 1989, p. D1; "A Dashing Way to Dine," *Time,* Sep. 18, 1989, p. 96; "Menus' Hot Item: Home Delivery," *New York Times,* Sep. 5, 1989, p. 27; "Pizza Makers Slug It Out for Share of Growing

Eat-at-Home Market," *Wall Street Journal,* Jan. 12, 1988, p. 39; "Restaurant Delivery Services Offer Operators New Options," *Restaurant Management,* June, 1988, p. 17; *Clustering America,* M. J. Weiss, New York, Harper and Row, 1988; Takeout Menu, *Takeout Taxi,* Fairfax, VA., 1990; "Finding and Targeting the Optimal Market for (Restaurant Food) Delivery, *George Mason University, School of Business Administration,* April, 1990.

**THE RESTAURANT EXPRESS**

**EXHIBIT 1-1**

**Brainerd/District Map**

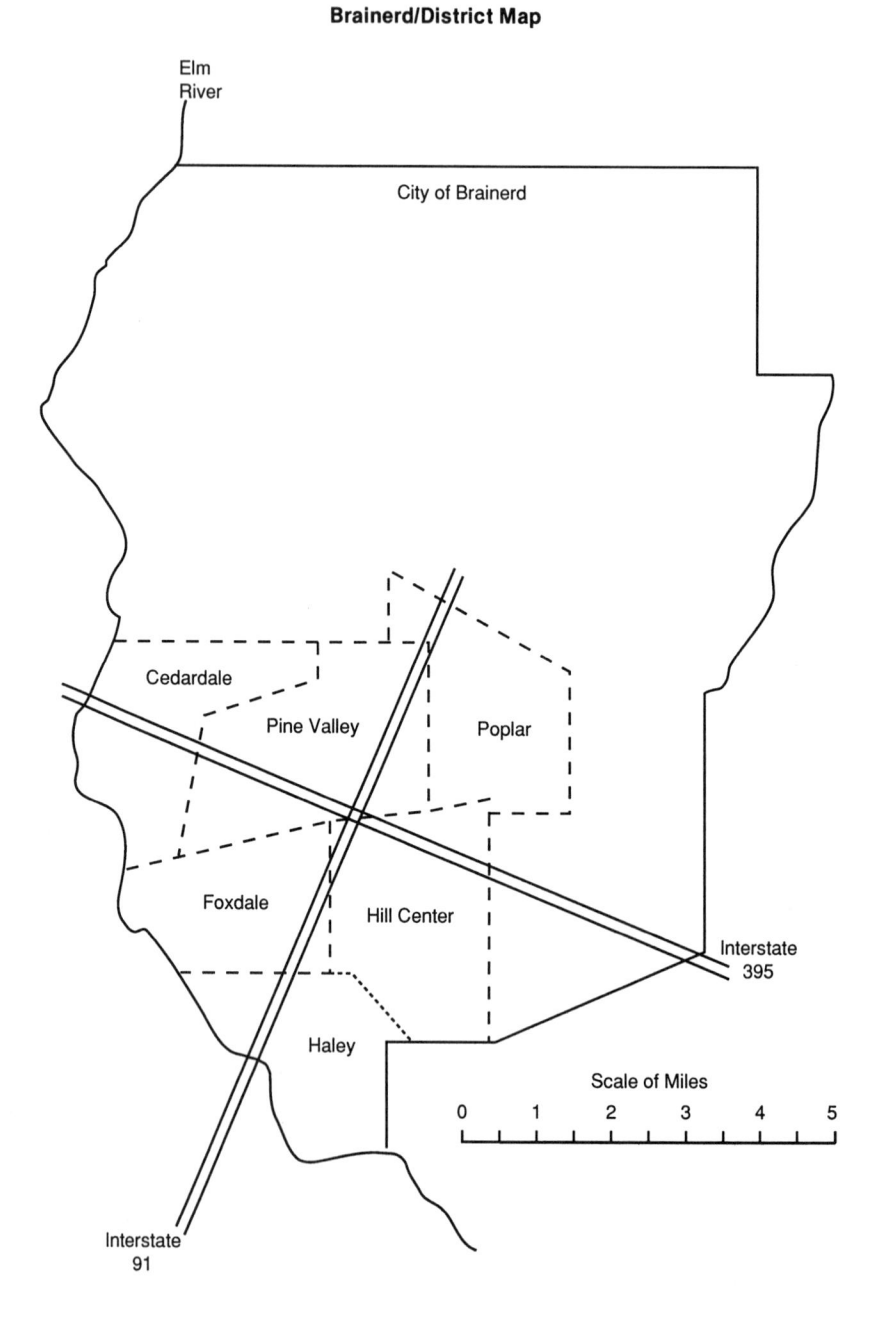

## THE RESTAURANT EXPRESS
### EXHIBIT 1-2
### Typical Resident Characteristics

A typical resident of the zip code area has one or more of these characteristics:

1. College-Educated Adult, Age 20-35

   Over half (57%) have college degrees. Of those, nearly a third (31%) have some type of post-baccalaureate degree. This is 3 times higher than the national average.

2. Married with no children, or single with no children.

3. Employed in a white-collar, primarily managerial or professional occupation.

   | | |
   |---|---|
   | 42.0% | Managerial/professional |
   | 26.4% | Administrative support |
   | 12.8% | Technical/professional sales |

4. Income significantly higher than the national average.


## THE RESTAURANT EXPRESS
### EXHIBIT 1-3
### Average Household Size by Type of Dwelling Unit

| Area | Single Family | Town House | Multifamily | Overall Average HH Size |
|---|---|---|---|---|
| Cedardale | 2.94 | 2.69 | 1.49 | 2.37 |
| Haley | 2.75 | 1.90 | 1.82 | 2.15 |
| Poplar Crest | 3.27 | 2.40 | 1.79 | 2.48 |
| Foxdale | 3.25 | 2.44 | 1.81 | 2.50 |
| Morton | 2.73 | 2.50 | 1.78 | 2.33 |
| Pine Valley | 3.59 | 2.80 | 2.50 | 2.96 |
| Hill Center | 3.50 | 2.65 | 2.16 | 2.77 |

## THE RESTAURANT EXPRESS
### EXHIBIT 1-4
### Median Household Income, 1980 and 1991

| Area | 1980 Median Household Income | 1991 Median Household Income | Percent Increase |
| --- | --- | --- | --- |
| Cedardale | $55,100 | $67,950 | 23.3% |
| Haley | 37,200 | 55,750 | 49.9 |
| Poplar Crest | 41,600 | 52,400 | 26.0 |
| Foxdale | 50,900 | 59,300 | 16.5 |
| Morton | 38,600 | 61,050 | 58.2 |
| Pine Valley | 55,400 | 71,750 | 30.0 |
| Hill Center | 48,700 | 62,900 | 20.0 |

## THE RESTAURANT EXPRESS
### EXHIBIT 1-5
### Number of Multiple Dwelling Units, by Type, in the Brainerd Area

| Area | Town House | Multiplex | Garden Apartments | Mid-Rise | High-Rise | Total |
| --- | --- | --- | --- | --- | --- | --- |
| Cedardale | 3,027 | 255 | 4,848 | 513 | 471 | 9,114 |
| Haley | 674 | 81 | 4,898 | 1,603 | 4,702 | 11,958 |
| Poplar Crest | 4,548 | 1,326 | 1,424 | 0 | 0 | 7,298 |
| Foxdale | 2,276 | 289 | 4,066 | 510 | 0 | 7,141 |
| Morton | 2,013 | 117 | 5,456 | 0 | 899 | 8,485 |
| Pine Valley | 12,716 | 522 | 1,336 | 0 | 0 | 14,574 |
| Hill Center | 10,426 | 738 | 7,040 | 421 | 285 | 18,910 |

## THE RESTAURANT EXPRESS
## EXHIBIT 1-6
### Excerpts from Consultant's Report

The home delivery market appears to be growing rapidly. One New York research analyst estimates that although home delivery accounts for only about $3.5 billion of the $40 billion take-out market, it is growing almost twice as fast as take-out or drive-thru sales. Restaurant on-premise sales have been relatively flat for the past few years, with more consumers opting for delivery or carry-out. Another food specialist predicts that the delivery market will grow 10 percent or more annually for the next three years.

Types of Delivery Services

There are a number of different types of full-restaurant delivery services in larger cities throughout the United States. The operating methods differ widely from store-owned to completely independent delivery operations. The successful ones are the independent delivery firms that are fully automated and depend primarily upon rapid and accurate communications.

Delivery services in this context are food-service middlemen, bringing the customer and restaurant together through the use of fast transportation. Unlike the restaurant, delivery services can locate anywhere to keep the overhead low, and they require very little space. The major expense is for the computer hardware and unique software suited to this type of service.

The role of the order-taking and delivery service is rather simple. The delivery service makes arrangements with a group of restaurants; six or eight seems to be the norm. The service is promoted by distributing tabloid-size flyers describing what a consumer has to do to order complete meals from the restaurant menus printed in the flyer. Other types of advertising are relatively ineffective since the customer must have a menu from which to order. Flyers are inexpensive to print (about 3 cents a copy) and distribution is often handled by youth groups such as boy and girl scouts who want to make money for the organization. About 42,000 menus are handed out at one time by one suburban Chicago service. This distribution method is also very cost effective because it is limited to the zip code areas where deliveries are made.

Order and Delivery Procedures

Procedures differ, but many work something like this: You want the daily special from the Marina Restaurant. You call the service and an operator enters your name, address, and phone number into the computer order screen. You name the restaurant and the operator punches a letter code which brings up a number-driven menu. As you order, the appropriate numbers are punched and the items are stored. When you have finished, the complete order is faxed (or called) to the restaurant, the bill is calculated, and map coordinates for your address are provided. Then, the current order is added to your history file in the comptuer.

When the restaurant receives the order, the chef usually advises the dispatcher when it will be ready, almost down to the minute in most cases. Then the dispatcher alerts the nearest delivery vehicle. This close control defines the territory which can be served and permits most orders to travel no more than five miles, taking an average of 12–14 minutes. Delivery services work most efficiently in residential "blocks," such as high-rise and other apartment complexes, or town-house areas. This is because people who live in those units are more likely to buy delivered food than those in freestanding homes and also because these units are more concentrated.

Food is packed in heat-insulated packages, then loaded into heavy insulated bags lined with heat reflective fabric developed for the space program. Drivers and dispatcher keep in close contact through 2-way radio so customers can be advised if there are any delays—a vital component of the service.

Contracts and Operations

The delivery service really has two customers, the food buyer and the restaurant. Contracts are negotiated with restaurants under which the service is billed for the food delivered at 30 to 35 percent off the restaurant retail price. Customers are charged the retail price plus a $3–$6 delivery charge, but many services make no such charge for orders over $50–$60. Drivers are usually free agents who pick their own shifts and work on commission plus tips (the order-taker advises customers that tips are not included in the overall price). Services also have corporate accounts for luncheons and dinners, which provide added visibility. Several services have placed large bowls at the cashier's counters of contract restaurants where patrons can drop their business cards. Once a month a drawing is held, and the winner receives a delivered meal for two. The cards are also a source of names for a mailing list.

Service Is Paramount

Efficient and polite customer service is at the top of the list of success factors for most services. The quality of food provided by contract restaurants must be constantly monitored, as must the delivery time and food temperature. One service-manager said that one or two dissatisfied customers can begin a negative word-of-mouth network that can seriously hurt business. Other problems include expanding outside the optimum delivery area, which is bound to result in excess transportation time and luke-warm dinners.

Most delivery-service owners say that they started with a capital investment of around $100,000. One service, opened about 18 months ago, did $18,000 in repeat business during its first month, and sales reached $1 million by the end of the 18 months. Sales for 1991 are estimated at $2 to $3 million, with about 80,000 customers served annually through private and corporate accounts.

Attached is a copy of the front page of an ad distributed in a section of another city. The inside pages contain instructions along with complete menus from each of the participating restaurants.

# Now We Bring FAIRFAX To You!

## TAKEOUT TAXI SUPERMENU

- Crystal Palace Chinese Restaurant
- Chesapeake Bay Seafood House
- Picco's
- PoFolks
- Yen Cheng Chinese Restaurant
- Mama's
- Topkapi Restaurant
- Thursday's
- Rick Walker's Scoreboard Fine Food & Beverage
- Hunan Lion III
- Sagebrush
- Pepper's Texas Bar-B-Q
- Tippy's Taco House
- Chili's Grill & Bar
- China East Restaurant
- Silver Plate

## We Bring The Restaurants To You!

## THE RESTAURANT EXPRESS
### EXHIBIT 1-7
### Descriptive Segments of Market from Survey Results

Segment 1: Dual Income Couples with No Children (DINKs)

This is the youngest group of those surveyed, with a mean age of 27. They tend to live in apartments and are the only segment of predominant apartment dwellers. DINKs have a larger than average proportion of discretionary income and order food from delivery services an average of 2.5 times a month. Although the countywide data reveal that two-person households are decreasing overall (probably caused by Empty Nesters moving away and DINKs having children), they are increasing in Cedardale, Haley, Morton, Thatcher, and Hill Center, but not in the other two sections. DINKs are willing to pay more than the average delivery fee ($3.20–$4.20) and spend the most per person of the segments ($8.75). These households are not necessarily married.

Segment 2: Empty Nesters

As the oldest segment, with a mean age of 51, empty nesters are distinguished from DINKs since they are likely to own their home, and as the term implies, their children are grown and have left home. They tend to use food delivery services less often than DINKs and are not as willing to pay a higher price for delivery. This segment is the only one to express interest in other delivery service items such as groceries or dry cleaning.

Segments 3 and 4: Three- and Four-Person Households

These two potential target markets are very similar in age, with means of 34.9 and 39.8 years respectively. Both are also likely to be home owners with median household incomes between $50,000 and $60,000. The three-person household tends to spend more per take-out/delivery order ($6.50 per person) than the four-person ($5.00). However, there is a significant difference in the amount each would pay for delivery; $3.00 for the three-person, and $4.50 for the four-person household.

# CASE TWO

# THE OLDE ODEON THEATER

It was a Friday afternoon and a beautiful September day in the foothills of the Appalachian Mountains. But not much sunlight crept into the dingy inner office of the Olde Odeon Theater where the governing board of the Preston County Cultural Association was holding a special meeting. Bob Kozaki, president of the association, had called today's meeting because he and others were concerned about the mounting losses from operating the Olde Odeon. Since it had been renovated and opened under the sponsorship of the association last year, it had operated in the black for only about half of the 16 months it had been running.

At least five of the eight-member board were anxious to close what they saw as a worthy but unsuccessful venture that they had hoped would bring motion picture entertainment (some of it cultural) into Preston County. But Bertrand (Bat) Weaver, who had spearheaded the project, was equally determined to keep the theater running, at least through the coming winter season. He had come prepared to make a proposal, and while he listened to the various members drone on about why the theater ought to be closed, he thought about it. He would have his say when they finished.

## PRESTON COUNTY—THE NEW AND THE OLD

Preston County, North Carolina, is located in rolling hill country near the Virginia border, roughly an equal distance (about 60 miles) from the Raleigh/Durham and the Winston-Salem/Charlotte metropolitan areas. It is mainly a community of small to medium-sized farms, with only three small towns—Wingate, Sutterville, and Monson—none of which has a population over 500. The farms had provided comfortable, if not outwardly profitable, livings for the families that worked them. But the 1940s and 1950s had brought economic changes that had adverse effects on smaller farms, particularly those from several hundred to a thousand acres. They could no longer provide enough income to pay for the necessities and conveniences that the U.S. population was beginning to demand. While older county farmers continued to work their land and lived in reduced circumstances, younger men and women often took seasonal or full-time jobs in stores, construction, or factories in one of the metropolitan areas. Most of them continued to live in Preston County, commuting the 50 to 70 miles each way to work. They continued to operate their farms, with the help of their children and other family members, or rented their land to others.

In the late 1960s, as the next generation moved out of its teens and was ready to form its own households, two things happened that were to make irreversible changes in the character and life-style of Preston County. First, as members of the new generation began to follow their fathers and mothers into the stores and factories of Durham and Winston-Salem, they quickly tired of the hundred-odd–mile daily drive. In addition, many of them had carried the brunt of farm work as they were growing up, and they had little interest in continuing it as a part-time occupation. So they began to move to the cities and the exodus from Preston County began. Over the next ten years, their parents grew older, some farms lay fallow and when the old folks died, with only limited demand for land in the county, farmhouses sat empty.

At the end of the 1970s, Preston County was "discovered" by an increasing number of older families from the large metropolitan areas in central North Carolina. Land prices were quite low compared to those closer to the cities and most of the farmhouses were salvageable. For example, a 400-acre farm with an older brick house could be had for not much more than $35,000. But for many, the price was secondary to the idyllic countryside with its rolling hills, the many picturesque small farms that were still operating, and the pleasant, generally mild climate.

Among the first "outsiders" to buy property in Preston were Bat and Elsie Weaver, who bought a decrepit farm from its absentee owner who worked at Bat's metal cabinet factory in Charlotte. The brick house had been empty for about five years and was basically sound although it needed some extensive repairs. The Weavers, who were both in their early fifties, planned to use the farm as a summer home and a place where their children and grandchildren could spend summer vacations. But in 1980, Bat received an attractive offer for his business, and after some family discussion, he and his wife decided to sell and move to Preston County.

They had lived there about six months, the remodeling of the old house was nearing completion, and Bat was getting restless. He was accustomed to working long hours, but now he had more leisure time than he really wanted. So it was only a matter of time until he began looking for a new occupation. Both he and Elsie noticed the increasing demand for Preston County real estate. Yet only one realtor from Wingate handled most of the property that was for sale.

After investigating the potential of the real estate business, Bat and Elsie took some courses in Charlotte and passed the examination for their broker's licenses. He set up a small office in Sutterville and she shared space with a stationery and gift store in Wingate, about 12 miles away. They were aggressive in tracking down owners of vacant farms and houses and visiting them to get listings of the property. The summer of 1981 was successful beyond their wildest dreams, with over 30 properties sold, most of them at asking prices. Many of the buyers were about the same age as the Weavers, or slightly older, and they were all thinking of eventual retirement, since few were interested in commuting to the larger cities. Also, prices had risen considerably and the area was attracting a number of well-known and prominent people from the two heavily populated areas to the south. One of the well-known ones was Georges Lyes, a long-time friend of Bat's, who had owned and operated the successful Paris Soir restaurant in Raleigh for many years. At lunch there one day, Georges confided in Bat that he was losing his location to an urban renewal project and wanted to locate in the country where he could run a small, quiet restaurant. Bat was quick to see the advantages to the real estate business of a first-class restaurant in Preston County, and he quickly convinced Georges that it was the spot for his peaceful country restaurant. But this was not to be. Because of Georges's culinary reputation, people from the metropolitan areas flocked to "quaint" Sutterville on weekends to dine at his excellent but expensive table. They often drove around the county and recognized the attractive possibility of buying property there.

## THE PRESTON COUNTY CULTURAL ASSOCIATION

By 1982, Preston County had become one of *the* places to live, and it was even attracting some business executives whose hours were flexible enough to permit commuting. Real estate sales statistics showed nearly 225 property sales in the past two years, most of them to "outsiders," and the extensive remodeling of old farmhouses made the countryside resemble an old-time Hollywood movie set.

But as these new arrivals settled down, Bat could see that they, too, needed some activity to occupy themselves. Many were interested in music, books, the theater, and art but had to make "expeditions" to the cities for them. So Bat and Elsie took it upon themselves to do something about it. With a few well-planted suggestions, these uprooted urban families decided to band together in a group where they could discuss cultural topics and other things of interest. Although it began with informal small group meetings at each other's homes, it soon evolved into a formal organization with officers, a board of directors, and dues-paying members. By early 1983, the "cultural association," with Elsie as president, had helped to renovate the small Wingate library and to buy 250 new books, had organized a small chamber orchestra from its own membership, and had put on a Christmas play in the high-school auditorium to a full house.

## The Olde Odeon Theater

Flushed by these successes, the association members looked around the county for other projects that would benefit the community and would absorb their spare time. Bat Weaver, who succeeded Elsie as president, came up with the answer. Over in Sutterville, which was about in the center of the county and which had once been a much larger town, was an old, 230-seat movie theater. Although it needed paint, a little carpentry work, and a monumental cleaning, the screen seemed to be in fair condition, as were the seats and heating plant. The town had taken the theater for unpaid taxes several years ago and had made several unsuccessful attempts to sell it. Bat thought the association could use it, for the price of cleaning and renovating. "There's no movie or any place else to go around here, except for the drive-in at Ravenal, 30 miles away," he pointed out."If we could get some good films, we should be able to attract a sizable number of customers if our price is right, even here in Preston County."

Committees were formed and work schedules were set up. With mops, paint brushes, and hammers, an ex-corporation president worked alongside an electronic engineer and the retired editor of a national women's magazine. There was no lack of expertise; one member designed the lobby, while another experienced retail chain executive set up the concessions. The film committee, chaired by an ex-theater owner, contacted a distributor and arranged to rent second- and third-run films at prices that would bring the estimated total cost per showing to about $50–$75. The house committee found that the screen was in much poorer condition than was apparent on first inspection and needed to be replaced. Projection equipment was also needed and the cost for both these items was estimated at about $5,500. The association's treasury could cover most of the renovation costs, but $5,500 was far beyond its capabilities, so the committee asked the board of directors to launch a fund drive to buy the screen and equipment. The full amount was subscribed in only a few weeks, and a date was set for the opening ceremony, in April 1984. The following is a quotation from the association's May newsletter:

> The opening day ceremony was a whopping success. We were all delighted at the number of dignitaries and other well-known personalities from Charlotte, Durham, and Winston-Salem who were there, not to mention our Senator who came all the way from Washington. The unexpected television and newspaper coverage certainly helped to put Sutterville and Preston County on the map. All this is a gratifying tribute to those who put so much work into the project.
> 
> Our new pair of 16mm projectors worked perfectly, having been checked over and over by Mary and Paul Steinberg. (They just *knew* something would go wrong.)

The 12 by 16 foot screen gave us an excellent picture and the stereo sound system, donated by Grant Haskell, was ready to go about the same time the paint dried in the lobby. But the popcorn was hot and buttery and the whole theater shone like a new penny.

Altogether, our audiences have been cooperative and enthusiastic during our "shakedown" period while we try to get everything working in unison. Our projector operators have learned quickly and we hope to continue to play to the large groups we have had during our first month.

If we are to make a success of our venture, we need your help in getting the word around. As you know, we are able to rent such high-quality films at low prices because we are a nonprofit group and because we agree not to advertise or otherwise compete with commercial theaters. So we cannot use radio, TV, or print media. But we must let our audience know what movies we will show, and when. We can get "publicity" announcements in the *Preston Weekly Banner* and on local radio stations, but we cannot include the names of the films. So we need to have everyone "Talk it up" whenever you go.

We thank all those who helped, and we appreciate the active and constant support of the Association Board.

## THE THEATER IN OPERATION

As the season progressed into summer, attendance remained high, and the association was able to sell a number of season tickets for 12 performances, mostly to its own members. Initially, Sheila McBride, head of the theater committee, noticed quite a few local residents (as distinguished from the "newcomers") at the showings. May and June continued to be successful, although the number of "locals" declined and association members and their friends made up most of the audiences. At the end of the series, however, the Olde Odeon showed a respectable profit of nearly $1,000. Exhibit 2-1 shows the attendance and selected financial data for the 1984 spring season.

Sheila and all those involved in the Odeon were quite pleased with the results of their labors. But the problem of attracting more local customers still needed some work. So in her planning for the fall and spring series, she decided to target the younger group in the county—those who might want films with more action, and who would be most likely to travel some distance to an out-of-town drive-in theater. She also faced other problems, not the smallest of which was the growing shortage of volunteers to staff the performances. At least three were needed to sell tickets, run the concession stand, and clean up afterward. And they were needed on weekend evenings when many people had other things to do.

The fall series started off quite well, probably because of the widespread publicity the Olde Odeon received in several mid-state cities as a result of publicity releases (and influence) from a former editor of Raleigh's major newspaper. Although a few of the younger local group came initially, their numbers soon tapered off. One high-school senior and his date were surprised to find her grandparents in the seats behind them during one performance. "That sure wouldn't happen at the Ravenal drive-in," he sheepishly remarked later.

As the series went on, overall attendance was spotty and it became increasingly difficult to show a reasonable profit. This was an important consideration because the association's objectives in opening the theater were not only to provide a local entertainment center, but also to generate profits that could be used for other community projects such as the health clinic and the library. This season, the Odeon was not doing very well. Exhibit 2-2 shows data for the 1984–85 series.

Sheila was concerned about overcoming these difficulties when she began planning the fall season in August 1985. She had tried a number of different strategies, none of which had done much to increase the local attendance, and she was hampered by the restriction on any advertising that mentioned the film names. It was common practice for distributors to rent films to nonprofit organizations for fund-raising purposes, but there could be no direct advertising of film names and dates so as not to compete with regular theaters that paid much higher rental fees. Nonetheless, she was still enthusiastic about the theater and was ready to plead with the board to approve it for yet another year. Her only hope was that Bat Weaver would have enough support to force that decision.

## THE BOARD'S DECISION

At the board meeting, the debate finally dwindled down. Bat Weaver rose and said:

> I tend to agree with most of what has been said. But there has to be something more involved in this attendance pattern than we have been able to find up to now. Maybe there is something else we can do. Maybe not. But I'd like to make a suggestion. I've been talking with Eric Swenson who just moved here from Charlotte where he had an ad agency and market research business for 25 years. He can't put his finger on the problem either, but he agreed to run a small research project on his own that should suggest what we should do. He says he can do this by early October, so why don't we go ahead and start the fall series. If Eric then suggests we fold, we can vote on that. If he suggests we try another strategy or other tactics, we can vote on that. I put this in the form of a motion to the board.

The motion was seconded and approved by a majority vote.

## ERIC SWENSON

In the year since he and his family had moved to Preston County, Eric Swenson had been intrigued with the wide gulf that separated the long-time residents from the newcomers. So his first task was to collect basic demographic data to see what changes had occurred in the county in the past ten to 20 years. Also, he wanted to get an idea of the characteristics of the area and of the people in it. The information he collected is shown in Exhibit 2-3. In addition, with the help of several long-time residents, he was able to get information on the entertainment habits and attitudes of their friends and relatives toward the Olde Odeon. This was done in casual conversations rather than by formal interviews, so he had to get the information second hand. The results are shown in Exhibit 2-4.

He knew that this research was neither extensive nor exhaustive, but he believed it gave him a clear picture of the consumers in the target market the Olde Odeon wanted to attract. Although he had lived in Preston County a relatively short time, he fully realized how important it was to the "new" residents that the Olde Odeon remain in business and show some profit. So he was ready to make suggestions to the board at its next meeting.

## CASE ANALYSIS QUESTIONS

1. From case information, and in terms of goals and needs, why did Eric Swenson believe the continued operation was so important to the new Preston County residents?
2. In general, would you think the selection of films should appeal to most of the "old" residents as well as the "new" ones?
3. Has the Olde Odeon been reasonably successful in its objective? Support your answer with case information and data.
4. What should the board recommend?

## REFERENCES

Original case. Name and location of area disguised. Actual data from local theater committees.

## THE OLDE ODEON THEATER

### EXHIBIT 2-1

**Theater Attractions, Revenue, and Expenses, Spring 1984**

| Date | Film | Gate[a] | Receipts[b] | Expenses | Net | Cumulative |
|---|---|---|---|---|---|---|
| Apr. 9, 10 | Arthur | 86 | $117 | $134 | ($17) | ($17) |
| Apr. 16, 17 | Diva | 132 | 246 | 183 | 63 | 46 |
| Apr. 23, 24 | Diner | 177 | 289 | 158 | 131 | 177 |
| Apr. 29, 30 | Ragtime | 87 | 119 | 134 | (15) | 162 |
| May 6, 7 | Time Bandits | 149 | 271 | 134 | 137 | 299 |
| May 13, 14 | My Favorite Year | 163 | 280 | 158 | 122 | 421 |
| May 20, 21 | Atlantic City | 76 | 103 | 159 | (56) | 365 |
| May 27, 28 | Pippin | 63 | 94 | 108 | (14) | 351 |
| June 3, 4 | Reds | 152 | 285 | 159 | 126 | 477 |
| June 10, 11 | Limelight | 184 | 318 | 74 | 244 | 721 |
| June 17, 18 | Gallipoli | 119 | 167 | 134 | 33 | 754 |
| June 24, 25 | Last Metro | 54 | 87 | 105 | (18) | 772 |
| July 1, 2, 4 | Days of Heaven | 221 | 361 | 158 | 203 | 975 |// Net Income: $975

[a] Gate includes number of box office sales, number of prorated season tickets, and number of complimentaries.
[b] Receipts include amount of box office sales, amount of prorated season tickets, and concession sales.

## THE OLDE ODEON THEATER

### EXHIBIT 2-2

**Theater Attractions, Revenue, and Expenses, 1984–85 Series**

| Date | Film | Gate[a] | Receipts[b] | Expenses | Net | Cumulative |
|---|---|---|---|---|---|---|
| *Fall Series 1984* | | | | | | |
| Sep. 29, 30 | Tender Mercies | 191 | $335 | $130 | $205 | $205 |
| Oct. 6, 7 | Year of Living Dangerously | 153 | 297 | 158 | 139 | 344 |
| Oct. 13, 14 | Last Metro | 204 | 377 | 183 | 194 | 538 |
| Oct. 20, 21 | Local Hero | 157 | 288 | 130 | 158 | 696 |
| Oct. 27, 28 | Four Seasons | 137 | 231 | 112 | 119 | 815 |
| Nov. 3, 4 | Gallipoli | 142 | 244 | 184 | 60 | 875 |
| Nov. 10, 11 | King of Hearts (incl. matinee) | 223 | 315 | 158 | 157 | 1032 |
| Nov. 17, 18 | Night of Shooting | 131 | 196 | 183 | 13 | 1045 |
| Nov. 24, 25 | Say Amen | 112 | 153 | 208 | (55) | 990 |
| Dec. 1, 2 | Gandhi | 149 | 231 | 197 | 34 | 1024 |
| Dec. 8, 9 | Bingo Long | 99 | 128 | 130 | (2) | 1022 |
| Dec. 15, 16 | Days of Heaven | 87 | 112 | 159 | (47) | 975 |

(continued)

### EXHIBIT 2-2 Continued

| Date | Film | Gate[a] | Receipts[b] | Expenses | Net | Cumulative |
|---|---|---|---|---|---|---|
| Spring Series 1985 (through April) | | | | | | |
| Feb. 2,3 | Bro Sun | 111 | $163 | $178 | ($15) | $960 |
| Feb. 9, 10 | Missing | 94 | 128 | 191 | (63) | 897 |
| Feb. 16, 17 | Chariots of Fire | 214 | 297 | 273 | 24 | 921 |
| Feb. 23, 24 | Sting | 83 | 102 | 110 | (8) | 913 |
| Mar. 2, 3 | Mao To Mozart | 115 | 168 | 228 | (60) | 853 |
| Mar. 9, 10 | Tess of the D'Urbervilles | 110 | 159 | 145 | 14 | 867 |
| Mar. 16, 17 | Muppets | 76 | 110 | 80 | 30 | 897 |
| Mar. 23, 24 | Honey Rose | 45 | 62 | 56 | 6 | 903 |
| Mar. 30, 31 | Jimmy's Hand | 57 | 77 | 110 | (33) | 870 |
| Apr. 6, 7 | Breaker | 151 | 228 | 249 | (21) | 849 |
| Apr. 13, 14 | Das Boot | 137 | 203 | 259 | (56) | 793 |
| Apr. 20, 21 | Graduate | 62 | 97 | 93 | (4) | 789 |
| Apr. 27, 28 | Sophie's Choice | 121 | 184 | 177 | (7) | 896 |

[a]Gate includes number of box office sales, number of prorated season tickets, and number of complimentaries.
[b]Receipts include amount of box office sales, amount of prorated season tickets, and concession sales.

### THE OLDE ODEON THEATER

### EXHIBIT 2-3

### Demographic Data for Preston County

| Age Distribution (1983) | | Income Distribution (1983) | |
|---|---|---|---|
| Under 5 | 361 | Total households | 2,250 |
| 5–14 | 1,005 | Under $5,000 | 353 |
| 15–24 | 1,053 | $5,000–9,999 | 418 |
| 25–34 | 1,072 | $10,000–19,999 | 661 |
| 35–44 | 881 | $20,000–24,999 | 254 |
| 45–54 | 925 | $25,000–34,999 | 260 |
| 55–64 | 765 | $35,000–49,999 | 127 |
| 65+ | 853 | $50,000+ | 177 |
| Median Age: 32 | | | |

| Population | | Workers Commuting Outside County | |
|---|---|---|---|
| 1960 | 5,587 | 1960 | 590 |
| 1970 | 5,289 | 1970 | 746 |
| 1983 | 6,250 | 1980 | 1,100 |
| Percent change 1970–83: 10.6% | | Percent of population 1980: 50.1% | |

(continued)

**EXHIBIT 2-3  Continued**

| *Employment (1982)* | | *Retail Sales (in millions)* | |
|---|---|---|---|
| Total labor force | | 1975 | $4.7 |
| Number unemployed | | 1977 | 5.5 |
| Unemployment rate: 10.6% | | 1979 | 6.5 |
| | | 1980 | 6.8 |
| | | 1983 | 8.2 |

| *Type of Employment* | | *Commercial Bank Deposits (in millions)* | |
|---|---|---|---|
| Manufacturing | 489 | 1975 | $7.6 |
| Construction | 431 | 1977 | 9.1 |
| Wholesale and retail | 354 | 1979 | 10.6 |
| Service | 745 | 1980 | 11.4 |
| | | 1983 | 12.9 |

| *Housing Values* | | *School Enrollment* | |
|---|---|---|---|
| Median owner value | $47,100 | 1977–78 | 1,207 |
| Median rent | 222 | 1979–80 | 1,175 |
| | | 1981–82 | 1,135 |
| | | 1982–83 | 1,071 |

| *Total Housing Units* | | *Crimes Committed* | |
|---|---|---|---|
| 1970 | 2,024 | 1977 | 105 |
| 1980 | 2,704 | 1978 | 88 |
| Percent change: 33.6% | | 1979 | 76 |
| | | 1980 | 103 |
| | | 1983 | 70 |

| *Residential Building Permits Authorized* | | *Sources County Revenue* | | |
|---|---|---|---|---|
| | | | Amount | Percent |
| 1981 | 52 | | | |
| 1982 | 37 | Local | $1,096,126 | 41.4 |
| 1983 | 30 | State | 1,175,602 | 44.3 |
| Percent change 1982–83: −42.3% | | Federal | 384,344 | 14.4 |

| *Net Migration* | |
|---|---|
| 1960–70 | −473 |
| 1970–80 | +807 |

# THE OLDE ODEON THEATER

## EXHIBIT 2-4

### Interview Information from Preston County Residents Obtained by Mr. Swenson

Note: Mr. Swenson gave a list of six questions to seven local residents who agreed to bring the questions up in conversations with friends and relatives when they could, and to keep a record of the replies or expressed feelings of each person. Even though Mr. Swenson believed that the general trends shown by the replies are reliable, he recognized that there were likely to be some errors in recording and interpreting the information by the interviewers.

|  | \multicolumn{4}{c}{AGE GROUP} |
|---|---|---|---|---|
| n = 38 | 16–24 | 25–34 | 35–44 | 45+ |
| 1. About how often do you go to the movies: | | | | |
|   More than once a month | 3 | 4 | 1 | 0 |
|   About once a month | 5 | 4 | 6 | 1 |
|   Four or five times a year | 1 | 2 | 2 | 4 |
|   Once or twice a year | 0 | 0 | 0 | 1 |
|   Very seldom or not at all | 0 | 2 | 1 | 1 |
| 2. Where do you usually go? | | | | |
|   Ravenal Drive-In | 7 | 8 | 5 | 1 |
|   Randal Twin Cinema | 2(7) | 1(6) | 2(4) | 4(1) |
|   Raleigh or Charlotte | 0 | 2(2) | 3(1) | 2 |
|   Other | 0 | 1 | 0 | 0 |
| Note: Parentheses are winter choices of drive-in patrons | | | | |
| 3. Have you ever heard of the Olde Odeon? | | | | |
|   Yes | 7 | 10 | 7 | 2 |
|   No | 2 | 2 | 3 | 5 |
|   If you know it, have you ever gone? | | | | |
|   Yes | 6 | 8 | 5 | 2 |
|   No | 1 | 2 | 2 | 0 |
|   If you went, would you go again? | | | | |
|   Yes | 1 | 3 | 3 | 2 |
|   No | 5 | 5 | 2 | 0 |
| 4. When you do go to a movie, how important is the movie itself? | | | | |
|   The movie is the main reason I go | 2 | 5 | 7 | 6 |
|   I go just to go someplace | 2 | 1 | 0 | 1 |
|   The drive-in is most important | 5 | 6 | 0 | 0 |

5. Those who said they would not go to Olde Odeon again were asked, Why not?
   a. We'd rather go where there is something to do afterward.
   b. I'd rather go to a bigger theater.
   c. I don't want to go with my date where people know me.
   d. We'd rather be by ourselves at a drive-in.
   e. The kids like the drive-in.
   f. We don't feel comfortable at the Odeon with kids.
   g. We like to go to Randall or Ravenal for something different.
   h. A lot of older people go to the Odeon.
   i. It's hard to find out what's playing there.

# CASE THREE

# NIKE, INC.

In the early 1980s, Nike had just outpaced Adidas as the best selling running shoe in the United States. It had also become the status brand for both joggers and nonjoggers. Nike held a slight lead until 1986, when its sales slipped about 14 percent, and the upstart Reebok moved to the head of the line in terms of both sales and market share. The newcomer's sales had soared from a mere $66 million in 1984 to nearly $850 million two years later. By 1989, however, Nike was back on top in market share and was running ahead of Reebok in retail sales. See Exhibit 3-1 for sales data.

**EARLY HISTORY**

The relatively short but sparkling history of Nike, Inc., is symbolized by the vapor trail simulation of its own distinctive "swoosh" logo. The firm was started in the early 1970s by a former University of Oregon runner, Philip H. Knight. He and a bevy of former athletes guided the firm's growth from a small importer of athletic shoes in 1972 to a major manufacturer with a spectacular $618 million in sales for the fiscal year ended in August 1984.

The Nike shoe had not only become the largest selling running shoe, but it had dislodged Adidas as the status brand. An unusual management team orchestrated Nike's success and seized opportunities offered by the zeal with which U.S. consumers adopted fitness activities. Many members of the company team were also former members or associates of the University of Oregon's track and field teams, including founder Knight, former President Robert Woodell and Deputy Chairman Bill Bowerman. Together, they not only brought a wealth of running expertise to Nike, but they also had an uncanny knack for successfully riding the country's cultural currents.

## CULTURAL CONDITIONS AND PROMOTION STRATEGY

If the United States hadn't undergone the health and fitness craze of the 1970s, Nike might have jogged along by itself, selling to a small market of serious runners. But not even the wildest visionaries could have predicted how all-encompassing the pastime would become. By the mid-1970s, Nike shoes had become a major part of the official uniform of the "Me Generation," and around-the-block runners bought them by the millions. Even nonrunners sported Nikes as an effortless way to partake in the mystique of running.

Nike's initial product, running shoes, fit naturally into the succession from the self-infatuation syndrome to the immersion into health foods and physical fitness activities. Advertising was directed to the solitary runner, the "detached" personality, the self-involved spirit that transcends the stifling bonds of society. One such ad, shown in Exhibit 3–2, depicted three runners on a muddy track with the caption:

> The Race Is Its Own Reward
> There was a time when people didn't run to collect T-shirts.
> Or race numbers.
> When the finish line was drawn in the dirt with a stick.
> And all the winner collected was a cold beer and a thumbs-up.

In another ad labeled "Man vs. Machine," a radiant woman is running past two creeping lanes of exhaust-laden traffic, where the drivers are gray and faceless.

## THE JOGGING MYSTIQUE

Although not as all-encompassing as the sport was in the 1970s and 1980s, jogging is still very popular. It is a highly personal, solitary, ego-building activity closely related to self-concept. What you wear while doing it sends a message to others about it and about you. A status-brand running shoe, for example, says the wearer is physically fit and that the mind is on higher things. Named for the Greek goddess of victory, Nike symbolizes the achievement and success that its users pursue. Nike also uses ad captions such as "Machines have put our bodies out of a job" and "Sooner or later the serious runner goes through a special, very personal, experience unknown to most people. Some call it euphoria, others say it is a new kind of mystical experience." These expansive, cultlike statements appealed to joggers and nonjoggers alike. They also appealed to unruly high-school and early college-age adolescents. For them, the statements captured the essence of their yearnings and rebelliousness. Nike successfully seized the opportunity to exploit this new culture and its new concepts but did it in a supportive rather than an aggressive way.

**A Tie-In with Athletes**

To attract attention to its advertising messages and the product, Nike also concentrated on the use of big-name athletes. The firm also solidified its position in the industry by asking athletes to help design shoes and signed large numbers of professionals to exclusive promotional contracts. Although payments couldn't be made to amateur athletes, Nike donated shoes and other equipment to them and their organizations, all clearly featuring the famous vapor trail logo. Nearly 75 percent of the firm's advertising and promotion budget went for this type of sales promotion.

Early on, Nike firmly allied itself with amateur athletics, and with the Olympics in particular, by sponsoring Athletics West. This supportive and training operation was the first large-scale corporate program to train potential U.S. Olympic participants. Of the 90 U.S. World Track and Field participants at Helsinki in 1983, 22 were from Athletics West. At that time, Athletics West saw itself as a free enterprise alternative to the Eastern Bloc's regimented programs, and Nike made a contribution of as much as $2 million a year to it. Athletes there got stipends, but only in their roles as Nike endorsers. Younger athletes who were brought in for their potential received a few hundred dollars a month and part-time jobs. Leaders in their sport, however, often got contracts that ran into six figures. The close ties between Nike and the participants in Athletics West provided an aura of confidence in the products the firm sells. Nike's help to athletes was also demonstrated in its advertising, and one such ad offering posters is shown in Exhibit 3–3.

## THE BATTLE FOR MARKET SHARE

Since 1986, when Reebok took the lead in market share, the two companies have competed fiercely to hold the market segments they have, and to attract others. Exhibit 3–4 shows comparative shares for Reebok, Nike, and a recent runner-up, L.A. Gear.

Oddly, the battleground between Nike and Reebok was not only the upscale youth market, but youths from the inner city; the modern sneaker has become a miracle of space-age technology and ultra-hype marketing. What blue jeans were to the children of the 1960s and 1970s, athletic shoes are to both kids and parents of the 1980s and 1990s. These shoes are statements of fashion, rebellion, life-style, and celebrity worship. They are also a lucrative vehicle for firms to sell self-image, in a rainbow of colors and a spectrum of styles.

But the market is a fickle one. Youths from 15 to 22 buy over 30 percent of all sneakers and exert direct influence over the purchase of another 10 percent. Contrary to the diffusion of innovation process for many other products, however, acceptance of an athletic shoe brand or design in the inner city is perceived as a symbol of authenticity. The life of fashion products such as these, however, is usually rather short.

As examples of the power of the inner city market segment, *The Wall Street Journal* reported recently that Nike paid the air fare to Chicago for a group of inner city sporting goods store owners. There, they were dressed in tuxedos and treated to a lavish banquet, with entertainment. Incidentally, Nike solicited their views on how the company could interest inner city kids in buying the company's products. Other producers, such as Reebok and Converse, ask the kids themselves or question coaches and gym teachers.

In the mid-1980s, Nike was the front runner in a multibillion dollar industry. The company's position was fueled mainly by the Air Jordan basketball shoes, promoted by Chicago basketball star Michael Jordan. Because of his influence, inner city kids wouldn't wear any other brand. Like all fads and kid's fashions, sales began to slow by 1985, and Nike had no new, innovative shoe to take its place.

In 1987, Reebok captured first place in the market-share battle by successfully producing and marketing colorful running shoes that appealed to trendy, fashion-conscious consumers. What Paris is to high fashion, Harlem and other inner city areas are to sneakers. But, of course, they aren't called sneakers. Instead, they are Alphas, Air Nikes, 830s, or Pumps—their model names or numbers. Fashion starts in these areas and spreads to other inner cities, to suburbs, and to the rest of the country. Today, the "athletic shoe" is a status symbol. Teens say, "The first thing a dude will look at is your sneakers."

Reebok, of course, had the styles, colors, and design to attract that market. Nike's reputation was related more to performance, physical activity, and status than it was to fashion. Reebok had moved rapidly ahead to fill Nike's product void. However, its victory was short-lived. By 1989, Nike had regained a slight lead, and the two adversaries are expected to run neck-and-neck through 1991, as shown in Exhibit 3-5.

## PRODUCT STRATEGY

Spurred by the success of its uniquely designed running shoe in the early 1970s, Nike moved rapidly into basketball, tennis, and other shoes used in court sports. As sales grew, Nike moved its production from Japan to South Korea and Taiwan where costs were considerably lower. This move enabled the firm to introduce a moderately priced line of shoes that quickly became a status product for the teen-aged market, and an intermediate line that provided trading-up steps for novice runners.

Initially, Reebok specialized in the production of aerobic and basketball shoes. The aerobics were made of soft, garment leather in pastel colors and were aimed at women, a segment that had not been approached by competitors. To gain and hold market share in this segment, Reebok gave free shoes to aerobics instructors and sponsored a new certification program for them.

The design, colors, and comfort of these shoes set them apart from aerobics made of regular leather, and they rapidly gained in popularity. But if the shoes were worn for sports or other activities, they tended to come apart. Eventually, if Reebok were to move into the sports activity market, new designs would be needed.

**The Reebok Products**

By the mid-1980s, changes were taking place in the marketplace. Aerobic participation dropped sharply, and jogging was no longer a growing activity. Also, researchers found that walking three times a week at a brisk pace of 4 miles per hour (vs. 3 mph normal walking speed) could strengthen the cardiovascular system, improve endurance, tone muscles, and burn calories. In other words, keep the walker in shape.

To move more directly into the walking and general sports shoe markets, Reebok introduced a line of white running shoes in early 1988. This was just about the time when consumers were demanding fashion shoes in wild colors, so the product failed and was taken off the market.

By then, the entire market was shifting away from the Reebok-type of limited use shoe and demanding more performance. Recognizing the trend, Reebok introduced The Pump, a $170 basketball shoe. This model inflated the upper part of the shoe by pushing a round button on the tongue. The injected air stiffens the collar and provides more support for the ankles.

Reebok also introduced athletic shoes with an "Energy Return System" using a mass of plastic tubes in the sole. Their purpose was said to be to allow energy to return to the wearer. How this actually happened was less clear, and retailers thought serious athletes might think the shoes were too "gimmicky."

In mid-1991, in an effort to revitalize the sagging interest in aerobics, Reebok introduced a line of Step Reebok shoes, promoted as lighter and cooler than regular aerobic shoes. They also provide greater flexibility through a "hinge" design in the front. The line is designed to accompany Reebok's new "Step Reebok" aerobics program, which features choreographed workouts where participants step on and off an elevated bench, in cadence with music.

**The Nike Products**

As mentioned earlier, Nike had no shoe to take the place of the Air Jordan when consumer tastes changed. However, the company had been using a new technology called Nike Air in most of its lines for several years. The Air was a gas-filled sac imbedded in the heel of the shoe. The sac cushioned the wearer's feet as they pounded against the pavement, making walking or jogging easier. The heel also keeps its spring much longer than the conventional rubber or foam. But Nike had not promoted this feature in its current lines, so it introduced the "Visible Air" model which had windows on each side of the heel so that customers could see the sac and watch it work. An ad showing a light shining through the windows has been very effective in selling the model. Nike's $175 Air Pressure shoe is similar to Reebok's, except for the window and the need for its wearers to carry a separate small inflation pump. Realizing that this appurtenance was a negative feature compared to Reebok's design, Nike introduced its own built-in pump shoe in the fall of 1990.

In early 1991, Nike introduced its latest model, the Air 180. Replacing the side windows of the Air is a large urethane window on the shoe bottom, revealing a much larger air bag for greater cushioning. Although glitz alone may sell the shoe, Nike is also conducting extensive tests of its durability. Athletes wear the Air 180s, covering at least 45 miles a week over all types of terrain. They also keep track of shoe comfort and performance. After 90 days, the shoes and notes are returned to Nike where their condition is examined. The company wants to be sure that this product will hold up for 500 miles or more.

### Diversification

As early as 1978, Nike began diversifying into babies' and children's shoes, in an attempt to imitate the appeal its products had in the adult market. Brand-conscious parents bought the status shoes for their youngsters as extensions of their own self-concepts, and they still do so. Nike's move in the early 1980s to introduce a line of sports apparel aimed at lower middle-class consumers (instead of its usual group of upscale income—education, downscale age buyers) lasted only six months before it was replaced by a new look trading on Nike's image. Today, apparel accounts for a sizable proportion of Nike's U.S. income.

Covering all bases, Nike has recently introduced separate brands for women and girls. The first, called i.e., is a line of casual women's shoes. The second, brought out in the fall of 1990, is Side One, a junior girls' fashion, athletic shoe. Through this strategy, the company hopes to have a stronger presence in the women's market.

## ADVERTISING COMPETITION

In 1988, Reebok and Nike embarked on advertising campaigns, both designed to appeal directly to inner city trend setters. Nike began with a group of roughly dressed teenagers emerging from a subway exit. Cameras focused on their feet, all shod in Nikes. This campaign was followed up with the "Just Do It" theme—ads showed serious-looking athletes puffing and sweating while working out. One ad pictured a runner, in Nikes, who stood exhausted at the end of a race, drenched with water.

Reebok's campaign was designed to appeal to individualism, with a do-your-own-thing connotation, using the symbol "Let U-B-U." TV spots featured various people engaging in odd pursuits, such as vacuuming a rug on a lawn, or hanging up laundry in the backyard.

But it didn't seem clear what it was that the ad was letting "U" be. Experts wondered if this type of message might simply go over the heads of most teenagers. An athletic shoe consultant suggested that the message was too abstract, too intellectual and too vague. He didn't even know what it was about.

Nike's "Just Do It" commercials, on the other hand, were more artfully and tactfully presented and their meaning was quite clear. The message was direct and easily understood by the market Nike wanted to reach. Some observers believe that this ad campaign was the turning point for Nike's return to first place. An example of one "Just Do It" ad is shown in Exhibit 3-6.

Not to be outdone, however, in 1991, Reebok aired episodes chiding both Bo Jackson and Michael Jordan for their endorsements of Nike. In one, Atlanta Hawks player Dominique Wilkins ends by saying, "Michael, my man, if you want to fly first class, pump up and air out," while he throws out a Nike Air. In another, Bengals player Esiason says, "Boomer knows something (about shoes) that Bo don't know." also tossing out a Nike. Neither Jordan nor Jackson were asked if their names could be used. While the ad created a minor flurry in advertising and endorsement circles, Reebok said it would continue to use the "Pump Up and Air Out" slogan, with athletes tossing away Nike shoes.

## PROMOTION

Nike has been especially adept in linking its brand to sports celebrities. The Air Jordan shoe sailed through the early 1980s, promoted by basketball idol Michael Jordan. The shoe was the first choice of trend-setting, inner city teens.

As the market waned for the Jordan design, a new celebrity had to be found, and Bo Jackson was an ideal replacement. From the catchy theme, "Bo Knows," to the tongue-in-cheek portrayals of him as an "expert" in at least 15 sports, Jackson has become synonymous with Nike. The company attributes a large part of its recent market gains to the Jackson commercials and the way they are presented. Ad agency executives agree, saying that if Jackson had only been shown using the shoes or talking about them, the commercial would have been lost in the clutter. The whimsical overstatements, together with Jackson's personality, are responsible for the commercial's success. One of Bo's most famous episodes is his attempt to play hockey on a gymnasium floor. It ends with a shot of Wayne Gretzky, who smiles slightly and simply says, "No."

To err is human, and so is Bo. So, also, are most consumers who wear Nike shoes. They aren't great runners or basketball players. Realizing this, Nike makes the celebrity stand for the idea. Bo Jackson "Just Does It." Using athletic celebrities is a risky business, especially when consumers identify them closely with the product, through classical conditioning. Bo Jackson's injury in 1991 will reduce his media exposure, and extinguish the product-image relationship.

## FUTURE STRATEGY

Although many Americans have diversified their fitness programs, Nike executives believe the market will continue strong. Their future strategy will include a sharpening of the company's identity, following an image that has been somewhat downgraded by its use on a proliferation of apparel and shoe products. Using individual brands on the women's line is an example of this strategy. From now on, the "swoosh" label will be less of a widespread family brand and more of a quality or status symbol.

Although large numbers of people continue to jog through neighborhoods, others are joining physical fitness centers where they run a few laps around the track before heading for indoor tennis or racquetball courts. Heeding this recent tendency toward diversification of fitness programs, Nike will promote itself as a total fitness company. Deemphasizing its wide lining in shoes, it plans to cut the number of Nike shoe models by 30 percent, and its recent acquisition of a maker of home lifting and other equipment will help it diversify.

The company also hopes to increase foreign sales from the present 16 percent to 20 percent during the next year, and it will continue its use of major athletes to promote its products. The question is whether or not the attributes that skyrocketed Nike to first place in the United States are those that are needed to compete on the three-front market of Europe, Japan, and the United States. Clever management and the ability to take advantage of United States cultural trends were the hallmark of Nike in the 1970s and 1980s, but both new strategists and strategies may be needed to map international attacks. One executive remarked, "Nike should know that marketing strategies that led to success in the United States will not necessarily work in Europe."

## CASE ANALYSIS QUESTIONS

1. How does "diffusion of innovation" seem to operate for athletic shoes? How does it differ from the normal diffusion process for most consumer products? Why does it work that way?

2. Reebok was the "fashion" and Nike was the "performance" shoe. Considering that Reeboks were not initially suited to sports activity use, how do you account for its overtaking Nike in the late 1980s?

3. What part do reference groups and self-image play in consumer buying decisions for athletic shoes?

**4.** Why did Reebok choose the "U-B-U" theme when the ad episodes themselves seem to have no relationship to the product or its users?

## REFERENCES

"Reebok Puts Big Push Behind New Aerobics," *Wall Street Journal,* Apr. 13, 1991, p. B-1; "Where Nike and Reebok Have Plenty of Running Room," *Business Week,* March 11, 1991, p. 56; "New Reebok Ads Enrage Rival By Taunting Nike's Star Endorsers," *Wall Street Journal,* Feb. 6, 1991, p. B-6; "L.A. Gear is Tripping Over Its Shoelaces," *Business Week,* Aug. 20, 1990, p. 39; "Step By Step With Nike," *Business Week,* Aug. 13, 1990, p. 29; "The Sneaker Steps Out," *Washington Post,* July 22, 1990, pp. 1–44; "Can Paul Fireman Put The Bounce Back in Reebok?", *Business Week,* June 18, 1990, p. 181; "Reebok Chief Looks Beyond Nike," *Advertising Age,* May 20, 1990, p. 16; "Nike Joins Literacy Fight," *Advertising Age,* Apr. 23, 1990, p. 4; "Once a Canvas Shoe, Now a Big Time Player," *New York Times,* Mar. 11, 1990, p. 1; "Reebok Splits U.S. Business Into Units Focusing on Fashion, Athletic Shoes," *Wall Street Journal,* Jan. 22, 1990, p. B-8; "Pumped Up Reebok Runs Fast Break With New Shoe," *Wall Street Journal,* Jan. 15, 1990, p. B-1; "Nike Posts Big Gains in Sales and Profit; Reebok Hopes Pump Will Help It Keep Up," *Wall Street Journal,* Dec. 19, 1989, p. B-10; "L.A. Gear, Highflier in Sneakers, Discovers Perils of Shifting Fads," *Wall Street Journal,* Dec. 8, 1989, p. 1; "Paul Fireman Pulls On His Old Running Shoes," *Business Week,* Nov. 6, 1989, p. 46; "Jackson's Nike Performance Proves He's Simply Irresisti-Bo," *Advertising Age,* Jul. 16, 1989, p. 85. "Nike is Bounding Past Reebok," *New York Times,* July 11, 1989, p. D-1; "Just Do It," *Washington Post,* Feb. 6, 1989, p. C-5; "Pricey Sneakers Worn in Inner City Help Set Nation's Fashion Trend," *Wall Street Journal,* Dec. 1, 1988, p. 1; "Nike Catches Up With The Trendy Frontrunner," *Business Week,* Oct. 24, 1988, p. 88; "Reebok Trails Nike in Fight for Teens Hearts and Feet," *Wall Street Journal,* Sept. 28, 1988, p. 21.

## NIKE, INC.

### EXHIBIT 3-1

**Producer's Athletic Shoe Sales by Brand, 1983-90 ($ millions)**

|          | 1983 | 1984 | 1985 | 1986 | 1987 | 1988 | 1989 | 1990 |
|----------|------|------|------|------|------|------|------|------|
| Reebok   | 13   | 68   | 295  | 850  | 1001 | 1790 | 1800 | 1950 |
| Nike     | 640  | 618  | 630  | 540  | 685  | 1200 | 1450 | 2200 |
| Converse | 206  | 254  | 190  | 200  | 260  | 240  | 216  | 225  |
| L.A. Gear|      |      | 11   | 15   | 40   | 220  | 617  | 880  |
| Adidas   | 210  | 185  | 150  | 160  | 165  | 172  | 181  | 186  |

*1989 Retail Sales ($ Millions)*

| | |
|---|---|
| Reebok   | 2300 |
| Nike     | 2400 |
| Converse | 500  |
| LA Gear  | 1000 |
| Adidas   | 320  |

**NIKE, INC.**

**EXHIBIT 3-2**

**Three Runners**

# THE RACE IS ITS OWN REWARD.

There was a time when people didn't run to collect T-shirts. Or race numbers.

When the finish line was drawn in the dirt with a stick. And all the winner collected was a cold beer and a thumbs-up.

That's how this revolution got started. And while it may be time to get runners and races organized, too much organization screws up the whole thing.

Because if you can't stay a little crazy, it's damn hard to remain sane.

**NIKE**
Beaverton, Oregon

*Source*: Photo courtesy of Nike, Inc.

NIKE, INC.    **37**

## NIKE, INC.

## EXHIBIT 3-3

### "Help an Athlete" Poster

A. Roadrunning, Deschutes River, Oregon.
B. "Battle of Atlanta," the Peachtree 1978.
C. Rono.
D. Finish, N.Y.C. Marathon 1978.

# BUY A POSTER. HELP AN ATHLETE.

You can have any of these big, (22"x36") full-color posters for only $2.50 apiece.

They're made from pictures of real athletes caught in the act of being themselves.

And the money goes for a good cause. We're donating the profits to the people and organizations that will best serve the interest of giving equal treatment for women athletes in the Olympics.

Simply put, we want to help convince the IOC to allow women to run the 3K, 5K, 10K, and marathon in the Olympic games.

The money will only be given to those dedicated to the runner's cause. It will be used wisely for athlete travel to some of the key foreign countries that remain unconvinced. For speaking tours and anything else that's necessary to persuade the IOC to give fair treatment to women.

We're putting up $5000 right away, and will donate any profits from the sale of these posters beyond this amount.

Send for one or more of these posters, and join our Operation Bootstrap: Athletes helping athletes.

If you don't help, who will?  **NIKE**

Dear Nike:
Please send the poster(s) I've checked below. I've enclosed my check or money order in the amount of $_____ ($2.50 per poster).
☐ A.
☐ B.
☐ C.
☐ D.

Name_____
Address_____
City_____
State_____ Zip_____

Mail to Posters/Blue Ribbon Sports, 8285 S.W. Nimbus Ave., Suite 115, Beaverton, Oregon 97005

*Source*: Photo courtesy of Nike, Inc.

**NIKE, INC.**

**EXHIBIT 3-4**

**Market Share: Top Three Brands, 1986-89**

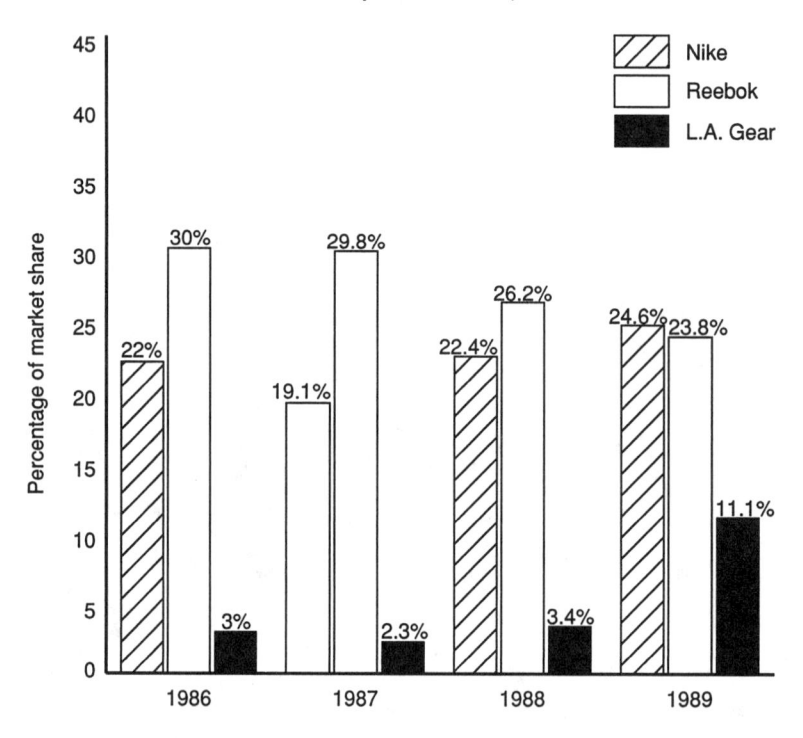

| Year | Nike | Reebok | L.A. Gear |
|---|---|---|---|
| 1986 | 22% | 30% | 3% |
| 1987 | 19.1% | 29.8% | 2.3% |
| 1988 | 22.4% | 26.2% | 3.4% |
| 1989 | 24.6% | 23.8% | 11.1% |

**NIKE, INC.**

**EXHIBIT 3-5**

**Market Share—Two Largest Companies**

**1987-91**

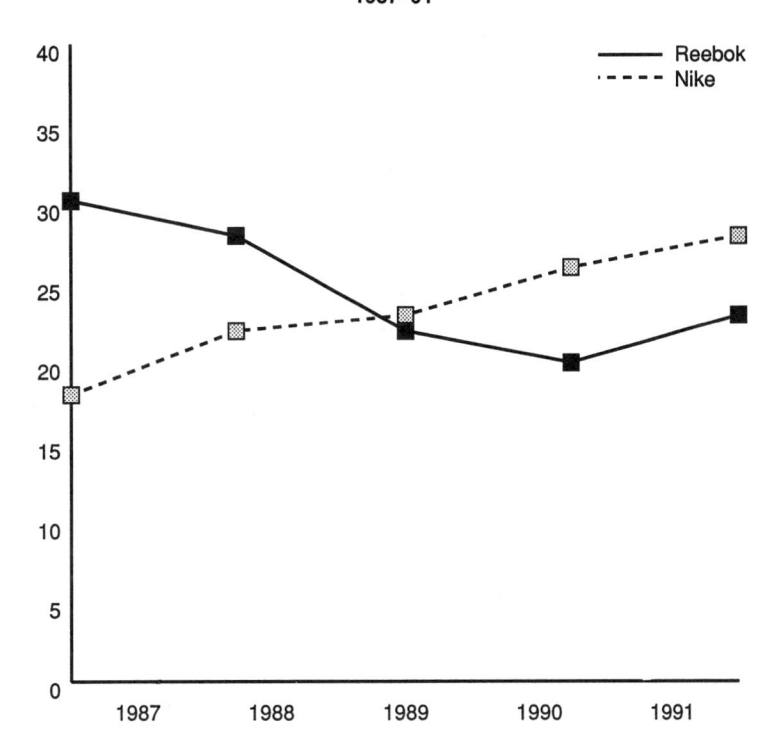

NIKE, INC.

EXHIBIT 3-6  Nike "Just Do It" Campaign

# "JUST DO IT."

*Just as Nike's hard-nosed ad slogan suggests, the company has hit the ground running after fumbling its lead to Reebok.*

BY BRYAN IWAMOTO

Nike is showing its strength down the back stretch"... are to be in a race for the top."... headed for a photo finish." The racing metaphors are predictable, but the media has Nike's number: "Some fast footwork has put it on Reebok's heels," says *Business Week*.

The championship for the athletic shoe title is on, and Nike is back in the fast lane. Philip Knight, Nike Inc.'s bearded chief executive officer, has brought his company out of a slump that had employees and analysts shaking their heads. Nike was leading the athletic shoe market through the '80s with high-performance shoes characterized by the Air Jordan basketball shoe promoted by superstar Michael Jordan.

The competitor came from nowhere. "Reebok began marketing the white aerobic shoe, and it especially caught on with women," says Ron Nelson, Nike vice president and 13-year company veteran. "We had a tradition of being a leader, but when this happened, we tried to follow Reebok, which was a mistake."

Nike has rebounded for several reasons, says Nelson. "Consumers demand change. They are tiring of the Reebok fashion look. Tech is real. Innovative research and development like NIKE-AIR® (a gas-filled sac embedded in the heel that Nike developed in the late 70s) always has been a strength and a Nike trademark."

In the Nike Sport Research Laboratory John Robinson, a Nike researcher, measures the characteristics of a cushioning system with a mechanical device. "As part of our research we have studied the structure of more than 5,000 feet," says Robinson, dressed informally like a university researcher, complete with Nike shoes. "The bottom line here is to build shoes that protect the athlete from injuries and also allow optimum performance."

Technology and safety aside, Nelson acknowledges that fashion underlies the industry. "Fashion is not a dirty word around here. We have four designers in the non-sports area and seven designers in footwear. Consumers want variety, and fashion plays to another strength — our ability to quickly transform marketing ideas into prototypes for the manufacturing process."

More than 600 Nike shoe models are complemented by the company's athletic apparel and accessory line. "We have always prided ourselves on guaranteed delivery and price," says Nelson. "Our delivery time has been trimmed from a week to overnight with our 'Nike Next Day' service to retail stores."

Retailers can place shoe and apparel orders with Nike's Memphis office until 7 p.m. CST and, with the help of Federal Express, they can have delivery the next day.

In August, before the program went national, more than 2,200 Nike Next Day packages were shipped. Point of sale material for the program was specially designed and distributed to more than 12,000 retailers via Federal Express delivery service.

Nike Next Day is a boon to the smaller retailer who hasn't the space or the resources to stock all sizes and models. "If a basketball team wants a dozen pairs of women's Air Delta Force High® shoes that are not in stock, the retailer can complete the order and guarantee the shoes will be delivered the next day to a home, office, school — or wherever they're needed," says Nelson. "The store doesn't have to lose the sale to one of its competitors and customers don't have to wait to get the shoes they want."

Spearheading Nike's second wind is a get-down-to-brass-tacks message to itself and its customers. "Just Do It," admonishes commercials and ads to perpetual procrastinators and excuse makers. It's a message that Nike has taken to heart. In response to Reebok's U.B.U. ad campaign, a Nike in-house newsletter proclaims the company's comeback: "So, let them be them and we'll continue to Just Do It." □

Gary Nelson

> "Fashion is not a dirty word around here. Consumers want variety, and fashion plays to another strength — our ability to quickly transform marketing ideas into prototypes for the manufacturing process."

# CASE FOUR

# SOURCE PERRIER II — THE SEQUEL

Perrier had become much more than a mere product in the U.S. market in the early 1980s. The small, green bottles shaped like miniature bowling pins had become a symbol of the health-conscious and status-minded baby boomers. Self-proclaimed as "nature's own soft drink," it turned millions of people away from alcoholic beverages.

But in early 1990, an ominous alarm was sounded in Vergeze, France, where Perrier has been bottled for nearly a century. Tests revealed that bottles of the water contained more than the recommended level of benzene—about the worst thing that could happen to a product whose reputation was based on natural purity. Unchallenged in the market for many years, it now appeared that Perrier was vulnerable.

## HISTORY AND MANAGEMENT

In the early 1900s, it was Dr. Louis Perrier, from the nearby city of Nimes, who first saw the potential of the bubbling, effervescent spring in Vergeze and devised a method of bottling the water. Later, the rights to the springs were acquired by Britain's Harmsworth family, headed by Sir St. John Harmsworth. He bought the rights with the proceeds from selling his stock in the family business, the *London Daily Mail*. In 1948, Gustave Leven, the firm's president until 1990, bought the rights to Perrier from the Harmsworth family.

Mr. Leven, in his mid-seventies by 1990, was not a typical business executive. He believed in a three-day workweek for himself, and sometimes disappeared for a week or two at a time. He made no provisions for a successor in the business, although in the 1980s, most of the company executives were in their sixties and seventies. The firm had no real structure at the top and made no attempt to do any analytical financial accounting. The French business magazine, *L'Expansion,* reported that, "Finance man Maurice Epry, had the reputation of calculating his sales prices by hand, just as he did in 1947."

In 1954, the firm acquired Contrexville, a French mineral water with a pronounced bicarbonate of soda taste. Nevertheless, it is the leading mineral water sold in France. Since 1968, the firm Source Perrier has functioned as a holding company for the various subsidiaries. Altogether, it operates some 18 bottling plants and warehouses throughout France. In 1969, the company took over Preval, an ailing French producer of dairy products, placing a severe strain on Perrier's resources through the early 1970s. Perrier also has the franchise to distribute Pepsi Cola and a European product, Gini, in France.

Erratic or not, Gustave Leven reshaped Perrier into a major worldwide producer, and the brand became a household word in the United States. Through a series of moves in 1975 and 1976, he rid the company of about 70 percent of its miscellaneous holdings, thereby substantially cutting losses. From these moves, he generated some $250 million. By adding $50 million more from internal funds, he was able to double the company's bottling capacity to about two billion per year. Now, he was ready to enter the potentially lucrative U.S. market.

## PERRIER IN THE UNITED STATES

U.S. distributors were not particularly interested in Leven's "Coca Cola without Sugar" when he made initial overtures. It was not until he hired Bruce Nevins, fresh from a successful career at Levi Straus, that things began to happen. Using a $2 million advertising budget, his strategy was to capitalize on the fitness-health fetish of the baby boomers. By stressing the natural properties of Perrier, and promoting it as a chic drink with no calories, he was surprisingly successful in weaning them away from sweet soft drinks and alcohol.

## PRICE AND MARKET SEGMENTATION

The prime strategy, however, was price. As an obscure, premium, imported product prior to 1976, Perrier's U.S. price was as much as $2.00 a bottle. Nevins cut it to about 69 cents, or 50 percent more than the price of an average bottle of a soft drink or carbonated water. This move had the effect of maintaining the premium niche and giving the product an appeal to affluent young adults, or those aspiring to this group. The approach was clear. Perrier implied status, and this snob appeal was aimed exclusively toward adults. This was an entirely new direction, since there had never been an attempt by any brand to segment the soft drink market on a price basis or to tap only the adult market to any great extent.

## ADVERTISING AND PROMOTION

Another one of Nevins's tactics was a cleverly designed advertising campaign using both print and electronic media. On national television, Perrier used the lofty tones of Orson Welles, an early radio, television, and film actor, who proclaimed the "miracle of Perrier." While he narrated the miracle, "In the south of France, near the village of Vergeze, stand gates which guard a single spring . . . blessed with waters of unusual purity and clarity," the sound of gas and bubbling water provided a tantalizing background. Print advertising featured details of how the product is naturally carbonated, how nature protects its purity, and why it is enjoyed for healthful reasons. Exhibit 4-1 is an example of an early Perrier ad, and Exhibit 4-2 is a recent one. After you have finished reading this case, you may want to compare the two. Appealing to the health-oriented market, another ad told why Perrier is "the natural conclusion to strenuous exercise."

There was also a rash of word-of-mouth advertising, and society page photographs showing affluent younger adults drinking Perrier on various occasions. It was fashionable to wear Perrier T-shirts and to flaunt Perrier beach towels, proclaiming the owner's membership in a status group. To combat rumors that the product was actually bottled in Brooklyn, Perrier flew a group of journalists to Vergeze to show them that the water was "naturally carbonated."

As the publicity hype ebbed, the company embarked on a third campaign to coin an ad "punch line" that would revive interest in the brand. The new campaign, begun in 1981, used historical or literary characters in vignettes related on radio by Orson Welles. In the one using Dracula, Welles tells how the vampire kneels beside a beautiful sleeping woman and lovingly sinks his long teeth into her white throat. This, and other stories, end with the words that Perrier hoped would become a household phrase: "It is good. But it is not Perrier."

## PRODUCTION AND SALES

The sales push in the United States was forced by the need to cover the heavy expense of the new bottling plant Leven built. Estimates are that the firm needed to produce and sell at least 800 million bottles a year of the plant's two billion bottle capacity in order to break even. And sales in the United States were expected to account for a large proportion of this figure. In Perrier's 1978 fiscal year, U.S. revenue was around $30 million, up from under $1 million two years earlier. Over 100 million bottles were bought in the United States in 1978, and the number grew to over 180 million in 1979, or about 27 percent of Perrier's total sales. Although the company predicted strong increases in the early 1980s, actual results in 1980 were flat with 1979, and there was only a slight increase in 1981. In 1989, U.S. sales were 350 million, about a fourth of Perrier's total bottle sales of 1.4 billion.

To offset the failure to meet early 1980 predictions in the United States, Perrier used advertising blitzes in Britain and Germany. These campaigns brought about a 60 percent increase in British sales to 12 million bottles. In Germany, where heavy advertising was steered by the Benton and Bowles agency, annual sales reached about 12 million. In 1982, Perrier conducted test markets in Italy and Spain. It also counted on U.S. sales of close to 300 million bottles, and French sales to stay at their normal level of about 400 million in order for the company to easily reach the break-even point. Financial data for the company, which include all of Perrier's products, are shown in Exhibit 4–3.

## COMPETITION

In addition to the naturally carbonated Saratoga Water, a number of artificially carbonated products began appearing on the U.S. market in the mid to late 1970s. Among these was Premier, which was introduced in Chicago in November 1978 by Hinckley & Schmitt, a long-time bottler of still spring water. Premier was simply a carbonated form of the regular product and was marketed with the slogan, "Let your guests *think* it's imported." Nestle's Deer Park division also began selling its Sparkling 100% Spring Water in New York in the fall of 1987. At the same time, Cadbury Schweppes test marketed its Schweppervescence carbonated mineral spring water in California. Even though this was a new product to the United States, it had been sold internationally for many years. Exhibit 4-4 shows the increasing total consumption of all bottled water in the United States and the portion of it that represents imported products.

There are also many still-bottled waters produced in Europe that are acclaimed by experts. Among these are French Evian, Italian Fiuggi, and Belgian Spa. It is interesting that in a test of sparkling waters conducted by *Savor* magazine, Perrier was placed third after Ramiosa, an obscure Swedish product, and the famous German Appolinaris.

## GLOOM IN VERGEZE

When the alarm sounded in early 1990, it didn't take much imagination to realize that disaster was imminent, and the town was shrouded in gloom since over 15 percent of the 3,500 inhabitants were Perrier employees, a percentage similar to that of other nearby towns. With the media screaming "benzene contamination," consumers would probably taste it in the product even if there weren't a measurable trace. On the Paris stock exchange, Perrier shares fell sharply and an investigative committee of the exchange was inquiring into the possibility of insider trading.

## THE "SOURCE" OF THE TROUBLE

The trouble occurred in a low concrete building where the naturally gaseous underground water enters the Perrier equipment. Only a handful of top engineers and their helpers are permitted to enter. The water comes into stainless steel vats where the gas is separated through a drip process. The extracted gas then runs through special coconut charcoal filters that remove microscopic impurities, including, says the company, benzene.

These filters are supposed to be checked regularly to make sure they are clean. But for several months, say company executives, the engineers "overlooked" the filters, and benzene began to clog them. Eventually, particles seeped through with the carbon dioxide gas. So when the supposedly filtered gas was reunited with the water, benzene was also present. The leakage apparently continued for several months. The process is illustrated in Exhibit 4–5.

## A SLIGHT MISREPRESENTATION

For years, Perrier had maintained that carbon dioxide was removed from the effervescent water which bubbled from the underground spring so that impurities could be removed. Once this was done, the gas was reintroduced into the water. But as more questions were asked about the process by the media and health authorities, the company admitted that additional gas from a separate well that was drilled deeper into the spring was introduced along with that which had been extracted from the water. This gas accounts for about half of the carbon dioxide content of the Perrier product. This process is shown by the dotted lines in Exhibit 4–5.

When North Carolina regulators first found traces of benzene on February 9, 1990, Perrier officials maintained that the contamination was an isolated incident confined to the United States and Canada. After that disclosure, the company recalled all bottles of the product in those countries. But on February 15, tests in Denmark and the Netherlands also found traces of the substance. It was only then that Perrier admitted small amounts of benzene had seeped into an unknown number of bottles that had been shipped to destinations around the world. This disclosure led to the pullback of all worldwide stocks.

## 12 TO 19 PARTS PER BILLION

Up to 72 million bottles were removed from shelves in the United States beginning on February 9. The North Carolina tests, and subsequent ones in Georgia, found 12.2 to 19.9 parts per billion of benzene in some bottles, according to the U.S. Food and Drug Administration. A spokesman said, "If you drank about 16 ounces of Perrier a day, your lifetime risk of cancer might increase by one chance in a million." The FDA set a permissible limit of 5 parts per billion units of water, based on an EPA finding that any more of that substance creates an increased risk of cancer. However, on February 15, 1990, France's Hygiene Council recertified that Perrier, even with the microscopic benzene traces, was safe to drink. Perhaps this is why Perrier's management seemed to have difficulty in explaining what actually happened. First, the chief spokesman said only the U.S. production had been contaminated because a benzene cleaning product had left traces on an individual bottling machine. Then, Gustave Leven, Perrier's president, said seepage through the filters caused the problem but, again, only on one line. He later admitted that it occurred on an unknown number of lines. While making this last announcement, he emphasized that all filters had been replaced and that tests since then had disclosed no presence of benzene. In the early stages of the problem, however, Perrier officials appeared nonchalant and unconcerned, even maintaining that all the publicity could only help brand recognition.

## SCIENTIFIC QUESTIONS AND LABEL CHANGES

Some scientific experts were puzzled over Perrier's claim that the water and gas naturally contain benzene. "It is usually," they maintained, "a substance distilled from petroleum, although it does occur naturally in some foods." One consultant to the beverage industry suggests that "Benzene in certain concentrations is probably man-made pollution." Another technician observed that "The contaminant isn't something usually found in a natural, pure water source."

The six months following the contamination problem saw three progressive changes in the Perrier label. First, the words "New Production" appeared on bottles produced after the recall to distinguish them from the earlier shipments. Then, in April 1990, the U.S. Food and Drug Administration required that the word "Naturally" be deleted from the label that read, "Naturally Sparkling Mineral Water." Another change on November 1, 1990, affected the 12-country European Community, about 60 percent of Perrier's market. This change will replace "Naturally Carbonated" with "Natural Mineral Water Fortified with Gas from the Spring."

## A TARNISHED REPUTATION

The total recall cost is estimated at some $30 million after taxes. But the dollar amount may be only a small portion of the cost in terms of the image and sales in both the long and short run. If Perrier had been a standard, well-known brand, a fast recall action and quick replenishment might have been an unfortunate blip, soon forgotten. But the product's long-term emphasis on nature, purity, and "the Earth's First Soft Drink" focused more than normal attention on the incident. Also, the company's initial attitude and conflicting explanations did little to minimize the situation.

Source Perrier began shipments of the new water in about three weeks after the recall. But restocking on U.S. shelves was a slow process. In the interim, the company had the extraordinarily difficult task of keeping the brand before consumers, when it was off grocery shelves—out of stock and out of sight. Consumer insistence on the Perrier brand is vital in the U.S. market, which consumes fully one-fourth of the 1.4 billion bottles Perrier sells annually. Advertising expenditures for the postrecall blitz in 1990 were about $25 million, compared to only $6 million in 1989. The campaign says, "Perrier. Worth Waiting For" and is presented in a light, humorous tone.

One radio ad featured reporter "Jill Purity" on the "Perrier News Network." Reporting on how well Americans are coping with the shortage, she interviewed a traveler at the airport. "Sir, how are you surviving?" she asks. "Not very well," he replies. "That's why I'm here at the airport. I'm flying to France so I can get the pure Perrier right at the spring." She concludes, "Don't worry America! You'll be able to refill those swimming pools soon!"

## PERMANENT LOSS OF #1 POSITION?

At the close of 1990, it appeared that Perrier was in trouble. A number of rival brands moved into its market, such as Pepsi Cola's H20h!, Coor's Rocky Mountain Sparkling Water, and Quibell. But the top beneficiary was Evian, produced by Evian Waters of France, which has replaced Perrier as the top seller of imported bottled water. See Exhibit 4-6 for comparative market shares of the two brands. Overall, Perrier's sales were only about 60 percent of those before the recall, and its market share has dropped from 44.8 to 20.7 percent. Nonetheless, The Perrier Group of America expects a 1990 gain of about 4 percent. Most of it, however, will come from the increased performance of its other brands such as Poland Spring and Calistoga waters. Exhibit 4-7 shows sales of the Perrier brand to wholesalers from 1985 to 1990.

Perrier has had considerable difficulty in returning the product to bars and restaurants, which accounted for about 35 percent of its prerecall sales. Today, only about two-thirds of those outlets that stocked it before, carry it. The company maintains, however, that sales are substantially better in supermarkets, but some large chains estimate that shelf space and sales are only 60 to 75 percent of the prerecall levels. Perrier was able to retain much of its shelf space only by stocking it with its own Poland Spring and Arrowhead brands.

Industry analysts attribute the brand's failure to recover rapidly to two factors. First, even before the benzene problem, Perrier was already being jostled by new brands in the U.S. market, and sales had reached their peak. To make things worse, the offhand, whimsical, and even joking reaction to the contamination, as described earlier, put consumers off. The interim ads, too, were lighthearted and airy, saying nothing and promising nothing. This procedure was in sharp contrast to Tylenol's fast recall action after the tampering scare, when a full-scale public relations campaign was launched, and a tamper-proof package was developed, both of which quickly restored consumer confidence.

Second, a sizable part of the brand's major losses was caused by the lengthy delay in restocking the U.S. market. Initial announcements promised the brand would be back in May, but because of production problems, it did not arrive until July, and stores were not fully stocked until near the end of the year. Despite the company's expensive advertising campaign to maintain visibility, the brand was out of sight too long. There was also the lingering question of the attributes "natural" and "purity" that disappeared from the product label. As one ad man put it, "When Tylenol came back, people still felt they could have their headache cured, but consumers are not too sure that Perrier is still a special product."

## DISCOUNTING THE MYSTIQUE

A key element in Perrier's initial strategy was not only to endow the product with the mystique of its source "deep in the caverns of the earth," but also to give it a premium image by pricing it about double that of other sparkling waters. To help regain its market, Perrier embarked on a highly visible discount strategy, with a buy-one-get-one-free offer.

In today's market, Perrier seems to be gathering increasing middle-class appeal, although its postrecall advertising has returned to the "Earth's First Soft Drink" theme. Many market specialists believe that the mystique and upscale image will never be fully regained. Now that consumers have discovered alternatives, the automatic "Perrier with a twist" bar order may be given less frequently.

## CASE ANALYSIS QUESTIONS

1. During the initial contamination crisis and in the postrecall period, company statements and advertising were light, whimsical, and humorous. Why do you think Perrier took this approach in communicating with its customers?

2. Considering that both French and U.S. health authorities said that Perrier was safe to drink, even with the small traces of benzene, what communications approach might have been more effective than the one the company used?

3. Was Perrier's attitude or the delay in resupplying U.S. markets after the recall primarily responsible for the change in Perrier customers' habitual purchase behavior? Or were there other reasons?

4. How might the price-quality concept affect the likelihood that Perrier will regain all or most of its U.S. market?

## REFERENCES

"Perrier's Vincent Plans Wave of Change As A Fresh Regime Displaces Old," *Wall Street Journal*, Feb. 14, 1991, p. B-1; "Perrier's Market Share Fizzles In the Aftermath of Its Recall," *Washington Post*, Feb. 2, 1991, p. F-3; "Perrier Finds Mystique Hard to Restore," *Wall Street Journal*, Dec. 12, 1990, p. B-1; "Carbonation Flap Forces 3rd Perrier Label Change," *Washington Post*, Aug. 29, 1990, p. 3; "Source Perrier Searching for Stronger Leadership," *Wall Street Journal*, July 2, 1990, p. B-2; "You Can Lead a Restaurateur to Perrier, But . . ." *Business Week*, Jun. 25, 1990, p. 25; "Perrier's Relaunch is Behind Schedule in U.S.," *Wall Street Journal*, Apr. 12, 1990, p. B-8.; "Can Perrier Purify Its Reputation?" *Business Week*, Feb. 26, 1990, p. 45; "Quibell's Booming Fiz Biz," *Washington Post*, Feb. 16, 1990, p. B-1; "Perrier News Hits Hard at the Source," *Washington Post*, Feb. 16, 1990, p. B-1; "Perrier Calls Problem More Serious Than Was Believed," *Washington Post*, Feb. 15, 1990, p. D-1; "Perrier Expands North American Recall to Rest of Globe." *Wall Street Journal*, Feb. 15, 1990, p. B-1; "Perrier's Strategy in the Wake of Recall: Will It Leave Brand in Rough Waters," *Wall Street Journal*, Feb. 12, 1990, p. B-1; "Perrier Recall Extended and Production Halted," *New York Times*, Feb. 11, 1990, p. 32; "Coors to Take Plunge to Sell Bottled Water," *Wall Street Journal*, Mar. 2, 1989, p. B-1; "Perrier Hopes It Has Tapped a Spring of Growth in the U.S.," *Washington Post*, Sept 10, 1989, p. D-1; "Perrier's Unquenchable U.S. Thirst," *Business Week*, Jun. 29, 1987 p. 46; "Water: Where Profits Spring Eternal," *Business Week*, Sept. 15, 1986, p. 75; "A New Zip to Bottled Water," *New York Times*, May 28, 1986, p. 34; "Natural Soda: From Health Food Fad to Supermarket Staple," *Business Week*, Jan. 14, 1985, p. 72.

**SOURCE PERRIER II**

**EXHIBIT 4-1**

**1982—Earth's First Soft Drink**

EARTH'S FIRST SOFT DRINK.

When the earth was new, mountains rose and valleys were carved and there was created, in what is now called France, a spring that is now called Perrier.®

All the Perrier in the world is born in that spring.

Still clear, pure and sparkling, and minus all those additives that civilization has invented. There's no sugar. No artificial sweetener. No calories. There's no caffeine, no coloring. And Perrier is recommended for salt-free diets, as well.

In modern times, when most beverages are made with water that's been disinfected, softened, oxidated or chlorinated, it's nice also to know that Perrier is naturally filtered as it rises to the surface from its deep underground source.

And so our only concession to civilization is the green Perrier bottle. Because without it, you would never get to enjoy Perrier.

Perrier. Earth's first soft drink.™ Not manufactured, but created by the earth when it was new.

© 1982 Great Waters of France, Inc.

*Source*: Courtesy of Perrier/Great Waters of France, Inc.

SOURCE PERRIER II—THE SEQUEL 51

**SOURCE PERRIER II**
**EXHIBIT 4-2**

# WHEN IT COMES TO THE HOLIDAYS THE EARTH ALWAYS RISES TO THE OCCASION.

Long before man had holidays to celebrate, the earth was already preparing for the festivities. In what we now call France, the mountains shifted and a subterranean spring burst forth. Delivering the pure, clear holiday cheer we now call Perrier.

An eon of New Year's Eves, and a millennium of Yuletides later, the excitement of the holidays is still heralded in with the hustle and bustle of Perrier bubbles. Perrier's merry green bottles are brimming with a drink as crisp, clean and pure as the day the earth first popped its cork.

EARTH'S FIRST SOFT DRINK

## SOURCE PERRIER II

### EXHIBIT 4-3

### Consoildated Income Statements for Selected Years

### (in French Francs—millions)

|  | 1983 | 1986 | 1987 | 1988 | 1989 |
|---|---|---|---|---|---|
| Sales, net | 3,483,596 | 12,452,300 | 11,518,700 | 15,147,800 | 16,671,900 |
| Other revenue | 192,700 | 111,600 | 329,700 | 335,600 | 513,500 |
| Total revenue | 3,676,300 | 12,563,900 | 11,848,400 | 15,483,400 | 17,185,400 |
| Material and supplies | 1,180,460 | 8,390,000 | 7,708,600 | 7,346,900 | 7,461,300 |
| Salaries and wages | 352,465 | 2,534,000 | 2,349,100 | 2,981,900 | 3,395,100 |
| Other expenses | 2,113,713 | 1,377,400 | 1,220,400 | 4,127,200 | 6,072,400 |
| Net income | 29,662 | 262,500 | 570,300 | 1,027,400 | 256,600 |

1991 exchange rate: 5.7 FF = $1.00 U.S.

Source: Company statements

## SOURCE PERRIER II

### EXHIBIT 4-4

### U.S. Sales of Bottled Water

|  | Total Sales ($ million) | Imported Sales ($ million) |
|---|---|---|
| 1978 | $ 400,000 | 13,000 |
| 1980 | 610,000 | 11,000 |
| 1982 | 925,000 | 12,000 |
| 1984 | 1,200,000 | 16,000 |
| 1986 | 1,450,000 | 31,000 |
| 1988 | 1,780,000 | 49,500 |
| 1989 | 2,150,000 | 67,000 |

| Leading Brand Shares—U.S. Market 1988 ||
|---|---|
| Arrowhead | 7.7% |
| Sparkletts | 5.9 |
| Perrier | 5.7 |
| Poland Spring | 3.5 |

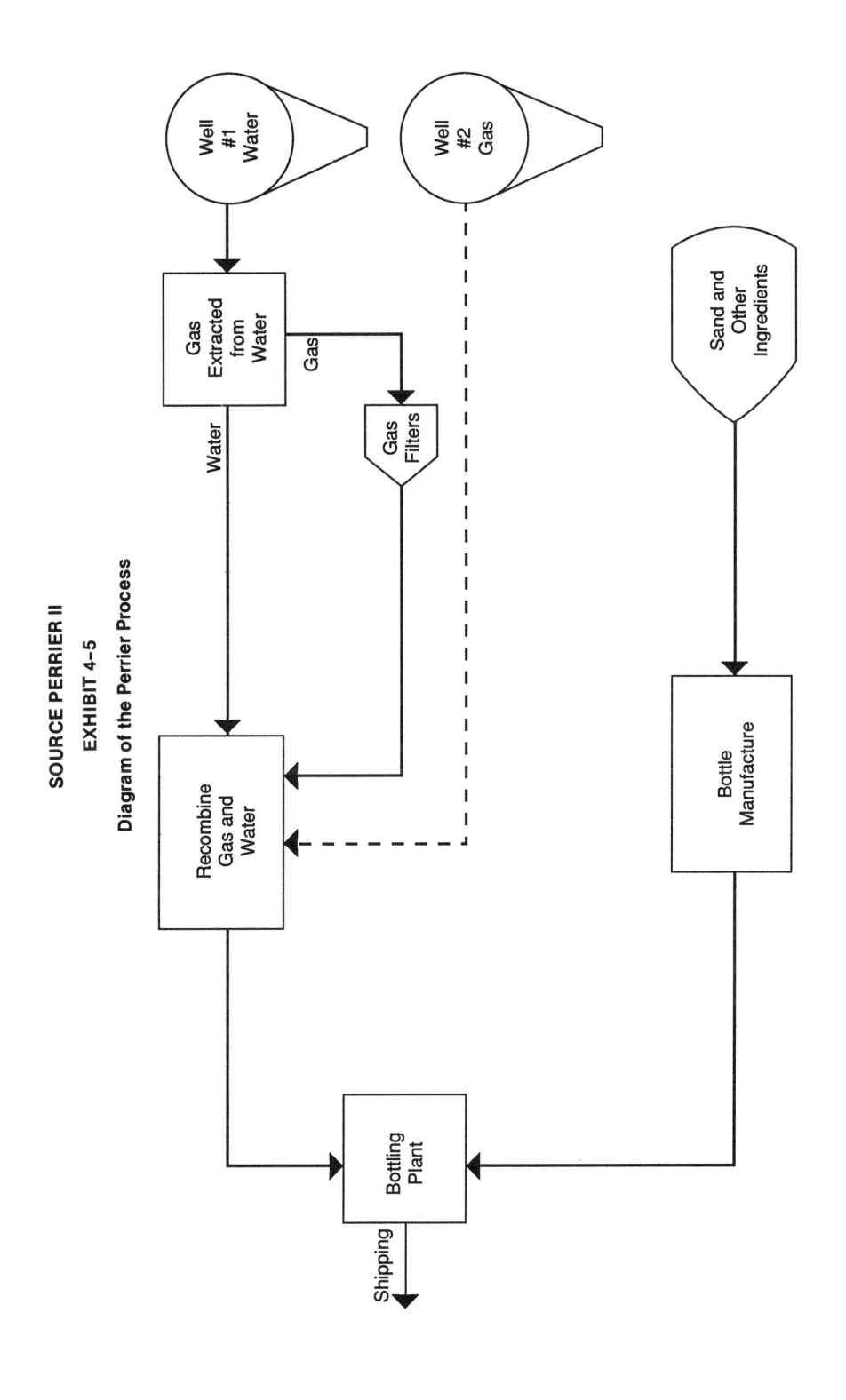

**SOURCE PERRIER II**

**EXHIBIT 4-5**

**Diagram of the Perrier Process**

53

## SOURCE PERRIER II
### EXHIBIT 4-6
**Percent Sales of Top Brands of Imported Bottled Water, 1986-90**

|      | MARKET SHARE | |
|------|---------|-------|
|      | Perrier | Evian |
| 1986 | 64%     | 8%    |
| 1987 | 58      | 11    |
| 1988 | 49      | 17    |
| 1989 | 45      | 29    |
| 1990 | 20.7    | 33    |

## SOURCE PERRIER II
### EXHIBIT 4-7
**Perrier Brand Sales of Bottled Water to Wholesalers, 1985-90 ($ millions)**

| 1985        | 64,000  |
|-------------|---------|
| 1986        | 83,000  |
| 1987        | 91,000  |
| 1988        | 102,000 |
| 1989        | 103,000 |
| 1990 (est.) | 49,600  |

# CASE FIVE

# THE NEW FRAGRANCE INDUSTRY

> In 1987, Leslie Saunders invested in what was then a small cosmetics and perfume manufacturer, L'Endanger Laboratories. At the time, she was an officer at a medium-sized Chicago bank. Her initial interest in L'Endanger was kindled by a new perfume product called Sextette.

Sextette, and other similar products, were called "communicative scents" because they contained pheromones, substances that have been shown to prompt a kind of sexual response in animals. Some tests had suggested a similar effect might be triggered in humans. Sextette was sold as a L'Endanger brand by the company, primarily through drug and other specialty wholesalers. Pheromone-laden perfume in other scents was also bottled under private brands for small and medium-sized firms. Most of the pheromone brands had been advertised on a small scale; none of the firms had resources to mount even a regional campaign. Sextette sold well for about six months after it was introduced, then sales declined to a moderate level. The brand is still carried by some discount chains. L'Endanger conducted some local research to determine why Sextette did not produce the sexual attraction consumers hoped it would. The findings may be summed up in a statement made by one younger respondent, "I put enough of it on, but when I walked into the party, nothing happened."

The company had a number of other profitable lines, so Ms. Saunders's investment had more than doubled in value in the past four years. Today, she is Vice President for Operations at a larger bank, and L'Endanger's account moved with her. Because of the knowledge of the scent business that she acquired when she first investigated L'Endanger's loan application at the previous bank, she was asked to serve on the L'Endanger Board of Directors. Shortly after she accepted the offer, she began to refresh her memory of the fragrance business and recent developments in it.

**BACKGROUND**

Perfumes, or fragrances, are usually mixtures of many different ingredients in solution. The solution most often consists of about 80 percent alcohol and up to 15 percent water. The remainder is the perfume itself. It, in turn, may contain more than 30 different ingredients of vegetable, animal, or synthetic origin. Most perfumes today contain some of each.

Essential plant or vegetable oils come from flowers, roots, stems, or seeds and include lavender, rose, sandalwood, citronella, and rosemary. These oils are extracted from flowers primarily by using a highly volatile solvent such as petroleum ether. In this process, flower petals or other parts are mixed with the solvent in closed containers for a lengthy period of time. The essential oils dissolve into the liquid, which is then fully evaporated, leaving the oils. In recent years, however, scents that previously involved crushing and extracting a thousand rose petals to get one ounce of expensive essence are being faithfully reproduced in the laboratory. Most of these synthetic fragrances, however, are used in soaps, lotions, room fresheners, and similar products, and they will be discussed in more detail shortly.

The best perfumes also contain ingredients of animal origin, such as musk, obtained from the glands of deer; civet, from the glands of the civet cat; and ambergris from sperm whales. These ingredients impart a warm quality to a perfume's scent and intensify the fragrance of other substances.

*Perfume* is the most expensive of all scents; it is the strongest and it lasts the longest. High-quality perfume, nonetheless, should be bought in small quantities and should not be exposed to direct sunlight or extreme temperatures. Once a bottle is opened, it should be used; otherwise, its potency will fade with time.

*Eau de parfum* is a more recent, less concentrated product and contains only about half as much of the perfume compound as regular perfume. It lasts longer than toilet waters or colognes when it is sprayed or smoothed over the body just before dressing.

*Eau de toilette* contains 5 to 8 percent of a perfume compound, with no other fragrances added. The higher proportion of distilled water makes it lighter than perfume or eau de parfum. It is used as a base for perfume application, or sprinkled onto accessories. It is sometimes sprayed about a room, or added to lingerie rinse water.

*Cologne* is the lightest fragrance, with only 2 to 4 percent of perfume oils, so more of it may be used at a time. Originally, it was simply fragrant citrus water, but today colognes contain fragrances from citron, ferns, molasses, lavender, and rosemary, as well as diluted perfumes. They are packaged in larger quantities and may be used more lavishly than the other fragrance versions.

Appendix 5–1 describes perfume use in different cultures.

## SYNTHETIC SCENTS

Most of the scents used in consumer products are put in simply to make the products smell better. And better fragrances are constantly appearing on the market because of technological advances in reproducing natural ones. As previously mentioned, a rose scent that requires crushing over a thousand rose petals to extract a single ounce of a very expensive essence can now be faithfully reproduced in the laboratory. This reproduction is accomplished at such a comparatively low cost that artificial fragrances are now available for use in mass-produced products.

The maturing perfume market has also driven producers such as International Flavors and Fragrances (IFF) to try to educate American consumers toward expanded uses of scented products, thereby stimulating demand. One of the newest technologies embeds fragrances in plastic for use in furniture, automobile interiors, Glad bags, toys, and plastic shoes. Fiat of Turin, Italy, has been experimenting with interior parts made of perfumed plastic for its cars. Sunlight liquid detergent from Lever Bros. depends on a special scent to enhance its image. New scents and chemical techniques are positioning, or repositioning room fresheners. Formerly these products were used to cover up undesirable odors, but they are now being introduced as "atmosphere enhancers," much as incense has been used for centuries. Furniture polish, too, may have a mood aroma of its own, now that good, cheap, synthetic fragrances are available. Henry G. Walter, the former chairman of IFF, believed that people from poorer countries liked stronger smells and flavors, and he cited the heavy-handed use of spices in Third World foods as an example. He believed that as more Hispanics come into the labor force, synthetic perfume and aroma sales will benefit.

Still another use of synthetics has been the development of aromas that tempt the palate as well as other senses. IFF and other firms have succeeded in imitating such mouth-watering aromas as candy, pizza, chocolate chip cookies, and baking ham. But the marketing and packaging of these aromas is the clever part. Some of them are packaged in aerosol cans that come with a timing device ($35 extra) that periodically releases a burst of the scent into a shopping mall. "We tried venting our cooking odors into the mall," says one restaurant manager, "but grease and other material came out, too, and they made us stop. These canned aromas are the ideal solution and they sure help bring customers in."

A boon to used car dealers has been canned, synthetic, "new car aroma" which can be sprayed inside a five-year-old heap to make it smell as though it were just driven off the showroom floor. The car's performance isn't helped much, however. One brand, Velvet Touch, made by a Massachusetts firm, has been a good seller to both owners and dealers who want to rid the car of undesirable odors such as those from a dog or a cigar.

> At the first board meeting she attended, Leslie Saunders had a sense of déjà vu, since the discussion was reminiscent of one she had with company officers when they applied for their first loan. L'Endanger was ready to embark on a second major expansion program. The present production facilities could barely support the demand, and there were several innovative products being developed in their own, and other, laboratories that appeared promising. The first item on the agenda was a presentation of the "state of the industry" by L'Endanger's president, Peter LeMoine.

## THE INDUSTRY TODAY AND COMPETITION

"With over 800 fragrances on the U.S. market today," began Mr. LeMoine, "competition abounds. Over 60 new products are introduced each year, and the pattern of distributing good perfumes only in upscale locations is changing." Avon products, the leader in women's fragrances for over 25 years, has just been replaced by Unilever, N.V., the Anglo-Dutch conglomerate producer of consumer goods. Since the 1980s, Unilever has been acquiring such old-line firms as Faberge, Elizabeth Arden, and Calvin Klein Cosmetics. These, and other firms, have created a powerful, diversified group that is number one in *both* men's (a 15.8 percent market share) and women's (12.6 percent) fragrances. Exhibits 5–1 and 5–2 show market shares for leading producers of both types.

Of the top ten fragrances in the United States, half were introduced in the past five years. All of them were pushed with the utmost in media hype, to assure that consumers always perceive a need for something new. "Very few perfumers are interested in perfume," commented one producer. "It is the launching, marketing, and advertising that is vital to the success of a brand."

For several decades, fragrance consumers have become less and less brand-loyal—they are purchasing, using, and switching to new products at an increasing rate. More than that, the bizarre and suggestive names of women's perfumes, such as Obsession, Poison, and Passion, along with their heavy, heady aromas, are being abandoned by consumers. In their place, buyers are beginning to favor more moderate semantics and performance in scents. Beneficiaries of this growing new attitude are old favorites such as Shalimar and Chanel No. 5. Both of these brands were introduced in the 1920s and flourished until the 1960s. By then, they were sold in every K Mart, drugstore, and duty-free shop. Nothing, industry experts say, kills a classy, snob-appeal perfume faster than overavailability. The sales decline that began in the 1960s continued until the early 1970s, when Chanel appointed Catherine Deneuve as its spokesperson. Sales then jumped from $15 million to $35 million annually. In today's market, updated packaging and advertising have also helped these brands regain favor.

Revlon, the industry's number three performer had not introduced a major new brand since its Charles of the Ritz subsidiary launched Charlie in 1974. In 1990, the company brought out the successful Unforgettable brand in a unique slim bottle holding 1.6 ounces and priced higher than most other Revlon scents. It was designed to be a part of Revlon's Unforgettable Women campaign, focused on Barbara Sinatra, actress Melanie Griffith, and others. Since Charlie, Revlon has been perceived in the industry as a stodgy company that relied heavily on the low-priced market. Unforgettable may have reestablished some of its lost market prestige.

## THE PRESTIGE MARKET

In 1990, U.S. perfume sales were about $2.7 billion, but much of the recent growth was caused by price increases and expansion of the men's market to about $860 million annually. The number of units sold has remained relatively constant, so like other saturated markets, growth of one brand must come at the expense of others. In the prestige market, the product itself must have appeal. The bottle and package must exude "class" and "status," but "the total package" is what is really being sold. It is the image that must be carefully created through advertising and other marketing devices. As one executive put it, "The beauty business deals in people's dreams and you have to be careful how you market dreams."

To make a splash in today's crowded market, a new brand must be accompanied by extra-heavy promotion. When Maxims de Paris appeared in late 1985, female models dressed as 1920s flappers passed out three million trial vials, while videotapes at cosmetic counters recounted the history of Maxims, the restaurant from which the perfume got its name. To top it off, Macy's held a masked ball in honor of the product's debut. "Glitzy campaigns certainly help," continued Mr. LeMoine, "but now, a brand may achieve a sizable market share by using only advertising and scent strips, as we will see later."

### Designing a Prestige Fragrance

Researchers do not ask men what attributes they would respond to in a women's perfume. They talk mostly to women. They don't talk about what women want in a fragrance but about their dreams and what it is they want out of life. They reply: luxury, adventure, and sex—mostly sex.

This method helped Charles of the Ritz to segment the perfume market, first with Charlie in 1974, designed for independent, carefree women. The next year, there was Jontue for the romantic and Aviance for the housewife. Two years later, the working mother could enjoy Enjoli. But there is apparently another type of modern woman to target for still another brand of perfume, Senchal. This woman is looking for some danger. She wants the passionate, adventurous life. She's a connoisseur of luxury. Men are part of her life, but she'll have a meaningful relationship with whom she wants, when she wants. The world is her toy, she's queen of the jungle. And she's not going to marry the boy next door. At least not in the ads.

Brenda Harburger, marketing vice president for Charles of the Ritz, points out that ads used to be able to say, "Wear this perfume and you'll catch a man." Today, the buyer must be convinced that a perfume brand matches her own attitudes and life-style. Lois Ernst, of the Advertising to Women, Inc., agency says, "We're talking about a stupid little perfume, but we're dealing with the whole texture of life and relationships."

> The purpose of this meeting was to decide which of several new product lines or target markets L'Endanger should consider as part of its expansion strategy. The company manufactured some products under its own name brand and other individual brands. It also produced and bottled other dealer's and manufacturer's brands and sold fragrance products in bulk. Therefore, the next presentation, by Bob Rijeka, the marketing vice president, would be concerned with products and niches in the market that might fit L'Endanger's capabilities. After the board had made its suggestions as to the proposals that might be considered, sales projections and financial aspects would be studied. The final proposals would then be presented at a future meeting.

"In a nutshell," concluded Mr. LeMoine, "that's what the fragrance business is all about."

*Emotion-eliciting fragrances.* Mr. Rijeka began with the early history of research into other uses for scents. In the early and mid-1980s, the International Flavors and Fragrances Corp. studied the future use of "control" fragrances. In its crystal ball, the corporation conceived of people who would control their health, and even their moods, with scents instead of drugs and alcohol. One scent could help them sleep; another could control high blood pressure. Others could induce relaxation, keep them awake, or cope with depression. The company's chairman predicted, "In 12 months, we will have a product on the market, probably a stress-relieving fragrance."

Although no such product has appeared, research in this area continues. It does so, however, under a new and less clinical or threatening name, "Emotion-Eliciting Scents." Today, researchers at IFF, Yale University, and Togasaga Institute in Japan are near a more complete understanding of how smell, the most mysterious of all the senses, affects humans.

We can detect over 10,000 different odors, and our sense of smell is quite precise. Yet it is almost impossible to describe how something smells to someone who has not experienced it—a new car, freshly cut grass, or a gym locker. Scientists know that if we hold a fresh lemon to our nose and inhale, the odor molecules move back behind the bridge of the nose where they are absorbed by the mucosa, containing receptor cells. In these cells are cilia, or microscopic hairs, which send impulses to the brain's olfactory bulb. The bulb signals the cerebral cortex and sends a message to the limbic system, a section of the brain where we invent, lust, and feel. Now, we know we have smelled something. If it is familiar, we know from stored information what it is. If not, we store the information so we will recognize it next time.

All smells can be placed into one of seven basic categories: minty (peppermint), floral (roses), ethereal (pears), musky (musk), resinous (camphor), foul (rotten eggs), and acrid (vinegar).

Although we know how the smell process works, researchers are trying to determine what effects odors might have on the other senses. In one study, people were connected to devices that measured tiny electrical impulses emitted by the brain, or "brain waves." While they were being measured, the subjects were given whiffs of different odors, from a relaxing lavender to an action-stimulating jasmine. Differences in impulses were then related to changes in the subject's moods. At Yale, studies have shown that the aroma of spiced applies reduces blood pressure in people under stress and actually averts a panic attack. Researchers hope that within the next several years they can produce hard evidence that certain fragrances have a significant statistical probability of creating specific moods in people.

Such mood changes, they say, will be rather small ones at first, such as those we experience while listening to certain kinds of music. As more is known about how reactions are triggered, smells may be potent enough to cause people to eat less, sleep soundly, study better, or drive more safely.

Other research indicates that preferences in smell may be established in infancy. Contrary to prior scientific belief, recent studies indicate that babies do respond positively to some odors, and negatively to others. Less is known about the latent effects that infant smell imprinting has on adults. Shalimar perfume makers believe it does have some effect. Although that product has a distinct oriental connotation and a heavy aroma, customers describe it as being "fresh and clean." The speculation is that women unconsciously associate Shalimar's powdery scent with purity, babies, and their own babyhood when they were dusted with baby powder.

There should be extremely heavy demand among consumers for fragrances that do something to, or for, you. The companies developing and selling effective aromas could carve profitable niches for themselves in the market. Some applications that come to mind are keeping truckers alert on the road, reducing anxiety in city subways, controlling riots, or providing scent systems for entire buildings.

## PERFUMES FOR MEN?

Georgette Klinger, a noted skin-care beautician, says she favors the use of both pre-and aftershave lotions as part of a treatment for her male clients. Until recently, though, her salons in New York and Beverly Hills had discreetly located separate entrances for men.

Ideas have been changing about men wearing fragrances. Ten or 15 years ago, aftershave lotion was a new and somewhat questionable male-directed product. But today, aftershave is a common item in male grooming, and cologne is gaining in acceptance. Moreover, the newer men's scents are more likely to be lighter and fresher smelling than women's perfume. Earlier ones were heavier and permeating, hence the joke, "I knew you were coming. Your aftershave got here ten minutes ago."

But the newest idea is that there is a link between good looks, good grooming, and success. So men, like women, are becoming concerned with such personal detractions as lines under the eyes and blotchy skin. Cosmetic makers are responding with such products as wrinkle removing eye cream, "color-correctors," and skin lotions. There is also a "Nails for Males" polish designed to remove ridges from nails, a process that is apparently acceptable to men.

Using masculine themes to name men's fragrance products is a major element in market success. Compete is supposed to attract the aggressive striver, while Entrepreneur is for men who would like to be one. *The Wall Street Journal* reveals that the latter product contains "a blend of exotic musk, amber, oriental spices and just a hint of cognac." Other macho-sounding names for men's fragrances or cosmetic products are the Gripper (football connotation), EC-17 (military), and Matrix Cellular Eye Creme (space and hi-tech). Although men seem more willing to accept lotions, colognes, and some creams, they balk at "cover-up" or color products. The only one with any degree of acceptance is a new bronzer. But it is packaged in an inconspicuous gray and white tube so it won't be noticed in the locker room. As the president of one major cosmetics firm observed, "The use of cover-up, eye shadow, or lipsticks by males is probably a generation away."

Locating men's fragrances and cosmetics has been a tricky decision for stores. Estee Lauder's Aramis affiliate prefers to use the spot where men's products of the English Leather variety have traditionally been sold. On the other hand, Clinique, which overtly features men's personal grooming products, sells in the women's cosmetics department. So far, according to store managers, the location seems to have very little effect on sales to men. Some give a slight edge to the women's location, since customers shopping there may pick up a man's product on impulse, as a gift.

The ultimate in men's fragrances is offered by Bijan Pakzad, a fashion designer, at $250 an ounce. The price for six ounces is $1,500 and it comes in a hand-blown, hand-cut Baccarat crystal bottle at no additional charge. The perfume is made up of rosemary, nutmeg, black pepper, vanilla, tangerine, and 17 additional plant and flower oils. Pakzad claims that Prince Mohamed ibn Fahad al Saud, heir to the Saudi Arabian throne, bought seven bottles to give to friends. Another customer says, "The perfume reminds me of the Arabian Nights. It's a heavier, spicy kind of scent. Something a man would wear." But men are reluctant to buy small bottles because they aren't masculine enough, which is why the Bijan perfume only comes in six-ounce containers. Up to now, very little psychographic research has been conducted to determine what fragrance male consumers want in a shaving lotion or cologne, or to investigate their inner motivations. That will come later.

Advertisements for men's perfume, oddly enough, are patterned after those of women's, in that they say very little, if anything, about the product. Consumers are supposed to read their own fantasies, meanings, and interpretations into the ad. Exhibit 5-3 is an example of a recent ad for men's perfume.

## BARGAIN-BASEMENT PERFUME

In 1989, Societe Bic, the French corporation that developed a low-priced market for cigarette lighters, disposable razors, and ball-point pens, embarked upon a similar strategy to sell perfumes in the United States. Four products, two for women and two for men, were packaged in quarter-ounce glass spray bottles which sold for $5.00 each. Bic hoped that the strategy that sold their other products would work equally well for perfume.

The company was banking on a $20 million ad campaign with the theme: "Bic Heritage: High quality at affordable prices. Convenient to buy and to use." They also had an established distribution system for razors and pens, including some 100,000 drugstores, supermarkets, and mass merchandisers. The four perfumes, Nuit, Jour, Bic for Men, and Bic Sport for Men, were sold on racks in plastic packages, and as impulse items at cash registers.

Bic had introduced similar products in Europe in 1988, but they will not discuss the results. Bristol Myers test marketed their Savvy brand perfume with its $5.00 price tag in the late 1970s. There was little market interest, and the product was withdrawn. Should the Bic perfume catch on, the market may look for expanded choices in the low-priced range, and there will be room for other producers. One consideration in this market is whether or not bargain-priced perfume will attract consumers the same way pens and razors do.

## THE SCENT STRIP

Thumb through almost any glossy magazine and you are likely to notice a penetrating smell. Even though you must pull back a tab in an ad to get the full effect, the aroma is certainly apparent. In one edition of *Town and Country* magazine, an ad invites the reader to "Open Here to Experience Oleg Cassini's Elegantly Persuasive New Scent."

For the relatively new strips, it might be said that "one scent is worth millions in advertising dollars." This proved to be true when the makers of Georgio Perfume pioneered the scent strip in the early 1980s. Earlier, when we discussed the prestige market, we said that launching a new, expensive fragrance required huge marketing and promotion outlays. In recent years, Revlon spent $18.2 million this way, Cosmair $13.8 million, and Estee Lauder $12.3 million. However, Georgio, one of the two major perfume successes of the 1980s, and still a top department store seller, spent only $2.2 million. By inserting scent strips in regional and national magazines, it avoided costly promotions and expensive television spots for the Christmas season. These weren't necessary when consumers could sample the fragrance at home.

The strip, itself, is a fairly simple device in which tiny amounts of a scent are embedded in a cohesive substance. This substance is coated in strips on magazine pages, and a strip of the page is folded over onto itself. By pulling a lightly sealed tab, and running a finger over the substance, an aroma is released. Fragrance producers supply the scent to magazine printers, who mix it with the cohesive substance in the production process. In one sense, this innovation permits small producers to provide relatively inexpensive advertising and sampling. In another sense, the proliferation of scent strips may blur the consumer's perception of product differences. Mr. Rijeka mentioned that there have been complaints about strip-released aromas causing headaches and asthmatic attacks for some people. In at least one state, legislation was introduced that would require fragrance samples to be sealed in odor-proof containers.

## FRAGRANCES FOR CHILDREN

In the past several years, at least four fragrances and toiletry products specifically for children have been introduced in the United States. Such products are commonly used in Europe, but U.S. interest has been limited until recently. In 1986, Givenchy, a well-known French perfume manufacturer, brought out a new children's scent called Ptisenbon, in cooperation with Catherin Painvin, a children's clothing designer. The product's citruslike scent proved to be so popular in France that it was introduced in the United States. Exhibit 5-4 is an example of U.S. advertising for this product.

Ptisenbon fragrance is marketed in the United States under the brand name Tartine et Chocolat. Translated, it means bread and chocolate, the usual after-school snack for French children. The product comes with or without alcohol because some parents are concerned about its effect on young children's skin. A 100-milliliter bottle sells for $30.

A U.S. company, however, claims to have predated Givenchy's entry by several months. PDF Enterprises, a company specializing in infants' and children's perfumes, introduced the Nouveau-Ne (newborn) brand, which also has a sweet, citrus-type scent and contains a small amount of alcohol. Many parents, however, spray the perfume or cologne on T-shirts or other clothing instead of directly onto the child's skin.

Children's fragrances are carried primarily in upscale department stores and children's boutiques. A girl's department buyer for Nordstrom observed, "We know how children want to imitate parents, but we were surprised how many mothers wanted the special fragrances for their children."

"Marketing of kid's products is tricky," cautioned Mr. Rijeka. Gregory's International Corp. promoted its new children's cologne using the president's four-year-old nephew as "spokesperson." The boy, dressed as a little adult in a black tie, or a white suit, stood beside a kid-sized Mercedes convertible in ads and in personal appearances. But many parents didn't care for this promotion and were turned off by it. Retailers saw the fragrance as a fad that sold well in the beginning but declined rather rapidly. They also observed that U.S. parents are not as interested in children's fragrances as Europeans are. "On the other hand," said Mr. Rijeka, "the same thing was said about men's perfumes only a few years ago."

> Mr. Rijeka's remarks concluded the presentations. Mr. LeMoine then opened the meeting for discussion and said, "You now have general information on the advantages, disadvantages, and competition for several new products and target markets we are considering. I hope that before we adjourn, we will have a consensus on those which you believe would be most useful for us to pursue further."
>
> Leslie Saunders began looking over her notes. She thought all the proposals had merit, but at this stage it seemed that the products themselves and potential consumer demand should be the main considerations in making her recommendations.

## CASE ANALYSIS QUESTIONS

1. How do perfume companies go about "designing" perfumes to match women's life-styles and personality characteristics? Consider the roles of both chemicals and promotion.

2. Which type of consumer "conditioning" do fragrance producers use in their attempts to change consumer behavior? How is it supposed to work for these products?

3. What social and ethical factors are involved in the so-called "emotion-eliciting" fragrances? From case information, do you think these fragrances will do what is being claimed for them?

4. What do you think about the future marketing possibilities for children's fragrances? What social factors are likely to be involved here?

5. Which *one* product do you think Leslie Saunders should recommend for L'Endanger Corp.? Explain why.

## REFERENCES

"Research Reveals How Marketers Can Win By a Nose," *Marketing News,* Feb. 4, 1991, p. 1; "Two Crucial Days in Scent Peddling," and "In Growth, It's a Man's World," *New York Times,* Dec. 23, 1990, p. F-5; "Our Most Mysterious Sense," *Parade,* June 10, 1990, p. 8;"The New Improved Unilever Aims to Clean Up in the U.S.," *Business Week,* Nov. 27, 1989, p. 102; "In Cosmetics, Marketing Cultures Clash," *Wall Street Journal,* Oct. 30, 1990, p. B-1; "Making Scents Of All Those Bottles," *Business Week Ad Supplement,* Oct. 20, 1989; "Firms Try to Flesh Out Sales of Tony Toiletries for Men," *Wall Street Journal,* Oct. 10, 1989, p. B-1; "Unilever is All Made Up, With Everywhere To Go," *Business Week,* July 31, 1989, p. B-5; "France's Bic Bets U.S. Consumers Will Go For Perfume on the Cheap," *Wall Street Journal,* Jan. 12, 1989, p. B4; "Revlon Buyers Incensed by Intimate Change," *Wall Street Journal,* Oct. 14, 1988, p. B-1; "Search is On For Emotion-Eliciting Scents," *Wall Street Journal,* Oct. 13, 1988 p. B-1; "Returning to Revlon's Glory Days," *New York Times,* Oct. 2, 1988, p. F-1; "Lauder, Hoping to Sell Men's Perfume in Japan, Looks for California Cachet," *Wall Street Journal,* Sep. 22, 1988, p. 44; "Trying to Make Scents of the Japanese Market," *Wall Street Journal,* Aug. 23, 1988, p. 23; "No Surprise: Modern Men Care About How They Look," *Marketing News,* Sep. 11, 1987, p. 18; "GC Technique Quantitates Odor-Active Substances in Food," *C&EN,* Sep. 28, 1987; "For Avon, Rodeo Drive is No Easy Street," *Business Week,* Dec. 28, 1987, p. 78; "The Make-Over at Estee Lauder," *New York Times Magazine,* Nov. 29, 1987, p. 32; "Creating Obsession and Making It Last," *New York Times,* Nov. 8, 1987, p. F-12; "Firms Push 'Aroma Therapy' to Treat Flat Fragrance Sales," *Wall Street Journal,* Mar. 20, 1986, p. 33; "Pheromones Discovered in Humans," *Washington Post,* Nov. 18, 1986 p. A-1; "Putting on a Renewed Face," *New York Times Magazine,* Oct. 26, 1986, p. 70; "Chemists Whip Up a Tasty Mess of Artificial Flavors," *Smithsonian Magazine,* May, 1986, p. 79. "Business Scents," *Washington Post,* Nov. 26, 1986, p. B-2.

## APPENDIX 5-1. PERFUME USE IN DIFFERENT CULTURES

Before 1800, perfumes were produced in tiny "laboratories" for small, affluent groups of people. Manufacture in bulk didn't begin until the 1800-50 period when companies were formed to provide larger quantities and to package the products, in response to increased demand.

The Victorian era, about 1850 to 1900, was noted for its austerity and strict morality. Those cultural qualities were reflected in the types of perfume used. They were predominately simple, based on natural flower essences. But perfume remained primarily a semiluxury item because of its high cost.

Along with the new era of technological development around the turn of the century, the way in which perfumes were presented became increasingly important. The name and package supplemented the perfumes themselves in the marketing process. After World War I came the emancipation of women, and the first of the great fashion designers arrived on the scene. Perfume was representative of their life-style and originality and became a true luxury product.

In the 1930s and 1940s, traditional perfumery houses lost their dominant position in the industry as the market sought greater individuality. This trend concentrated less on the floral base and more on perfume combinations. Around the mid-1950s, perfume products were well into the growth stage. The proliferation of products and the cost of launching new ones prohibited the positioning of fine perfumes solely for the elite. During this period and well through the 1960s, perfumery was primarily a French preserve. Although the number of fragrance producers was increasing in other countries, most of the world still looked to France for leadership.

Even so, the mass market was emerging in the United States where consumers' purchasing power was growing at a greater rate than in Europe. Avon, Max Factor, and Prince Matchabelli all offered what consumers wanted: medium-priced products, value for the money, performance rather than sophistication, and scents that were easier to "comprehend." This meant a return to familiar, strong fragrances with little originality—a "reassuring" product.

Beginning in the early 1970s, the U.S. perfume producers began to move away from French leadership and to develop products designed to capture their own prestige market. Yves de Chris of Naarden International Fragrance Center in Paris observed, "American designers were never able to impart, by their names alone, their tastes and ideas into [the U.S.] fragrance market." In part, this was because the American woman had begun to consolidate her status and, above all, her individuality. The success of tomorrow's products will be increasingly dependent on the quality of the concept developed and the fidelity of its translation into fragrance advertising, packaging, and color scheme—in other words, "a total package."

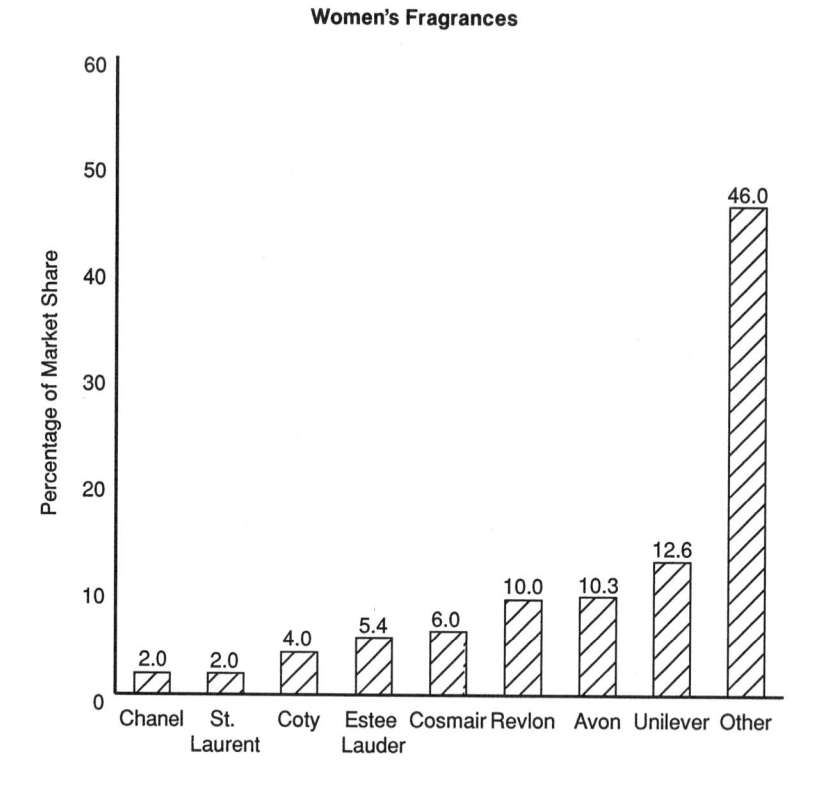

## THE NEW FRAGRANCE INDUSTRY
### EXHIBIT 5-1
#### Market Share: U.S. Fragrance Market, 1990
#### Women's Fragrances

| Company | Percentage of Market Share |
|---|---|
| Chanel | 2.0 |
| St. Laurent | 2.0 |
| Coty | 4.0 |
| Estee Lauder | 5.4 |
| Cosmair | 6.0 |
| Revlon | 10.0 |
| Avon | 10.3 |
| Unilever | 12.6 |
| Other | 46.0 |

## THE NEW FRAGRANCE INDUSTRY
### EXHIBIT 5-2
### Market Share: U.S. Fragrance Market, 1990
#### Men's Fragrances

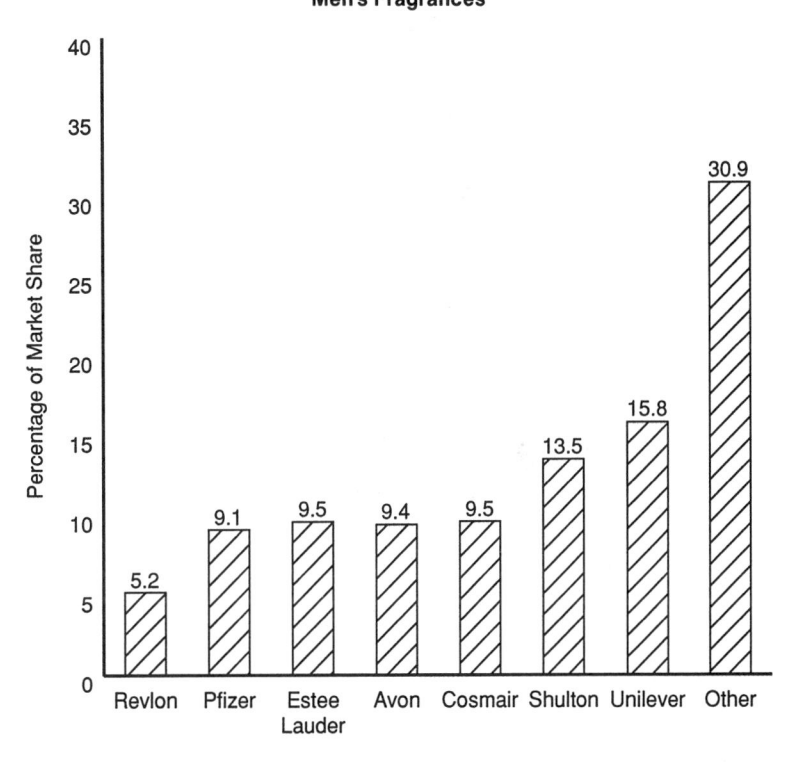

| Company | Percentage of Market Share |
|---|---|
| Revlon | 5.2 |
| Pfizer | 9.1 |
| Estee Lauder | 9.5 |
| Avon | 9.4 |
| Cosmair | 9.5 |
| Shulton | 13.5 |
| Unilever | 15.8 |
| Other | 30.9 |

**THE NEW FRAGRANCE INDUSTRY**
**EXHIBIT 5-3**
**Example of Men's Perfume Ad**

**EXHIBIT 5-4** Ptisenbon Children's Ad

# CASE SIX

# JACK DANIEL'S OLD TIME DISTILLERY

Every year, nearly a quarter of a million visitors trek to a tiny village (population 668) in a valley at the edge of the Cumberland mountains of Tennessee. They come to see the legendary Jack Daniel's distillery, founded by Jasper N. (Jack) Daniel in 1886, the oldest distillery registered in the United States.

**EARLY HISTORY**

Jack's grandfather, Joseph Daniel, was born in England before the Revolutionary War. In his early twenties, he became the coachman for the wealthy Calaway family and, in a storybook romance, fell in love with the young Elizabeth (Bettie) Callaway. In the face of stern opposition from her family, the couple eloped and shortly afterward sailed for America.
   Joseph served for a time in the revolutionary army, then the family lived for many years in New Burn, North Carolina, before moving to Franklin County, Tennessee. Their eighth child, Callaway Daniel, grew up there and married Lucinda Cook, who became the mother of ten children. The last of these, Jasper Newton (Jack) Daniel, was born just five months before Lucinda's death in 1847.

## THE YOUNG JACK

Several years later, Callaway Daniel remarried a younger woman, Matilda Van-Zant. It was on the occasion of his sixth birthday that Jasper Newton realized he was getting rather tired of being the "runt" of the family. On top of that, he had a few problems getting along with his new stepmother. After mulling over these difficulties in his six-year-old mind, "Jackie-Boy," as he was called, talked them over with his brothers and sisters and decided he would go to live with "Uncle" Felix's family who lived a mile or two over the hill. The two families mutually agreed that Jack would stay in Felix Waggoner's household for a while. Jack quickly made himself useful doing household chores and learning to ride horseback. He pulled his small weight in the home and got along well with the two young Waggoner daughters.

## THE MAKING OF A BUSINESSMAN

In September 1853, at a party Felix's family gave for Jack's seventh birthday, a young man named Daniel Houston Call was riding by the farm and stopped in to join the party. Call, at the age of 17, was already one of the most promising men of the community. He had inherited several hundred acres of good farmland and a country store and managed both quite well. He also made whiskey for sale at the store, but he did not allow drinking at the store or in his home.

Call noticed Jack playing in the yard and inquired about him. "Uncle" Felix described Jack as a lively youngster and "smart as a whip." Call thought a while and said, "I could sure use a boy like that at home and at the store. My wife is plumb tuckered out at night, doing chores and tending the baby. I wonder if Jack could live with them for a while. I'll pay him, of course, and he can learn about the business and how things are done in the outside world." Felix put the proposition to Jack, who was quite excited and accepted willingly.

## EARLY EDUCATION

During the following year, Mary Jane Call taught Jack to do basic arithmetic using coins at the store, to read words in the Bible, to write, and to be strictly honest. Jack also coerced Call into letting him work part-time learning the still operation, saying, "I don't mind chores at the house and running errands at the store, but I want to learn new things all the time. I'm little, and 'Uncle' Felix said I would always be little. I've got to make up for my littleness by being smarter in other things." This was a rather long and knowing statement for a seven-year-old.

## THE DISTILLING BUSINESS

Jack spent as much time as he could at the still, learning the slow and painstaking process of making a first-class whiskey. He was careful to save almost all the $10.00 a month he was paid, and he soon owned two mules and a high-backed wagon. He and "Button" Waggoner, a boy his age and a cousin to Felix, used them to peddle jugs of whiskey to nearby country stores.

When Jack was 13, an evangelist preaching whiskey prohibition visited the local church where Call was a lay preacher. After hearing a few of his fiery sermons reciting case histories of the evils of alcohol, Mary Jane Call and the congregation urged Call to abandon the still and stop selling whiskey at the store.

The result of all this was that, at the age of 13, Jack Daniel became the owner of Call's still, the largest in the area. Call offered it to Jack with liberal credit terms, but there was no ready market for its full output. Before he made any plans, Jack called on "Uncle" Felix for advice, which went something like this, "You can't be really successful just running a little country still. The government will control this business soon because of taxes, and the little business won't stand a chance. You also need to be close to transportation. You have to sell your product away from home to be profitable." Jack decided to take on the challenge.

## THE CIVIL WAR YEARS

Leaving three slaves who had run the still for Call to keep up production, Jack and Button began to make frequent trips to Huntsville Alabama, 50 miles away. In their high-backed wagon, they carried cured meat and whiskey. This became a profitable business and helped considerably to pay off Jack's debt to Dan Call. When the Northern Army moved in to hold Huntsville, the wagon trips continued although the risk was considerably greater and the product had to be concealed under hay and other farm products.

At the war's end, 18-year-old Jack moved the old equipment to a location near Lynchburg, Tennessee, called Cave Spring. The water from this spring was almost completely free of minerals—the type that makes the best whiskey. And its temperature was a constant 56 degrees, perfect for the special charcoal mellowing process.

## THE PROCESS

Jack Daniel was set on making the best whiskey possible and made it mostly from corn, with rye and barley malt. Whiskey is made in batches, and the old "yeasting back" process was used which meant that instead of starting each run from "scratch," a part of the mash from the previous run was used to start each new one. This is also known as the "sour-mash batch." Jack also used a traditional leaching process to smooth the new-made whiskey after it came from the still. It took about 12 days longer than most processes used at the time for whiskey to seep, drop-by-drop, through vats packed with hard maple charcoal. This "Lincoln County" process, together with the pure and constant-temperature water, produced an exceptionally mellow product, and its reputation spread throughout the area. Since the leaching removes the characteristic aroma and taste of "bourbon" whiskey, Jack Daniel's must be called Tennessee Sour Mash Whiskey. (See Case 23, The Merriwether Distillery.)

Although the federal government began a plan to tax and regulate all whiskey distilleries in 1860, it did not enforce the rules until 1866, when Jack Daniel's became the first registered distillery in the United States. Jack ran the business profitably, although the product was just one of many brands, without any particular niche in the market.

## LEM MOTLOW APPEARS

In June 1887, Jack's nephew, Lem Motlow, appeared at the office. "Uncle Jack, I want a job," he said. Having just finished the course at Lynchburg Normal Academy, he was dressed in overalls and carried all his clothes in a bundle tied to a stick over his right shoulder. He was given the jobs of slopping the hogs, attending to the cattle, and cutting cordwood.

But Lem had considerable native intelligence and a mathematical genius with the ability to add a long column of figures, up to four digits each, after just a momentary glance. In two years, he moved to the distillery office and four years later, he assumed the duties of manager.

Jack Daniel never married, so there were no children to carry on the business. In 1907, he deeded the distillery to his cousin Dick Daniel and to Lem Motlow. Dick later sold his share to Lem. As the story goes, Jack lost his temper one day and gave a powerful kick to the old office safe. For a while, he limped a little, but eventually the bruise became infected and he died six years later.

## THE LEM MOTLOW ERA

Lem was an excellent businessman, fair and generous. During the Prohibition era, from 1920 to 1933, he started a mule auction business, and Lynchburg became one of the largest mule-trading centers in the South. The distillery produced whiskey again until 1942 when the government required the company to make pure alcohol for military use.

Lem Motlow died in 1947 and the distillery passed on to his four sons. The oldest, Reagor, who had been general manager under his father, became president and the other three managed various operations and became known as the "shirtsleeve" brothers. Production increased, and the quality reputation was enhanced.

In the 1950s, the tax on whiskey in storage had to be paid before the product was sold. This required heavy cash investments, especially when the future sale price could vary widely. Also, there was a potential complex inheritance tax problem when any one of the brothers died. For these reasons, the Motlows sold the distillery to the Brown-Forman Co. in Louisville in 1956. The new owners made few changes, and the brothers continued to run the business for many years.

## TODAY'S MARKETING AND PROMOTION STRATEGY

Nearly 40 years ago, Jack Daniel's was just another brand in the group of U.S. premium whiskeys. It was then that the firm began its rustic ad campaign that portrayed the slow-paced, rustic life of the rural South, pursued it relentlessly, and transformed the product into a fast-lane seller.

Advertising is restrained. It uses a low-key, soft sell with black and white photography in print media. Real people are featured in the ads instead of actors and models or artists' conceptions. The copy is conversational with family-album glances into the charcoal mellowing process, along with bits of historical information. This consistent theme has built up an emotional involvement with the consumer and created an image of honesty and believability that is unique in the distilled spirits industry. Examples of the advertisements are shown in Exhibits 6–1 and 6–2. Note that in Exhibit 1, the ad suggests you "Drop us a line and tell us something about yourself."

### Reaching Target Markets

The primary advertising target is males 21 to 49 with household income over $35,000. Magazines delivering those demographics are the primary print media, although newspapers and outdoor boards are used in areas without adequate magazine coverage. Twenty new ads are created each year and the campaign runs in 80 magazines, but the same ad never runs twice in any one magazine. The current ad budget is about $5 million.

Promotion has always been a major part of Jack Daniel's strategy. Support of civic and service organizations, sponsorship of charities and participation in the National Trust for the Preservation of Historic Sites are examples of the company's activities. Another successful promotion has been the Jack Daniel Silver Cornet Band, a recreation of one formed by Jack Daniel himself in 1894. The band tours the United States regularly and has performed at the White House, in Disneyland, and on major television shows.

The Tennessee Squire Association was originated by the company as a noncommercial method of keeping in contact with Jack Daniel fans worldwide, as was the Ambassador's Program, a series of radio and TV interviews by Jack Daniel personnel. Dave Fulmer, leader of the Cornet band, and Lynne Tolley, manager of Bobo's Boarding House in Lynchburg, are two such ambassadors.

The personal contact with distillery tour visitors is a major part of the public relations image effort. Advertising invites consumers to visit Lynchburg, and the town is maintained in an old-fashioned motif. Slow-talking old-time employees escort visitors through the town and distillery with a series of one liners: "Last summer it was so dry I saw a bush chasing a dog."

The company uses direct mail extensively and sells a number of items carrying the Jack Daniel logo through regular gift shops nationwide. It also promotes the product through exposure in television and motion picture scripts, as well as in stories, books, and cases such as this one.

Decorative in-store promotions, bin signs, dealer incentives, and theme displays are used extensively. On-premise support in clubs, bars, and restaurants is mostly in the form of seasonal drinks such as "Lunchburg Lemonade" and "Tennessee Mud." Cooking with Jack Daniel's is also featured periodically by food and beverage editors in newspapers and magazines.

## THE PRODUCT

For many years, Jack Daniels made only two nationally marketed products, Black Label at 90, 86, and 80 proof, and Green Label at 80 proof. The alcoholic strength of whiskey is double its percentage of alcohol. Pure alcohol is 200 proof, and Green Label at 80 proof contains half that figure, or 40 percent alcohol.

In 1988, the distillery introduced Gentleman Jack, a new and completely different product from Jack Daniel's. It has its own unique formula and goes through the charcoal mellowing process twice. Both it and Green Label use selected distribution to a few domestic states while Black Label is sold throughout the United States and in over 100 foreign markets. Annual sales of all Jack Daniel's brands are about three million cases, with estimated revenue about $450 million, over one-third of the total sales of the parent company. Recent income statements of Brown Forman are shown in Exhibit 6-3. Competitive brands are not only all other bourbon and other types of whiskey, but *all* distilled spirits of similar type and price, both domestic and imported.

## THE COMPANY LEGACY

The rustic image, and the legend of Jack Daniel's early life, give the brand a crucial identity and differentiate it from other premium bourbons that may taste about the same. Year after year overwhelmingly male consumers reach for this "moonshine-related" brand that capitalizes on its hillbilly background.

## CASE ANALYSIS QUESTIONS

1. What aspect of U.S. culture is involved in the success of the Jack Daniel's Co.? Why is the "early history" important here?
2. How do consumer perception and involvement operate in maintaining the Jack Daniel's image and the product?
3. Since the company uses mainly black-and-white and old-time photos, why does it depend mainly on magazines for ad exposure? What is the advantage of never running the same ad twice in the same magazine?
4. Why does Jack Daniel's depend so heavily on promotion? How does this method help reach the target market, if that is its purpose?

## REFERENCES

Gowen, Edward (1954), "Sippin' Whiskey and the Shirtsleeve Brothers," *True Magazine*, p. 2-8; Green, Ben A., (1967), *Jack Daniel's Legacy*, Shelbyville, TN., Rich Co.; Bigger, Jeanne R. (1972), "Jack Daniel Distillery and Lynchburg: A Visit to Moore County, Tennessee," *Tennessee Historical Quarterly;* "Jack Daniel's Hopes the Other Guy's Liquor is Quicker," *Wall Street Journal*, May 18, 1990, p. B-2; Brown-Forman Corp., *Annual Report,* 1989, Louisville, KY, June 12, 1989. *Jack Daniel Distillery,* Information pamphlets: "Distillery Tours," "Brand History," "Tennessee Whiskey," "Historical Sketch," and "The Jack Daniel Character." undated.

**JACK DANIEL'S OLD TIME DISTILLERY**

**EXHIBIT 6-1   Example of Image Ad**

Are you a Jack Daniel's drinker? If so, drop us a line and tell us something about yourself.

A NEW MAN at Jack Daniel Distillery has a lot of listening and learning to do.

Sadly, the special skills of making old time whiskey have all but disappeared these days. But our own Jack Daniel Distillery pursues its ways of the past—mellowing each drop through hard maple charcoal burned right here on distillery grounds. Here, old hands have always taken care to guide new generations. And after a sip of Jack Daniel's, you'll know why we've kept it like that.

SMOOTH SIPPIN'
TENNESSEE WHISKEY

Tennessee Whiskey • 40-43% alcohol by volume (80-86 proof) • Distilled and Bottled by Jack Daniel Distillery, Lem Motlow, Proprietor, Route 1, Lynchburg (Pop 361), Tennessee 37352
*Placed in the National Register of Historic Places by the United States Government.*

**JACK DANIEL'S OLD TIME DISTILLERY**

**EXHIBIT 6-2   Example of Image Ad**

Consider this an invitation to visit our distillery sometime soon. We'd like to meet you.

VISITORS ALWAYS COMMENT on the sawmill at Jack Daniel's and wonder why on earth we need one.

The reason is that every drop of Jack Daniel's is smoothed through hard maple charcoal. (Mainly, that's how it gains its uncommon rareness). And the sawmill is where we buy, stack and burn our maple to char. Of course, other distillers don't take all this time and trouble. So no other distiller has a building so named. Nor, we believe, a whiskey so rare.

SMOOTH SIPPIN'
TENNESSEE WHISKEY

Tennessee Whiskey • 40-43% alcohol by volume (80-86 proof) • Distilled and Bottled by Jack Daniel Distillery, Lem Motlow, Proprietor, Route 1, Lynchburg (Pop 361), Tennessee 37352
Placed in the National Register of Historic Places by the United States Government.

## JACK DANIEL'S
## EXHIBIT 6-3
### Income Statements: Jack Daniel's Parent Corp., Brown-Forman

| | YEAR ENDED APRIL 30, | | |
|---|---|---|---|
| *(Expressed in thousands except per share amounts)* | 1989 | 1988 | 1987 |
| Net Sales | $1,287,079 | $1,354,598 | $1,404,465 |
| Excise taxes | 281,298 | 288,010 | 306,355 |
| Cost of sales | 433,735 | 510,763 | 534,689 |
| Gross profit | 572,046 | 555,825 | 563,421 |
| Selling, advertising, administrative, and general expenses | 363,566 | 364,141 | 381,295 |
| Operating income | 208,480 | 191,684 | 182,126 |
| Gain before income taxes on sale of Martell marketing rights in 1989 and ArtCarved in 1988 | 36,000 | 33,581 | — |
| Interest income | 6,172 | 1,513 | 1,814 |
| Interest expense | 24,821 | 18,399 | 22,125 |
| Nondeductible write-down of intangible assets | — | 33,000 | — |
| Income before taxes | 225,831 | 175,379 | 161,815 |
| Taxes on income: | | | |
| Taxes on operations | 67,668 | 60,373 | 72,231 |
| Taxes on sale of Martell marketing rights and ArtCarved | 13,666 | 16,875 | — |
| Nonrecurring tax benefit | — | (5,268) | — |
| Total taxes on income | 81,334 | 71,980 | 72,231 |
| Net income | $ 144,497 | $ 103,399 | $ 89,584 |
| Earnings per common share | $ 5.15 | $ 3.25 | $ 2.78 |

Source: Company records

# CASE SEVEN

# THE NEW L. L. BEAN

L. L. Bean was founded in 1912 by Maine hunter Leon L. Bean, who wanted to supply the "latest and best quality sporting equipment to sportsmen." "L. L." as he was called, grew up in the western Maine hills in the late 1800s. Orphaned at the age of 12, he worked on relatives' farms and made enough money from trapping to attend Kent's Hill Academy, supporting himself there by selling soap door-to-door. Afterward, he worked at various sales jobs but never stayed in one place long enough to get established. He did, however, develop a lifelong passion for hunting and fishing. The year 1907 found him near 40 years old, clerking for $12 a week in his brother's men's wear store in Freeport, Maine, where the L. L. Bean store is now situated.

A dedicated hunter, he couldn't stay out of the woods. On his frequent deer hunting trips, L.L. couldn't seem to find boots that would protect his feet in the damp, cold, Maine winters. He used the "sure-footed" leather boots that were popular in the early 1900s, but moisture seeped in so his feet were chilly and soggy. He tried rubber boots, but they were uncomfortable and gave poor footing. Discouraged with the available products, he designed a pair of boots combining lightweight leather uppers attached to rubber overshoe bottoms and had a local shoemaker sew the two together to make them both dry and comfortable to wear. L.L. had several more pairs made for his hunting group, who were delighted with them and encouraged him to manufacture the new boots for sale to others. Thus, the Maine Hunting Shoe and L. L. Bean, Inc., were born.

In 1912, he began the boot-making enterprise like a seasoned businessman. He was able to get a list of all holders of Maine hunting licenses and set up a manufacturing shop in his brother Erwin's basement. He mailed a printed brochure to all the names on the list. A copy of the brochure is shown in Exhibit 7–1. If he didn't get an order in a reasonable time, he sent a follow-up letter. A copy of one of the original letters is shown in Exhibit 7–2. Orders soon began to trickle in, but many of the first 100 were returned because the tops and bottoms came apart. The brochure offered money back if not satisfied and, true to his word, L. L. refunded the full purchase price. This early lesson taught him the need to personally test all his products and to keep customers satisfied at all costs.

He borrowed some money, perfected the bottom seal, and mailed more brochures. Consumers were captivated by the genuine enthusiasm and common-sense logic of his advertising appeal, so success had to come. Convinced of the potential of mail order marketing, L. L. began to expand by moving into his own building as soon as he was financially able. He resolved never to go into debt again, and from then on, company growth was always financed with retained earnings.

By 1924, he had added hand-knit socks and a few other hunting items to his line. There were 24 people working in the factory, producing sales of $135,000 a year. Fishing and camping equipment further extended the line in 1927.

## ADVERTISING AND CONSUMER SATISFACTION

The critical elements were word-of-mouth advertising and consumer satisfaction. His message was in the ever-expanding catalog: "We consider our customers a part of our organization and want them to make any criticism they see fit in regard to our merchandise or service." One employee remarked about L.L., "When he found out one of his products had failed, he would storm around the factory looking for the cause. Then he would write to the customer, refund the money, enclose a gift, invite the customer on a fishing trip, or do anything else necessary to make things right." Although L.L. didn't stint on the quality of merchandise, he had at least one pet economy. For years, customer inquiries were answered on the backs of letters, circulars, and bills the company got in its own mail.

The business was incorporated in 1934, and sales passed the $1 million mark in 1937, despite the Great Depression. In 1951, L.L. began his world-famous business hours; 24 hours a day, 365 days a year. They are still in effect today.

## THE END OF AN ERA

In 1961, L.L.'s grandson, Leon A. Gorman, was hired. He came with a liberal arts degree and four years' experience on a Navy destroyer, but L.L. "always had a soft spot in his heart for unemployed relatives," according to Gorman. In 1967, L. L. Bean died at the age of 94, and his style of management passed with him. At the time of his death, the company had fallen into the doldrums. During the Christmas rush, elderly clerks filling rush orders ambled slowly into the confusion of a systemless stockroom. They often stopped to pass the time of day, deliberating about the weather or deer hunting. Eventually they returned with a pair of Maine Hunting Boots or a chamois shirt. The catalog was out of date and sales were flat.

## MODERNIZING THE BUSINESS

Leon Gorman quickly picked up the reins of the business which now employed 200 people, mailed out 600,000 catalogs and had sales of $4.75 million. Total sales from 1924 on are shown in Exhibit 7–3.

Gorman also led the firm's response to the consumer movement of the late 1960s. Newer consumers wanted a number of attributes in Bean's products: lighter weight, longer wear, extra comfort, more safety, higher performance, easier care, and easier maintenance. Under Gorman's direction, each item in the product lines was reviewed and altered whenever possible to reflect the new consumer requirements.

## A NEW MERCHANDISE STRATEGY

During the 1970s, L. L. Bean prospered as a supplier of Shetland sweaters, tweed coats, and whale-design ties to what was called the "Preppie" fashion market. Like other fads, preppies, as a market, disappeared in the early 1980s, so the huge mail order retailer scrambled for a new merchandise strategy.

Unfortunately, this abandonment of Bean's mainstay fashions by the market came at a time when the catalog business was beginning to feel the first pangs of a shakeout. Many small firms were entering the market, attracted by profits and the low cost of entry. At the same time, consumers were being inundated by hundreds of undifferentiated catalogs featuring undifferentiated merchandise.

## COMPETENT MANAGEMENT

L. L. Bean, however, is a well-managed firm carrying highly specialized, quality merchandise, with a reputation for excellent service and for paying the postage on all shipments to customers. Its managers are also masters of inventories and mailing lists. Despite all the friendly, Maine woods, down-east images of the specialized catalogs and the Maine accents of telephone order takers, the company is run by a lot of MBAs. There are also computers and a few ex-executives of Sears, Spiegels, and other top merchandisers.

## MAILING LISTS AND CATALOGS

Unique and precise manipulation of mailing lists is one of Bean's keys to success. It is accomplished by entering names, addresses, and other information from rented lists or records of past customers into computers. Data from each name, such as age, zip code, and so on, are matched with likely purchases, and appropriate catalogs are sent. For example, a male aged 30 to 40 living in a zip code with a median income of $50,000 may be sent the sports clothing catalog in addition to the general one. The lists are updated each time a purchase is made and analyzed for frequency and size of the orders. If a name has not placed an order for two or three years, it is automatically dropped from the list.

Bean now mails more than 90 million catalogs to the active list names, in 22 different specialty groups. Most of its exponential growth has come from catalogs mailed to customers targeted by this detailed list analysis, and these sales account for 90 percent of the company's total sales. In 1979, Bean mailed seven different catalogs, 20 million times. In 1989, there were 116 million mailings of 23 different catalogs. These repeat mailings are part of its strategy and have paid off handsomely in additional orders.

Each individual catalog generates an average of $5.07 in sales, and many catalog retailers would break even with as little as $1.25 per mailing. Those Bean customers who do respond to catalogs spend about $67 per order, somewhat lower than other sporting and apparel mail retailers. Eddie Bauer, a subsidiary of Spiegel, realizes about $100 per order, but Bean makes up for its lower rate by volume; well over 9 million orders a year. And high volume is needed because profit margins are slim on many items.

## MERCHANDISE POLICY

Bean seldom makes changes in its lines. Its chamois shirt and Maine hunting shoes, for example, are mainstays, having led the best seller list for over 60 years. Along with a number of other items, these perennial sellers help the company to control inventory and mailing costs. They also give Bean an advantage over competitors who must update their lines frequently.

Over 99 percent of all orders are filled correctly, and the average time for filling orders was cut from seven days five years ago to a little over three days today. And its budgets are controlled as tightly as other costs. In a recent year, the company came within $20,000 of predicting the total mailing budget of more than $18 million.

## A DIFFERENT STRATEGY

With this background, and faced with the demise of its Preppie business, Bean's management considered, but rejected, a shift into different lines to capture some newly emerging market. Instead, the company decided upon an approach that downplayed its trendiest lines in favor of the traditional sellers. It also beefed up its services by adding a toll-free telephone order number, streamlining the order operations, and expanding the catalog mailing lists. As a result, 1988 sales were about $500 million, or 20 percent more than in the previous year. Some general information about the company is shown in Exhibit 7–4.

## RETURN RATES AND SLOWER GROWTH

In mid-1990, Bean decided its strategy would be to slow its growth to around 7 percent a year, down from the 23 percent it has experienced over the past ten years. Slower growth, according to Bean's president Leon Gorman, will allow the company to concentrate on its major problem: Customers returned $82 million worth of goods in 1989, or 14 percent of the $588 million total sales. The returns also cost upward of $2 million to mail the original order, as well as to send back the right items, since the company paid all postage. About 65 percent of the returns were for wrong sizes. In the spring of 1991, however, the company announced that it would make a flat postage and mailing charge of $3.50 per address, per order—a startling departure from the traditional, "postage paid" policy.

Nevertheless, 14 percent is the one of the lowest return rates in the mail order retail business, where about 15 to 18 percent of the merchandise is returned. To help customers get the right fit the first time, Bean is establishing uniform sizes for both vendors and customers, as well as updating size information in catalogs and in its own order takers' computers. There were other problems with vendor's shipments in addition to sizes. Not long ago a supplier delivered 999 pairs of dark green rubber boots. But Bean had ordered light green with a narrower heel and toe, as pictured in the catalog. Another problem experienced by all catalog retailers is from customers called "bracketters," who order three of the same item in different sizes or colors. After trying them on, they return two.

Very few products are returned because of defects, but several years ago the yoke on several of its Oxford shirts ripped. Bean recalled the entire lot of 25,000 but only a small number were sent back. The company, however, still mailed every buyer a new shirt free.

Today, Bean is retraining 3,200 employees in the use of new techniques to improve customer service and quality, as well as vendor performance.

## A FRIENDLY UNCLE

Quality products and easy returns are very nice, but what really sets L. L. Bean apart is the way customers feel about the company. It's as though Bean were an odd but amiable uncle up in the Maine woods who sends packages. People mail pictures showing themselves decked out in Bean clothes. They chat with order takers on the phone, wondering what Bean thinks about sending their teenager to Outward Bound. (They like it.) What should they take? (Bean has a list.) A California customer once called wondering what to name his Scottie pup. The department got together and called him back suggesting Chivas Regal or Blue Belle. And in 1984, a couple walked into the store with a justice of the peace and were married on the main stairway landing!

Often, Bean's employees meet anxious vacationers at the nearest Maine Turnpike toll booths to deliver outdoor equipment to them. Some years ago, L. L. Bean himself drove a truck 500 miles to New York, delivering a canoe to a customer who needed it in a hurry. "Costly service like this," commented one of Bean's consultants, "will certainly continue. It's a great way to keep a customer for life, and the word gets around fast." The Nordstrom Department Stores have gained nationwide attention because of the quality and consistency of their service. L. L. Bean has achieved the same reputation, but along with it is a close, friendly customer relationship.

## CASE ANALYSIS QUESTIONS

1. Unlike many catalog retailers, L. L. Bean has not opened retail stores in other locations. In terms of consumer perception, why do you think Bean has elected not to expand this way?

2. Sales of other catalogers, such as the giant Lands End, have declined because they have failed to follow current trends in apparel styles. Considering this, what do you think about L. L. Bean's "return to the basic products"? Was this a good move or not?

3. What degree of "involvement" do Bean's customers have with the company? Why is this important to Bean and how does the company develop it?

4. Although Bean has a lower return rate than other catalogers, it is trying to reduce it still further. Why is this rate of more concern to them? How does it relate to Bean's service image?

## REFERENCES

"King Customer: At Companies that Listen Hard and Respond Fast, Bottom Lines Thrive," *Business Week,* Mar. 12, 1990, p. 88; "L. L. Bean Scales Back Expansion Goals to Ensure Pride in Its Service is Valid," *Wall Street Journal,* June 18, 1989, p. B-8; "Shop-by-Mail Industry is Facing a Shakeout," *Washington Post,* Nov. 4, 1988, p. 1; *A Passion for Excellence,* T. Peters and N. Austin, New York, Random House, 1985, p. 95; *L. L. Bean, Inc., Outdoor Specialties by Mail from Maine,* Address by L.A. Gorman, New York, The Newcomen Society in North America, 1981. Company records, catalogs, news releases, public relations material. Used by permission, 1991.

## THE NEW L. L. BEAN
### EXHIBIT 7-1
#### Bean Hunting Shoe Brochure

Weight Only 31 Ounces (the pr.)

# MAINE HUNTING SHOE

Outside of your gun, nothing is so important to your outfit as your foot-wear. You cannot expect success hunting deer or moose if your feet are not properly dressed.

The Maine Hunting Shoe is designed by a hunter who has tramped Maine woods for the past eighteen years. They are light as a pair of moccasins with the protection of a heavy hunting boot. The vamps are made of the very best gum rubber money will buy. The tops ($7\frac{1}{2}$ in. high) are soft tan willow calf that never grow hard by wetting and drying. Leather inner soles keep the feet off the rubber and prevent "drawing" that is so objectionable with most rubber shoes.

Skeleton cork-filled heels keep the shoes from slipping and make them much more comfortable to one accustomed to wearing shoes with heels.

For those hunters who go just before the first snow it is next to impossible to find footwear that is adapted to both bare ground and snow hunting. The Maine Hunting Shoe is perfect for both. For bare ground, its extreme light weight and leather inner soles keep it from drawing the feet while the rubber soles keep it from slipping. For snow, by using a heavier stocking, you have warm light, dry footwear that is ideal for still hunting.

The light weight friction lining makes them easy to dry as a dish. Just roll down the the leather tops, set them where it is warm and they are dry in ten minutes.

With every pair we give a small repair outfit that we warrant to mend a cut or snag in five minutes.

For all-round hunting purposes there is not a shoe on the market at any price equal to the Maine Hunting Shoe. See guarantee tag that is attached to every pair.

Price $3.50 delivered on approval anywhere in the U. S.

## L. L. BEAN,
**MANUFACTURER**
### FREEPORT, ME.

## THE NEW L. L. BEAN

### EXHIBIT 7-2

**Copy of Early Bean Follow-Up Letter**

---

Freeport, Me.
Oct. 5, 1912.

F.N.Sawyer,
 21 Chesnut St.,
 Wakefield, Mass.

Dear Sir:-

Recently I sent you circular of my Maine Hunting Shoe. As I have not received your order I take the liberty of again calling your attention to my shoe. I am receiving so many compliments from all over the states that I am sure the shoe would please you and am willing to send you a pair on approval. Below are some of the good points not to be found on any other hunting shoe.

1st. Weight, lightest shoe made.
2nd. Leather Innersoles.
3rd. Made in whole and half sizes for both men and women also in F and E widths.
4th. Cork filled heels that keep them from slipping.
5th. Price, lowest of any sporting shoe on the market.
6th. A printed guarantee with every pair.

I enclose order blank and envelope for your convenience.

Yours truly,
L L Bean

**THE NEW L. L. BEAN**

**EXHIBIT 7-3**

**Total Sales, 1924-91**

| Year | Total Sales |
|---|---|
| 1924 | $     135,000 |
| 1937 | 1,050,000 |
| 1967 | 4,750,000 |
| 1975 | 29,500,000 |
| 1979 | 77,700,000 |
| 1985 | 305,000,000 |
| 1986 | 350,000,000 |
| 1987 | 415,000,000 |
| 1988 | 500,000,000 |
| 1989 | 588,000,000 |
| 1990 | 644,000,000 |
| 1991 est. | 673,000,000 |

Source: Company records

## THE NEW L.L. BEAN
### EXHIBIT 7-4
### General Company Information, 1989

Catalogs

In 1989, 23 different catalogs printed and 116 million mailed. About 3.5 million people visited the retail store.

Distribution

| | |
|---|---|
| Packages Shipped | 11.3 million |
| Outbound Postage Cost | $22.6 million |

On the busiest shipping *week*, Bean sent 648,600 packages, enough to fill 192 truck trailers.

On the busiest day, it sent 133,700 packages.

| | |
|---|---|
| Inventory on hand, average | $135 million |
| Peak Inventory | $168 million |
| Total Items (including sizes) | 46,000 |

Telecommunications

Over 10.5 million incoming toll-free catalog order and customer service calls received. Phone bill $5.5 million.

Mail

4.4 million pieces of mail received.

Products

5,500 different items stocked.
84% of Bean's products come from the U.S.
94% of Bean's products carry the L. L. Bean label.
$44 million of sales came from products it manufactures.

Employment

| | |
|---|---|
| Peak Employment | 5,663 |
| Off-Peak Employment | 3,558 |

Total Space Occupied (all locations)

1,667,000 square feet

# CASE EIGHT

# NEPTUNE KITCHEN AND BATH REMODELERS, INC.

Ken Gunther, president of Neptune Remodelers, wondered what strategy would be best for his firm to follow in order to expand the business substantially from its 1990 volume. He knew that Neptune's two specialties constituted an $18 billion nationwide market in 1990 and promised continuing expansion. Mr. Gunther listed some of the major reasons why the remodeling industry was experiencing strong growth:

1. The cost of newly constructed homes is escalating.
2. The present stock of homes is getting older.
3. The rising number of resale homes leads to remodeling, a common activity when people move into an existing home.
4. The current generation of buyers wants homes to be "personal statements" and has discretionary income to make them so.
5. The average age of homeowners is increasing, and such owners tend to be more stable and less mobile and prefer to alter present homes to suit a new life-style.

**CHANGING STRATEGY**

Neptune had been a medium-sized family construction business specializing in completely gutting and remodeling groups of older, well-constructed row houses into "luxury town homes." This had been a highly profitable operation for some years, but the supply of raw properties adjacent to upscale residential areas was running out, as was the supply of buyers of the remodeled homes in the $300,000–$400,000 range.

The firm altered its strategy in 1989 by specializing in kitchen and bath remodeling as the overall real estate market declined in its marketing area, but it continued to find some town-house opportunities. Neptune's success in the new venture had been limited because it was not as well known as some of the many competitors. One industry analyst predicted, "As remodeling continues to account for an increasing share of the construction business, we will certainly see more contractors and builders entering the expanding market."

In the past, residential remodelers were small entrepreneurial firms, many of whom were neither stable nor dependable. They were smaller businesses and over 75 percent had sales of less than $1 million. Because of new demand, national companies are expanding into remodeling and the industry is more stable, but also more competitive.

Ken Gunther realized that doubling the kitchen-bath business would require more employees and additional capital, which might cause the family to lose control of the business. Neptune had 25 employees, permitting them to complete five to six jobs at a time. The firm also had a 2,500-square-foot showroom in a storefront warehouse in a suburb of Shawnee, a large mid-western industrial city where Neptune was located. Since Gunther hoped to move to a more accessible location in the future, the showroom was only partly finished and displayed only a few of the remodeling options. However, it did give credibility to the business and testified that Neptune was not a fly-by-night company.

With a number of family members in the operation, installers have a stake in high-quality work and are perfectionists, so Neptune has a good reputation with its customers. Gunther controls the entire remodeling operation from design to installation, since no subcontractors are used. Also, the firm has considerable experience in plumbing, an integral part of the kitchen-bath business, from its townhouse remodeling.

## NEPTUNE'S PRODUCT

The firm's product is specialized residential remodeling done by professional contractors. Current kitchen-bath design trends follow those in newly built homes where baths are larger, more luxurious, and dramatic. They use more natural light and newer ornate fixtures and are more than just functional spaces. Kitchens, too, are multifunctional and incorporate social as well as other activities.

## NEPTUNE'S CONSUMERS

A typical remodeling customer is married, 41 years old, works in a white collar job, and has one or two children. The home is a single-family, detached residence, built in the early 1960s, with about 1925 square feet of floor space, and a market value of $101,000. The family has lived there a median of 12 years and has a household income of $65,000. Remodeling is usually paid for in cash, and the remodeling firm is most likely to have been chosen on the basis of referrals from friends.

**THE CONSUMER DECISION PROCESS**

Remodeling is usually an extensive decision-making process, and the cost is similar to that of an average car. The first step consumers take is to recognize that they have a problem. It could be the need for another bathroom, the kitchen is outdated, or one or the other isn't functioning properly. The desire for a different aesthetic look or for statement-making may also be factors. Although cost plays a large part in the decision, consumers would rather remodel than move, unless a lack of overall space in the home is a problem.

Once the remodeling decision is made, consumers search for a contractor to fill their needs. An overwhelming proportion of them, about 75 percent, choose a builder or remodeler over individual subcontractors (e.g., plumbers, carpenters, electricians). Almost the same proportion, 72 percent, choose the company based on referrals from friends or neighbors, and this method is ten times more common than the yellow pages, the next most used method. Homeowners say that reliability, reputation, and quality work are more important factors in their decision than is price.

Most customers know what they want before selecting a firm. Nearly all, for example, ask for a specific type and brand of flooring product they have seen in magazines or in other homes. However, the younger customers are, the more likely it is that their ideas have come from friends.

**THE MARKET AREA**

The population of the Shawnee metropolitan area was 1.3 million in the 1990 census. In the past 20 years, the median age changed from 27.8 to 36.2 years, reflecting national trends, as well as the aging of the baby-boom generation, the increasing life span, and the decline in the national birth rate. In 1991, nearly a third of the Shawnee population was over 45 years of age, with the proportion expected to grow to 44 percent by 2010. By then, 16 percent will be age 65 or older. The age distribution in Shawnee is shown in Exhibit 8–1.

Single-family homes represent the largest group in Shawnee, with 55 percent single-family detached, and 22 percent single-family attached town houses. In 1991, about 76 percent of these housing units were owner-occupied, with a mean market value of $144,300. In 1990, there were about 246,000 housing units. Of the single-family detached units, over one-third were built before 1970.

A majority of the population is employed primarily in skilled or semi-skilled industrial jobs, with a very high percentage of working women, as shown in

Exhibit 8-2. Thus, the proportion of families with two or more wage earners is quite high. Exhibit 8-3 shows median incomes for Shawnee.

## MARKET SEGMENTS FOR REMODELING

Ken Gunther believed that the basis for market segmentation should be the purpose the customer wants to achieve by remodeling. Such segments would break down as follows:

### Finishing Remodelers

The overall condition of the property is the problem underlying the need for remodeling. The home owners are interested in adding a bathroom to an unfinished area, a large closet space, or in the basement. These properties are usually the newest and have basic plumbing already roughed in. Usually, town houses are in this segment, and some other remodeling work is already being done at the same time by the owner, such as adding a basement room. There is no typical age group in this segment.

### Replacement Remodelers

This type generally involves older homes and the remodeling of bathrooms and kitchens to replace older or deteriorating appliances, fixtures, cabinets, and floors that have exceeded their useful life. The customers are more concerned with replacement of the existing facilities with new standard items, rather than a lavish upgraded installation. Price is a strong consideration in the decision. Customers who are remodeling their long-term home tend to be upscale in age, while those remodeling a newly purchased, older home are likely to be in their mid- to upper thirties.

### Upgrade Remodelers

There are three subgroups in this category.

*Upgrader I* These are the youngest remodelers, 35 or less, who are upgrading their older, first home—the only one they could afford. They need to modernize an older kitchen or bath to make it more functional and reflective of their life-styles and tastes.

*Upgrader II* These consumers are 35 to 44 years of age. They want more expensive furnishings and are willing to pay for them. They want "designer" kitchens and baths that will make personal statements for them and improve the quality of their lives. They are two-income households who like their present home, so they are remodeling it rather than moving. The houses have appreciated considerably since they were purchased, and the customers believe that upgrading important features like the bath and kitchen will make them more marketable later on. People in this segment depend heavily on peer groups for their choice of design and remodeling firms.

*Upgrader III* These consumers are 55 or older and at the peak of their earning power, often retired military or government employees who have returned home to Shawnee. They are united with other retirees who have high disposable income and are willing to spend it on remodeling older houses in convenient locations. They no longer have college or other child-related expenses and plan to stay in their current house for a long period of time. They want to make their home a showplace and have dreamed for years of building or remodeling a house to reflect their own tastes.

## THE COMPETITIVE ENVIRONMENT

Ken Gunther knew that there were about 25 firms in the Shawnee area that were competitors in the kitchen-bath specialty market. Some firms remodeled only kitchens or baths; others did both as part of overall home improvement work, such as adding rooms. Gunther considered about nine of them to be stable, direct competitors. Even though he knew quite a bit about these competitors, some of the information was old, and much of it was either incomplete or based on his own "feelings." To find out more about the competition, Ken's wife and his secretary phoned the nine firms posing as potential customers and asked questions customers might normally ask about the firm's background, size, and capabilities. The two "researchers" also looked for ads from the nine competitors in local media. The results of this "survey" are found in Exhibit 8–4.

### Market Area

Each of the nine companies described its market area as the overall Shawnee area and suburbs, although two firms were located well outside this area. This description indicates that some firms are willing to travel considerable distances for work and also suggests there may be competitors other than the ones Mr. Gunther chose. Many of the nine firms are small, independent entrepreneurs such as those described earlier. However, one is owned by a lumberyard, and another by a construction company. Some started as remodelers while others expanded from backgrounds in plumbing, construction, or electrical work.

### Customer Types

The firms generally described their customer types as (1) those upgrading present facilities, (2) those replacing old facilities, and (3) those wanting to finish a basement by putting in a bath. The person who answered the telephone in most of the firms seemed to warm up considerably when a more lavish upgrade was mentioned.

### Self-Described Attributes

All the firms seemed to stress two major attribute groups in describing themselves. The first included experience in the business, the number of years they had been in business, and when it applied, family ownership. The second involved high quality work, products, and service. Only one firm mentioned low price as an attribute, while another said, "Price is not an issue. We are not the place to come if you are shopping around."

### Sources of Customers

All of the firms said they used the yellow pages as their major advertising medium, followed by co-op ads for manufacturer product lines in local newspapers and magazines. None mentioned television, radio, or other such media vehicles. Thus, advertising seems to create awareness that remodeling firms exist. However, as much as three quarters of the remodeling business comes from personal referrals, according to replies from the firms questioned.

## EVALUATION OF MARKET SEGMENTS

Neptune can select all of the market segments that have been identified, or some combination of them. Ken Gunther evaluated each of the segments as follows:

### Replacement Remodelers

These are quite similar to customers Neptune has dealt with in its previous work, and employees have the technical expertise and know-how to solve repair problems. But these customers are the hardest to find, since they seek remodeling help only when their problem surfaces. Although the age of the house is a good predictor, many owners of newer houses are also good prospects.

This type of work is risky for Neptune. Because of problems hidden in the walls, pipes, and drains of older houses, it is not easy to make estimates that assure a desirable margin. Also, this is a highly cost-conscious segment since its problems are often unexpected, and such home owners are more likely to want a quick and economical solution than a well-planned and designed one. Nonetheless, with careful estimating, this segment can be profitable fill-in work if customers can be located.

### Finishing Remodelers

These customers tend to seek Neptune out. Not only is the work less risky, but it is easier to do since installations are in newer houses. Also, the customers live mostly in developments with others who have similar needs, so they are a good source of referrals. This market has good expansion potential.

Finishing customers, however, are quite price sensitive because the recent home purchase consumed a large proportion of their assets. Competition is keen, but the work typically involves installing standard equipment, so the remodeler who can buy the fixtures and supply labor at the lowest cost has the edge. Neptune's margins are low, and the work requires little creativity from Neptune's staff. Margins are margins, however, and these jobs contribute to them.

### Upgrade Remodelers II

This segment (U-2s) promises the greatest profitability, because the 35–55-year-old consumers represent nearly half of the remodeling market. Yet, this segment has been a much smaller proportion of Neptune's work.

As their discretionary income grows, the U-2s are likely to expand their present homes because newer and larger housing is too expensive. It would also be more difficult to sell present homes at current prices.

Whatever the cause, this group seems to do a lot of upgrading. It also plans to spend more, with an average cost of more than twice that of some other age groups. U-2s want to add something to their life-style and to make their kitchens and baths look like those in their friends' homes. They will be interesting challenges to Neptune's staff creativity. Also, because of the wide age range of U-2s, there may be more remodeling jobs in the future.

Ken Gunther realized that one drawback is that Neptune has relatively little experience with this type of remodeling customer. As a group, they may be less impressed with the family-oriented aspect of the business. They are more concerned with "professional" credentials and attracted to trendy design centers.

### Upgrade Remodelers III

This is Neptune's current market, and salespeople intuitively recognize customers in this segment when they walk into the showroom. Neptune knows how to handle them, and they are comfortable in the family-owned atmosphere. Perhaps this is why they sought out the firm.

Gunther knew that this is, by far, the largest segment, mainly because it tends to remodel more often. Over one-third of all people seriously considering remodeling are 55 or over, and the highest proportion of bath remodeling is done by people 65 and over. It is also a stable segment that is likely to have occupied a home over 15 years, and fully one-third are 50 years or older. Ken Gunther believed that the length of time at the same address was an important factor in the decision process, and also that the houses undergoing U-3 remodeling were part of a cohesive neighborhood. But there are fewer people in this age group, and the probability of more than one remodeling job per customer is low.

## WHICH WAY TO GO?

He knew that every day he delayed planning a strategy for expanding the business meant the longer it would take to get it started. At the same time, more competition was entering the business, establishing referral contacts and "freezing" out Neptune. Having looked carefully at all the information at hand, he wondered what he should do.

## CASE ANALYSIS QUESTIONS

1. Using a Consumer Decision Model, briefly sketch and explain the decision process for the kitchen-bath product.
2. How does the Family Life Cycle apply to this case? How could Ken Gunther use it in analyzing his market?
3. What techniques of advertising, promotion, or interpersonal communication should Ken Gunther use to expand his business, based on information in the case?
4. Which target market(s) should Ken Gunther concentrate on in order to expand his business?

## REFERENCES

"Increasing Kitchen and Bath Remodeling Sales," B. Crossan, L. Linder, J. Loveland and C. Malacarne, School of Business Administration, George Mason University, April, 1990; "Remodeling Surge Promises New Opportunities, D. Delano, *Professional Builder,* Feb. 1990, p. 13; L. Levine, "Building Out in a Crowded Market," *New Dominion,* Mar. 1990, p. 46; "The Business of Remodeling is Hitting Home With Builders," *Washington Post,* Feb. 17, 1990, p. E16; "What do They Want: How Homeowners Plan to Remodel Their Houses," C. Farnsworth, *Professional Builder,* Sept. 1989, p. 83; "A Profile of the $82 Billion Remodeling Industry," *National Association of the Remodeling Industry,* 1990. "Remodeling," J. Fletcher and R. Binsacca, *Builder,* Dec., 1989, p. 79; "The Changing Home Building Industry," K. Baker, *Professional Builder,* Dec., 1989, p. 73; "Opportunities in the '90s," D. Heinly and D. McFeister, *Professional Builder,* Oct. 1989, p. 108; "A Flushing Success," *Washington Business Journal,* Oct., 1989, p. 48; "Survey Points the Way to Future Business," *Professional Builder,* Sept. 1989.

## NEPTUNE

### EXHIBIT 8-1

### Age Distribution of Persons 20 and Older in Shawnee Metropolitan Area

|      | AGES    |         |         |         |         |         |           |
|------|---------|---------|---------|---------|---------|---------|-----------|
| Year | 20–24   | 25–34   | 35–44   | 45–54   | 55–64   | 65+     | Total     |
| 1980 | 116,713 | 273,994 | 239,351 | 171,114 | 121,659 | 66,269  | 989,100   |
| 1985 | 137,345 | 314,928 | 325,941 | 197,206 | 126,332 | 99,498  | 1,201,250 |
| 1991 | 147,250 | 313,100 | 334,670 | 187,300 | 153,550 | 101,150 | 1,237,020 |
| 1980 | 11.8%   | 27.8%   | 24.3%   | 17.3%   | 12.3%   | 6.7%    | 100%      |
| 1985 | 10.6%   | 26.3%   | 27.3%   | 16.5%   | 10.6%   | 8.5%    | 100%      |
| 1991 | 11.9%   | 25.3%   | 27.0%   | 15.2%   | 12.4%   | 8.2%    | 100%      |

## NEPTUNE

### EXHIBIT 8-2

### Labor Force Participation Rates—Male and Female, Greater Shawnee Area

| Year | Male  | Female |
|------|-------|--------|
| 1950 | 82.9% | 28.2%  |
| 1960 | 84.4  | 32.5   |
| 1970 | 85.7  | 43.4   |
| 1980 | 85.3  | 62.5   |
| 1984 | 85.8  | 66.8   |
| 1986 | 85.7  | 71.7   |
| 1990 | 82.1  | 72.2   |

## NEPTUNE

## EXHIBIT 8-3

**Median Family and Household Income—Shawnee Area, 1979 to 1983**

| Year | Median Family Income | Median Household Income |
|---|---|---|
| 1979 | $23,300 | $21,750 |
| 1983 | 37,100 | 33,250 |
| 1984 | 41,100 | 35,300 |
| 1985 | 44,800 | 39,150 |
| 1986 | 46,200 | 42,200 |
| 1987 | 52,100 | 44,500 |
| 1988 | 55,400 | 46,100 |
| 1989 | 56,100 | 47,800 |
| 1990 | 59,350 | 49,700 |
| 1991 est. | 61,000 | 50,500 |
| 1992 est. | 62,350 | 51,300 |
| 1993 est. | 64,500 | 52,400 |

Family Income: Income of related individuals living together.
Household Income: Income of singles and/or unrelated individuals living together.

**NEPTUNE**

**EXHIBIT 8-4**

**General Replies to Questions from the Nine Competitive Firms**

*1. General Information*

| Firm | How long in Business (yrs.) | % of Kitchen-Bath Work | # Jobs in Past Year | No. of Employees |
|---|---|---|---|---|
| Quality Remodelers | 15 | 80% | 50 | 3: use subcontracts |
| Remodel Center | 15 | 100% | 55 | 3 |
| Siegel Specialties | 50 | 100%<br>60 bath<br>40 kitchen | 200 | 25 designers |
| Grogan Kitchens | 50 | 100% | 5000 builders' work | 17 designers |
| Kitchen-Bath Specialties | 12 | 100% | 400 | 4 designers |
| South Shawnee | 6 | 90% | 50+ | 11 designers and installers |
| Nu-Kitchen | 12 | 100% | 100–150 | 4 |
| Robertson | 23 | 90% | 150 | Parent Co. designs |
| J&W | 27 | 95% | 75 | 15 |

*2. How did your remodeling business start?*

| | |
|---|---|
| Quality Remodelers | Started as plumbing firm. Recently bought by a partnership and focus changed to kitchen-bath remodeling. |
| Remodel Center | Family business selling custom cabinets to builders. Built showroom, now sell direct to home owners. |
| Siegel Specialties | As a family plumbing firm. |
| Grogan Kitchens | As a family business specializing in kitchens and baths. |
| Kitchen-Bath Speciallty | As an offshoot of a family-owned business, the Shawnee Lumber & Supply Co. |
| South Shawnee | As a family-owned electrical firm doing electrical work in kitchens. |
| Nu-Kitchen | As a family-owned home-building business that began specializing in kitchens and baths. |
| Robertson | Has been in kitchen design from the first. |
| J&W | Parent Co., Jay Construction, moved J&W into kitchens and baths five years ago. |

*(continued)*

**EXHIBIT 8-4 Continued**

*3. What are your areas of specialization?*

| | |
|---|---|
| Quality Remodelers | Strictly luxury installations. |
| Remodel Center | Depends on market economics. Customized new home kitchen business declining. Now doing kitchen remodels. |
| Siegel Specialties | We specialize in everything. |
| Grogan Kitchens | Beginning to target independent remodelers more than builders. |
| Kitchen-Bath Specialties | Custom kitchens, not stock items, high-end items. |
| South Shawnee | Mainly upscale kitchen and bath design and installation. |
| Nu-Kitchen | Work in all areas, majority is luxury/necessity work. |
| Robertson | All lines. |
| J&W | Work in all areas. |

*4. What facts about your business do you stress (e.g., price, workmanship, family owned, length of time in business, warranties, certified employees, etc.)?*

| | |
|---|---|
| Quality Remodelers | Full-service organization, including paint and wallpapering. |
| Remodel Center | Quality and service in what they are paying for. Service after the sale. |
| Siegel Specialties | Length of time in business. Quality, reliability, bonded/licensed employees, large firm. |
| Grogan Kitchens | Longevity, price, and service. |
| Kitchen-Bath Specialties | Use all ideas presented to us. |
| South Shawnee | Quality of work and service—price not important. |
| Nu-Kitchen | Family owned—longevity of business. |
| Robertson | Quality of products, design, service, and installation. |
| J&W | Number of years of experience employees have—product quality and highly trained staff. |

*(continued)*

## EXHIBIT 8-4 Continued

*5. Do you conduct any kind of postpurchase follow-up?*

| | |
|---|---|
| Quality Remodelers | Informally. |
| Remodel Center | Emphasis on service after the sale–informal postpurchase follow-up. |
| Siegel Specialties | Send evaluation form with warranty to determine consumer satisfaction. Call within first year to refresh customer's memory of the firm. |
| Grogan Kitchens | Salesperson keeps in touch and asks if everything is OK. |
| Kitchen-Bath Specialties | Evaluation forms sent out and designers check if the job was done correctly. |
| South Shawnee | Absolutely. Evaluation forms sent out and salesperson calls to ensure client satisfied. |
| Nu-Kitchen | Firm's main contact with customer calls after installation. |
| Robertson | In contact throughout the whole process. |
| J&W | Client given a punch-list similar to walk-through forms used when someone is buying or renting a house. |

# CASE NINE

# THE HOME SHOPPING NETWORK

In the early years of television, about the only direct selling was for a kitchen device called Veg-o-Matic. According to the fast-talking pitchmen, it would perform any number of miraculous operations such as deftly making paper-thin tomato slices, corrugating potatoes for French frying, or shredding carrots to be squeezed for fresh carrot juice. Unfortunately, the Veg-o-Matic didn't work nearly as well in the kitchen at home.

But a new era in direct sales emerged in the summer of 1985 when the Home Shopping Network began a national live program over cable stations, 24 hours a day. The network began as a radio merchandiser, then later switched to a cable TV channel. In the early 1980s, a number of companies attempted to enter the video market. Most of them, however, failed, including one attempt by the Knight-Ridder newspapers. Their channel supplied banking, shopping services, news, and other information through interactive keyboards working with home television sets. But the channel offered no entertainment, music, or pictures, just wordy commercials in black and white.

## THE NEW SHOPPING FORMAT

The new Home Shopping Network was a prototype for today's shows. The selling resembled techniques used by carnival barkers rather than normal television commercials—including hosts with names like "Budget Bob" Circosta. He, and others, endlessly pushed such glitzy merchandise as $13.95 Taiwanese cubic zirconium "diamond" earrings and Milanese 18-carat gold necklaces. These products became household items in the United States, closely associated with the early days of home shopping. In 1986, the earrings accounted for one-fifth of the Home Shopping Network sales, and the gold chain sold so well that the network claimed to be the nation's largest importer of that quality of gold. Other popular items were a rabbit fur coat, closeout Christmas ornaments (sold in January), and a $129 cat scratcher. Customers were high-pressured and told that they had only ten minutes to take advantage of "the opportunity of a lifetime."

Pushy hosts and hostesses presented an endless stream of electronic devices, chinaware, appliances, jewelry, and housewares, stressing the limited quantities and bargain prices. Many items were classified as "manufacturer's closeouts" at a fraction of their regular prices.

Viewers placed their orders by calling a toll-free number and joining the Home Shopping Club. Most transactions were by credit card since this type of payment was the spur that fostered development of television home shopping in the first place. There were also drawings for prizes or "cash" to buy displayed products.

## COMPETITION NOT FAR BEHIND

With a hot, profitable operation such as this, it did not take long for competition to move in. By the end of 1986, there were five 24-hour cable channels with a combined audience of nearly 40 million viewers. There were also seven part-time broadcast, cable, and satellite channels claiming 87 million potential viewers. Noting these figures, large U.S. retailers jumped on the bandwagon early. Sears Roebuck announced late in 1986 that it would sell products on the Pennsylvania-based QVC cable network to some 8 million subscribers. And in February 1987, J.C. Penney Co., the nation's third largest general merchandise chain, began working on a cable network advertising scheme which would enable buyers to push telephone buttons to order merchandise displayed on their TV screens.

At the end of 1986, results were mixed. Industry home shopping sales for that year were $450 million; the Home Shopping Network accounted for about $180 million. Some analysts predicted as much as a $2 billion market in 1987, while others wondered if video retailing wasn't just another fad like the hula hoop or pet rock. The nonstop shopping shows, they pointed out, provided no original programming or service to the local communities.

## PRICING PRACTICES AND COMPARISONS

But consumer advocates and retailing officials said that overall, customers appeared to be satisfied with the quality of home shopping goods and said that the goods were accurately portrayed on television. However, only about 17 percent of purchases were returned, compared to the average rate of about 5 percent at discount stores. One Better Business Bureau cautioned, however, that customers could not easily compare prices because few of the goods were in stock at local stores. Also, the quoted retail price on television may have been a "suggested" one, or the price an item sold for when it was introduced several years earlier. When identical merchandise was located, however, prices on the Home Shopping Network were competitive, before shipping costs which consumers paid. Nevertheless, in 1989 the New York Attorney General's Office said it considered the marketing practices of the Cable Value Network (CVN) to be deceptive. The office had examined all products promoted in a single week in 1987, and in many cases, the network could not adequately support the price comparisons it made. Although it did not admit or deny guilt, CVN agreed to change its marketing practices.

## CONSUMER ACCEPTANCE OF HOME SHOPPING

Early data from the Home Shopping Network indicated that it had a 6 percent response rate in terms of the potential audience, considerably better than the 2.5 percent average for other direct response media. The average purchase was about $25, but many customers were repeat buyers with about 15 purchases a year.

The quick acceptance of this new form of direct selling is not too surprising, considering that in seven out of ten homes there are no adults present during the day to go shopping. In these two-income households, teen-aged children often buy much of the family food and other convenience goods. When the adults get home, they may be too weary, or don't have enough time, to shop for other goods. This is why the mail catalog industry has expanded. As a logical extension to catalogs, television selling adds color, movement, sound, and entertainment to make both the process and the products exciting.

## CONSUMER BEHAVIOR CONSIDERATIONS

By 1989, there were three major competitors in the profitable home shopping business, the QVC Network, the CVN Company, and the Home Shopping Network (HSN). But in mid-1989, HSN posted its first quarterly loss since it went public in 1986. Company representatives attributed this decline to higher administrative costs and fees from a legal squabble with the GTE corporation.

Spurred by this reverse in fortunes, HSN altered its overall marketing strategy. While QVC continued to offer more sophisticated selling techniques and products, HSN continued the carnival, hucksterish approach that accounted for its double-and-triple digit sales gains over the past several years. CVN also followed this technique, but in a less aggressive mode. But there were signs that the segment of middle-aged, middle income women who responded to this approach was becoming saturated with the jewelry and collectible products that formed the core of HSN's merchandising. Realizing that it needed to penetrate other types of homes, HSN began to feature more classical items, including VCRs, CD players and computers. But the demand just wasn't there, and the network pulled the new items off after only a few weeks.

The other networks, such as QVC, used a more highly developed technique that attracted a number of different segments, instead of the single group HSN was courting. Instead of offering the endless chain of unrelated products, the competitors, such as QVC, separated their programming into individual blocks. For example, one hour featured home furnishings, another showed toys, and a third, clothing. Periodically, future segments were flashed on the screen, and product times were listed in some cable guides. The presentations were more low key. Instead of the pushy promoter, a host or hostess is seated comfortably in a living room or a kitchen, giving demonstrations of products, or showing the quality features of a lamp. Often, the segments feature short talks about how products may be used. In one of these, a camcorder was shown filming valuable possessions for insurance purposes.

While these events were going on at QVC and CVN, Home Shopping was offering a radar detector and a walkman-type radio receiver. The two products simply sat on a plain table in front of the camera. There was no visible person or demonstration—just the background voice of an announcer asking customers if they wanted to hear a "toot" or two on a toy horn that indicated a sale had been made.

## BROADENING THE SCOPE

Although broadening the scope HSN continued to maintain its regular format. It also decided to make what it called "incremental changes" to broaden the product line. A HSN executive observed, "At this time, spontaneous impulse buys, together with the entertainment element of the show, seem to work well enough for us." HSN did feature a line of women's clothes as well as a successful three-hour fashion program called "Designer Row." Next, it added beauty products, mail order drugs, and tickets for entertainment and sporting events in different parts of the country.

In 1990, HSN entered into a broad marketing agreement with *Family Circle* magazine to help bolster declines in video sales and readership. HSN will sell *Family Circle* subscriptions along with cookware and cubic zirconium rings and will insert subscription cards in each of its 70,000 daily merchandise shipments. The magazine will offer short HSN segments on such topics as "helpful household hints" and will run magazine ads offering products from HSN's catalogs. Industry observers believe that *Family Circle,* with its image as a traditional women's service magazine, will bring some degree of respectability to HSN. Video shopping channels, on the whole, have a rather tacky image among many consumers. Yet, the target markets for them and magazines such as *Family Circle* are similar. If HSN and *Family Circle* can penetrate only 1 percent of each other's customer base, Home Shopping would gain about $59 million in sales from that small percentage of *Family Circle's* 21 million readers. HSN estimates its members spend $285 each, annually. Similarly, *Family Circle* believes it could add some 450,000 subscriptions.

## COMBINING THE COMPETITION

The Home Shopping Network, together with its rivals QVC and CVN, control about 90 percent of all home shopping dollars spent. QVC and CVN have been gaining ground against HSN during the past several years. In an attempt to stem these inroads, the Home Shopping Network made an unsuccessful bid to merge with the C.O.M.B. Company (Close Out Merchandise Buyers). C.O.M.B. owned 50% of CVN, and the merger would have brought in about 11 million new cable subscribers, the market where HSN needs more exposure. Also, C.O.M.B., itself, would have provided expertise in buying larger merchandise inventories.

Instead, the QVC network acquired CVN in July 1989, dashing HSN hopes of controlling more of the market and moving into new segments without jeopardizing its core customer base. QVC has indicated interest in expanding into a second channel where large retailers such as Sears and Spiegel could lease time to offer their products. QVC is mailing coupons and other incentives to get CVN's members to shop with QVC, and the network has also copied CVN's policy of permitting customers to order any time. Both HSN and QVC are trying other gimmicks to outsell each other. QVC signed Joan Rivers while HSN features Farah Fawcett and Vanna White, all of whom have reportedly helped to boost sales. The major shopping networks and their subscribers are shown in Exhibit 9-1.

## THE FUTURE OF VIDEO RETAILING

Contrary to earlier predictions, home video retailing is alive and well, as shown in Exhibit 9-2. In the 1990-91 recession period, home video shopping continued to grow. The consolidation of two of the three competitors divided the market into two camps; upscale, lower-key and high-pressure, impulse-oriented. Some experts suggest that the video retailing business may evolve so that it mirrors some aspects of traditional retailing in the long run. The combined QVC and CVN will take the role of upscale, successful department stores, while the Home Shopping Network will resemble low-end mass merchandisers. HSN scoffs at this prediction, noting that there aren't all that many upscale video consumers, and today, "everybody has to deal pretty much across the board."

## CASE ANALYSIS QUESTIONS

1. What motivational factors are involved when consumers buy from HSN or CVN?
2. Why have HSN and CVN placed time limits for consumers to call and

make purchases? What effect does this limit have on the consumer decision process?

3. In what social class(es) are Home Shopping customers likely to be found? What class characteristics support your choice?

4. Do you agree that the two major home shopping networks will eventually look like the traditional retailing structure?

5. Ever since Home Shopping on television was first started in 1984, retailing and advertising experts have dismissed it as a "fad." Do you agree, or do you think it is here to stay? Why?

## REFERENCES

"This Home Shopper May Be A Bargain," *Business Week,* Jan 28, 1991, p. 67; "Home Shoppers Keep Tuning In—But Investors Are Turned Off," *Business Week,* Oct. 22, 1990, p. 70; "Family Circle, Home Shopping Set Link, *Wall Street Journal,* Oct. 22, 1990, p. B-6; "Home Shopping Finds a Bargain," Market Place, *New York Times,* Dec. 22, 1989, p. D-6; "Home Shopping Network Stumbles in Upscale Move," *Wall Street Journal,* Jul. 31, 1989, p. B-1; "CVN Cable Network, Law Firm to Pitch Legal Services Plan to Home Shoppers," *Wall Street Journal,* Jul. 25, 1988, p. 20; "Shop-at-Home Firm Looks to Diversification," *San Diego Tribune,* Apr. 12, 1988, p. 1; "One Home for Two Shoppers?" *Business Week,* Feb. 27, 1987, p. 34; "Shopping Is TV's New Hit Program," *Washington Post,* Feb. 22, 1987, p. H-1; "Home Shopping, C.O.M.B. Merger Talks Could Collapse If Cable Operators Resist," *Wall Street Journal,* Feb. 8, 1987, p. 34; "Big TV Retailer Helps Suppliers, Cable Firms, Damages Direct Sellers," *Wall Street Journal,* May 13, 1987, p. 1; "Home Shopping Bid for C.O.M.B. Said to be High," *Wall Street Journal,* Jan. 22, 1987, p. B-4; "Home Shopping, Is It A Revolution in Retailing, or Just a Fad?" *Business Week,* Dec. 15, 1986, p. 64.

**HOME SHOPPING NETWORK**
**EXHIBIT 9-1**
**Networks and Subscribers (millions)**

| Network | 1986 | 1990 |
|---|---|---|
| Home Shopping | 15.0 | 21.0 |
| QVC | 7.6 | 35.0 |
| Cable Value | 9.0 | (merged with QVC) |
| Shop Television | 5.0 | — |
| J.C. Penney Shopping | — | 10.0 |

**HOME SHOPPING NETWORK**

**EXHIBIT 9-2**

Home Video Shopping and Home Shopping Network Sales, 1984–1990

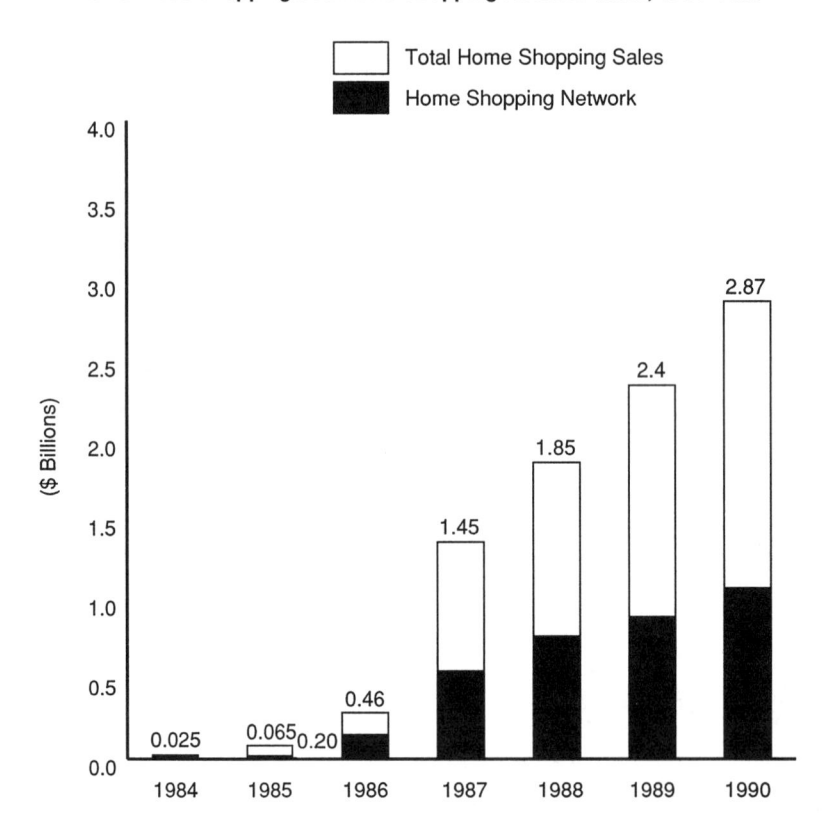

- ☐ Total Home Shopping Sales
- ■ Home Shopping Network

($ Billions)

| Year | Total Home Shopping Sales |
|------|---------------------------|
| 1984 | 0.025 |
| 1985 | 0.065 |
| 1986 | 0.20 / 0.46 |
| 1987 | 1.45 |
| 1988 | 1.85 |
| 1989 | 2.4 |
| 1990 | 2.87 |

# CASE TEN

# THE SPORT OF KINGS

In Shakopee, Minnesota, just outside of Minneapolis, the newest race track in the United States opened for business in late June 1985. It was only the second tract built in the nation in the past ten years, and it cost some $70 million. It was odd enough that this track was built in Minnesota, a state not exactly teeming with industrial and other blue-collar workers. This group, together with minorities, have been the mainstay of most race tracks throughout the country. But even more puzzling, it came at a time when horse racing was declining in popularity. Until 1984, horse racing was the best-attended spectator sport in the United States, but in that year it was edged out of its lead by baseball. Exhibit 10-1 shows that major league baseball attendance has increased close to 20 percent from 1983 to 1990, while horse racing attendance has remained flat. Baseball holds the number one spot, however, because other baseball leagues collectively, attract almost as many spectators as the majors. Horse racing holds second place, with football and basketball in third and fourth places respectively. Growth in attendance of all major sports except racing has been steady, but modest, since 1983. Exhibit 10-2, however, shows that net receipts from parimutuel betting have increased about one-and-one-half times since 1983. Parimutuel is a system of betting on races in which the winning bettors share the total amount bet, less a percentage for the track operators.

Canterbury Downs, the new Minnesota track, is supposed to contribute $150 million annually to the state's economy. But going to the races will be a new experience for many of its potential customers since only about half of those who

113

live in the Minneapolis metropolitan area have ever been to a track. And only a tiny percentage of those who have can define such common racing terms as *exacta* accurately. The question is whether or not this unique location with its nonracing demographics can attract the estimated 10,000 daily customers who will spend an average of $120 each.

## PROBLEMS AT OTHER TRACKS

Older tracks are having their own problems attracting customers, and the industry has been casting about for something that will rekindle the racing spirit. Noting the success of the Super Bowl and its phenomenal contribution to the coffers of professional football, the racing industry decided to stage a spectacular annual event called the Breeders' Cup. This extravaganza would feature about 100 horses, from which champions would be selected in a number of different categories.

Winners of the top seven races would be awarded a total of $10 million in cash prizes, the most ever in the history of horse racing. The first Breeders' Cup was held on November 10, 1984, at the Hollywood Park track in California, which had been completely refurbished for the event. The television blitz and the four solid hours of racing with the accompanying commentary and pageantry were supposed to reach 7 percent of all U.S. television households. It actually attracted 5.1 percent, while the Kentucky Derby reached about 12 percent that same year. The second annual Breeders' Cup was run at Aqueduct Race Track in New York on November 2, 1985, with limited success. In subsequent events, the Breeders' Cup has not done for racing what the Super Bowl does for football.

## UNDERLYING PROBLEMS

Marketing observers say that the hype and hoopla of this kind of event will do little to solve the real problems of the racing business. It merely extends the futile approaches the industry has taken in the past, such as lobbying state legislatures for more racing days and trying to get permission to take more profitable bets. But neither showmanship nor modifications to the same old track fare are likely to change the attitudes of the younger market that racing so desperately needs.

Racing's sellers and buyers are a study in contrast. On one side is a wealthy, cliquey, professional group of owners, trainers, and breeders. On the other are track customers: blue-collar workers, minorities, a few seedy touts (racing tipsters who hang around tracks), and some white-collar middle-class patrons. The former are beset by skyrocketing costs and the latter are upscale in age—the average age of a racing fan is 50. *Business Week* quotes a sports management consultant as saying, "The racing industry has not been innovative in marketing." One reason for this problem is that the sport is largely regional. Racing is closely regulated, usually by state racing commissions, which allocate an equal number of the available racing days to tracks in their jurisdiction. So when one track is running, the others may be closed. Another reason is that the sport itself is not too sure which market or markets it is competing against for fans. Are baseball, football, and basketball the main competition? Are off-track betting, state lotteries, and illegal gambling operations keeping customers away from the track? Are potential racing fans seeking other types of entertainment? Or is it all three? To some extent, they all compete for the customer's discretionary income.

## CONSUMER ATTITUDES

New York tracks tried to change attitudes toward racing by luring younger potential fans to the races with attractions these customers were already favorable toward—concerts featuring big-name bands and entertainers. The gimmick brought these customers in, but they came to hear the music. Apparently their attitudes toward racing were unchanged since they bet very little. If attitudes and behavior are closely allied, as they are supposed to be, then attitudes of the younger population are negative toward horse racing.

Exhibit 10-3 shows results of a semantic differential scale measurement of attitudes and beliefs about horse racing and Exhibit 10-4 depicts the perceived attractions of the four major spectator sports in the United States. The data in these exhibits were extracted from larger studies by the author on spectator sports. Overall, the exhibits suggest largely unfavorable attitudes to racing and visiting the track.

## CASE ANALYSIS QUESTIONS

1. Of the statements on the semantic differential image profile shown in Exhibit 10-3, which would you classify as overall attitudes (the affective component) and which are more related to beliefs (the cognitive component)?

2. What approach has the management of the Breeders' Cup event and the New York track concerts taken to attract younger customers? Why haven't either of these activities attracted more of the target group as active racing fans?

3. What approaches do you think the track owners might use to change attitudes or beliefs?

## REFERENCES

U.S. Government Printing Office, Bureau of the Census, *Statistical Abstract*, 1991, Washington D.C., U.S. Government Printing Office. Table 390; "Will It Ever Be Post Time Again for Hialeah?" *Business Week*, Mar. 5, 1990, p. 91 "What's New in the Horse Business," *New York Times*, Apr. 20, 1989, p. F18; "Popularity of TV Sports," *Washington Post,* Sept. 11, 1988, p. E8; "Race Tracks Gamble on New Strategy," *Wall Street Journal,* Jun. 2, 1988; "Riding High With Arabian Horses," *Business Week,* Nov. 25, 1985, p. 148; "In The Breeders' Cup Horse Race, Some Say an Industry Is at Stake," *Wall Street Journal,* Nov. 1, 1985, p. 33; "Horse Racing in Minnesota: Will It Take?" *Wall Street Journal,* Jun 26, 1985, p. 29; "Horse Racing Tries A Come-From-Behind Sprint," *Business Week,* Nov. 19, 1984, p. 82.

## SPORT OF KINGS
### EXHIBIT 10-1
### Attendance for Sports (000)

| Sport | 1983 | 1984 | 1985 | 1986 | 1987 | 1988 | 1989 | 1990 |
|---|---|---|---|---|---|---|---|---|
| Major League Baseball[a] | 46,269 | 45,262 | 47,742 | 48,452 | 53,182 | 53,808 | 54,200 | 54,950 |
| Horse Racing | 75,693 | 74,076 | 73,346 | 70,580 | 70,105 | 69,949 | 69,810 | 69,050 |
| Basketball | | | | | | | | |
|   Pro | 10,262 | 11,110 | 11,491 | 12,193 | 13,186 | 14,051 | 14,987 | 15,604 |
|   College | 31,471 | 31,684 | 32,057 | 31,645 | 31,911 | 32,504 | 33,069 | 33,891 |
| | 41,733 | 42,794 | 43,548 | 43,838 | 45,097 | 46,555 | 48,056 | 49,495 |
| Football | | | | | | | | |
|   Pro (NFL) | 13,953 | 14,053 | 14,058 | 17,304 | 15,180 | 17,024 | 17,298 | 17,772 |
|   College | 36,302 | 36,652 | 36,312 | 36,388 | 36,463 | 35,581 | 35,801 | 35,933 |
| | 50,255 | 50,710 | 50,370 | 53,692 | 51,640 | 52,605 | 52,099 | 53,705 |

[a] College baseball attendance is small.


## SPORT OF KINGS
### EXHIBIT 10-2
### Net Revenues from Parimutuel Betting 1985-90
### ($ millions)

| 1985 | 1986 | 1987 | 1988 | 1989 | 1990 |
|---|---|---|---|---|---|
| 2.64 | 2.93 | 3.22 | 3.50 | 3.76 | 3.91 |

## SPORT OF KINGS

### EXHIBIT 10-3

### Example of Use of Semantic Differential Scale in Attitude Research

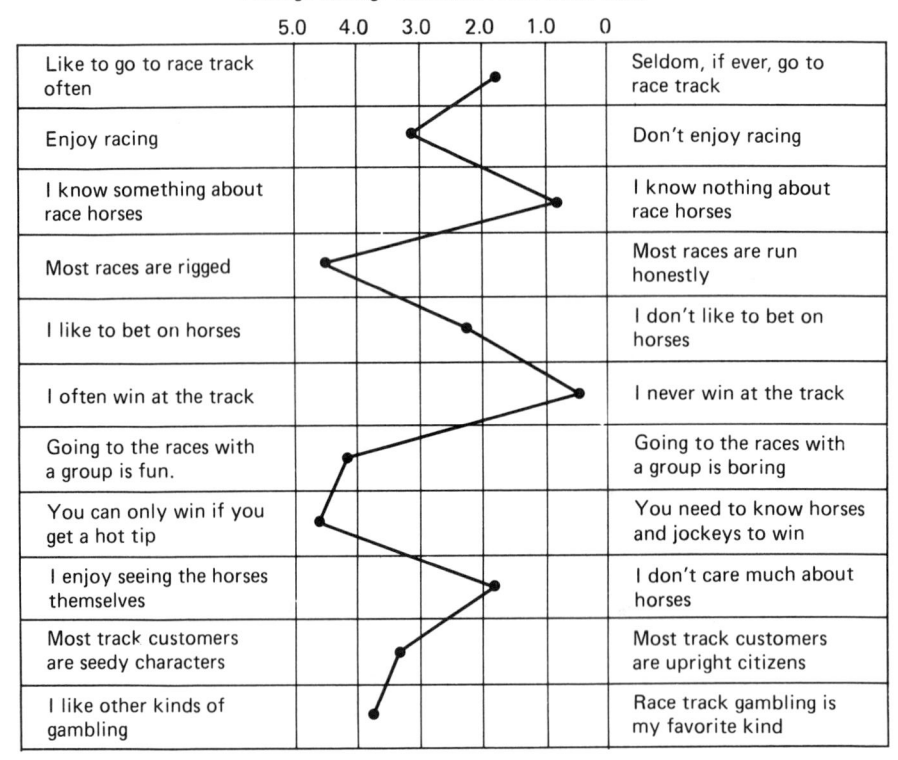

Average Rating: Semantic Differential Scale

| | 5.0 | 4.0 | 3.0 | 2.0 | 1.0 | 0 | |
|---|---|---|---|---|---|---|---|
| Like to go to race track often | | | | ● | | | Seldom, if ever, go to race track |
| Enjoy racing | | | ● | | | | Don't enjoy racing |
| I know something about race horses | | | | | ● | | I know nothing about race horses |
| Most races are rigged | ● | | | | | | Most races are run honestly |
| I like to bet on horses | | | | ● | | | I don't like to bet on horses |
| I often win at the track | | | | | ● | | I never win at the track |
| Going to the races with a group is fun. | | ● | | | | | Going to the races with a group is boring |
| You can only win if you get a hot tip | | ● | | | | | You need to know horses and jockeys to win |
| I enjoy seeing the horses themselves | | | | ● | | | I don't care much about horses |
| Most track customers are seedy characters | | ● | | | | | Most track customers are upright citizens |
| I like other kinds of gambling | | ● | | | | | Race track gambling is my favorite kind |

## THE SPORT OF KINGS
### EXHIBIT 10-4
### Perceived Attractions of Four Major Sports
### (Rank Ordered)

Question: If you enjoy any of these sports, please list the reasons why you do.

| Professional Football | Professional Basketball | Horse Racing | Major League Baseball |
|---|---|---|---|
| Action | Fast moving | Betting | Team play |
| Physical sport | Individual play | Know horses | Individual skills |
| Fast moving | Interesting to watch | Personal participation | Pennant race |
| Super Bowl | Strategy game | Know jockeys | |
| Colorful | | | |

# CASE ELEVEN

# PROCTER & GAMBLE — THE SIGN AND THE SYMBOL

Since it was founded in 1837 as a soap and candle-making firm, Procter & Gamble has been an American institution. Its Ivory soap, introduced in 1879, is probably the one product most people associated with the company, although it has a number of other noteworthy accomplishments to its credit. Procter & Gamble conducted its first market research in 1924 and, by acquiring an English soap firm, made its first overseas move in 1930. In 1932, P&G sponsored the first radio soap opera, called "The Puddle Family." Fourteen years later, in 1946, Tide was introduced, followed by Crest toothpaste in 1955, and Pampers in 1961. From 1980 through 1982, it embarked on a diversification program, acquiring Ben Hill Griffin Citrus and Norwich Eaton Pharmaceuticals.

Its 1924 expedition into market research marked the beginning of P&G's close relationship with its customers. This continuing dialogue between producer and consumer began, so the story goes, back in 1879 when a mixing-vat worker forgot to turn off his machine when he went to lunch. When he came back, instead of the usual creamy substance ready to be molded into soap cakes, he found a frothy mixture that appeared to be useless. But he and his foreman decided the soap had not really been harmed, and they were able to mold it well enough to sell. A few weeks later, P&G began getting pleas from storekeepers along the Ohio river for "more of that floating soap." Tracing back to the mistake, the firm found that air bubbles whipped into the liquid soap by the longer mixing process gave the soap a buoyancy that kept it afloat while its users were bathing or washing in the murky river.

This incident not only spawned Ivory soap, but it also gave life to a policy of being tuned-in to what consumers want. Today, P&G receives and replies to nearly half a million customer letters and telephone calls each year. About one-half of the calls and letters are requests for information, one-third are complaints, and one-sixth are positive comments. One result of P&G's close attention to this overwhelming volume is that, in 1981, P&G products held six places out of the top ten household products, three of the top ten in health and beauty aids, and two of the top ten in food products.

In addition to the contacts that are initiated by consumers themselves, P&G calls upon over 1.5 million people each year in research projects designed to find out what people think about its products and their packaging, effectiveness, and other characteristics. The research also includes inquiries into how people go about doing such household tasks as cleaning, preparing meals, and washing clothes. The firm's cautious entry into a toll-free telephone response program in 1974 helped with this research. The head of P&G's consumer services department describes results from the number on Duncan Hines brownie mix packages: "We learned that people in high altitudes needed special instructions for baking, and we added these to the package. We also found one of the box recipes was confusing and we changed that." Although consumers send in about 4,000 new product ideas a year, most of them do not usually amount to much. The real pay dirt comes from "basic" research where P&G asks the questions and observes people at their regular household chores.

P&G has also been a socially responsible firm. It reacted positively and rapidly to the discovery that its Rely brand tampons were related to toxic shock syndrome. Within about two weeks it had removed this product from the shelves, although this action prematurely ended 20 years of research and a $75 million program. And the company went even further, launching an educational campaign to inform women about the syndrome, the link between it and tampons, and the greater statistical link between it and the Rely brand. This positive and complete response was highly effective in preventing negative image connotations for the firm and its other products.

Although the colorful legend of the birth of floating Ivory Soap typifies P&G's diligent search for the views of those who contribute over 17 million purchase transactions each day for its products, another sinister and damaging legend has crept upon P&G more recently. Since 1976, the firm has been plagued by a spotty, nagging series of rumors that link Procter & Gamble with cults or religious subcultures. These rumors are all concerned with the trademark that the firm has used for over 100 years on all its products. This mark depicts a group of thirteen stars enclosed in a circle, in which a bearded man-in-the-moon is shown. According to P&G, this logo evolved from shipping practices along the Ohio and other midwestern rivers. Illiterate dock workers identified wooden crates of P&G's Star brand candles by placing crude plus marks on them so shippers would know whose product they were handling and where it should go. Later, when P&G began putting identifying stars on each box, artistic stevedores drew circles around them and added other decorations such as moon-faces—images that were popular at the time. P&G then made a stencil of the moon-man as a more elaborate crate mark. But when someone erased the face on several boxes, a New Orleans wholesaler protested that he would only trust shipments that had the full Procter & Gamble seal on them. Exhibit 11-1 shows the evolution of the symbol.

Quick to recognize an eye-catching symbol, William Procter, the firm's cofounder, suggested using 13 stars to represent those in the original U.S. flag. In 1882, the revised seal was registered as a trademark under number 9,829 and has appeared on all P&G products ever since. Nearly 100 years later, in 1976, rumors linking the logo with cult symbolism began to appear with increasing strength and frequency. The *Wall Street Journal* reported a rampant rumor in southern Minnesota that "the Moonies have taken over Procter & Gamble!" No one could trace how it got started, but someone apparently connected the moon symbol with the Rev. Moon's Unification Church, and P&G reported several inquiries about the supposed takeover in 1979. Early in 1980, a nursing home newsletter in Gaylor, Minnesota, published a note by one of its employees saying that the "Moon Church" owned Procter & Gamble. A few days later, the Lafayette-Nicollet (Minnesota) *Ledger* heard about the article and nearly printed an editorial commenting favorably on a boycott of P&G products. Fortunately, someone contacted P&G before it was printed, and the editorial that was actually published suggested that its readers check their sources before stirring up actions such as boycotts.

At the time, P&G thought the problem would go away and took no overt action. For a while it did, but two years later it reappeared, this time in full force and apparently among Protestant fundamentalists. Now the rumor became more specific, charging that P&G's president, John Smale, appeared on national television (on the "Phil Donahue Show" or maybe it was "Merv Griffin"—no one seemed to be sure) and supposedly linked the firm's success with the devil, avowing his membership in the Church of Satan and stating that P&G tithed to that church. Professor Martin Marty of the University of Chicago cites the following excerpt from one of the tract flyers that were circulated at the time (see the enlarged logo, Exhibit 11-2).

> Look for this emblem on all PROCTOR [sic] & GAMBLE PRODUCTS (a sorcerer's head & 13 stars). Which is a symbol of Satanism. One of the top officials of the PROCTOR AND GAMBLE COMPANY is an avowed Satanist. On national television recently, gave all of the credit for the success of the company to SATAN. He said that they have placed their satanist symbol on all their products, so they can get SATAN into every home in America.

Thus, in 1982, when the seal's centennial should have been celebrated, P&G found itself coping with 300 calls a day to the toll-free numbers it lists on its packages; the calls peaked at about 15,000 for the month of June 1982. Nearly all the calls were related to the logo and P&G's supposed links to the Church of Satan. P&G countered with six lawsuits against rumor spreaders, including a popular Atlanta weatherman and four Amway products distributors. It also enlisted the help of such well-known clergymen as Jerry Falwell, Billy Graham, Archbishop Joseph Bernardin, and even Donald Wildmon, who had been a long-time objector to P&G's television programming. The company also used a media blitz explaining the trademark and mailed thousands of letters to consumers citing the support of top religious leaders. By July, either because of these actions or because the rumors had run their course, the number of calls decreased and by the end of 1982, P&G quit keeping records on them and stopped worrying. During 1983 and early 1984, there were only about 35 calls a month related to these rumors.

But P&G's worries began anew in the fall of 1984 when Sister Domitilla Drobnsk, an elementary-school principal in Clymer, Pennsylvania, found an unsigned leaflet in her mailbox. It told the story of how the president of Procter & Gamble appeared on the "Phil Donahue Show" to declare his company's support for the Church of Satan. It also showed the man-in-moon trademark, which was said to be the sign of Satan. Interpreting it as her duty to spread the word, the sister sent copies of the leaflet home with her students, together with a personal note urging a boycott of P&G products, such as Crest toothpaste, Tide, and Ivory soap. Sister Domitilla's efforts and those of others were quite productive. In October, piles of leaflets were reported to be in the Hairworks beauty salon on Clymer's main street and in the shower room at a nearby coal mine. A local supermarket refunded the price of a can of Folger's coffee to a customer who refused to drink the "devil's brew." Apparently other copies of the same or similar leaflets were distributed in western Pennsylvania near Clymer because in October 1984, P&G's calls skyrocketed to 5,000 a month with 1,600 of them from that area.

The other calls came from such places as Milwaukee, where Virginia Meves, editor of a weekly newspaper (circulation 6,000) that usually reports on such topics as abortion and government regulation, ran the Satanism story; and Stamford, Connecticut, where Sister Noel passed out leaflets to women of the Villa Maria retreat. Both of them, as well as Sister Domitilla, have retracted and apologized for their actions.

But there are still some people who are not ready to completely discount the rumors. Most troublesome to P&G are clergy, such as Father Trongo, pastor of St. Anthony's church in Clymer. "You can't rule out a connection [between the company and the Church of Satan]," he says, "P&G could be using the Satanism rumor as a tax writeoff or a publicity gimmick. I wouldn't give a sermon [defending P&G]."

The 1982 rumors centered mainly around Protestant fundamentalists, but P&G attributed the 1984 sources to Roman Catholic nuns and priests, mostly in the Northeast. But calls also came in from certain regions in California, Wisconsin, western New York state (mostly around Buffalo), and Chicago, in addition to the areas already mentioned. The 1982 problem was national, but in 1984 it was more regional and was spread through flyers distributed in churches, schools, shopping malls, and workplaces. In 1984, a P&G representative said that the company knew of specific cases where "unauthorized persons connected with Catholic churches" in Buffalo and Nebraska had published false accusations in church bulletins. Catholic school children in Cleveland and Pittsburgh took home the same rumor.

Rumors of the type described here are passed through an informal yet efficient network by word-of-mouth, printed matter, and overheard conversations by people who really believe that P&G would put disguised symbols into their seal and tithe to a Satanic church. Although stars do show up in some Satanic systems, they appear in many other systems and symbols as well and have been universally used since primitive times. The "13" count has been associated with evil and bad luck. But it would take a dedicated symbol seeker to turn the seal upside down and look at it in a mirror to find the "666" that is supposed to be hidden in the curlicues of the beard of the man-in-the-moon. This number from the book of Revelations is a "mark of the beast" and an enemy of God. It is also a favorite occult emblem among superstitious Christians in America. But looking for such symbols and interpreting them in this way is excessive behavior, to say the least.

Examine any of the many Procter & Gamble products and the tiny seal will be found near the toll-free telephone number and patent numbers. Exhibit 11–3 shows reproductions of the seal from three consumer products. It is difficult to believe that it could be the center of so much rumor, controversy, and parental-like protection by P&G.

In mid-1984, Procter & Gamble appeared to be backing away from its coveted symbol. After considerable thought, the firm decided its moon-and-stars logos would not appear on its new twin-tower, 18-story office building in Cincinnati, although the original plans called for them. Eight of the seals had been made in bas-relief marble carvings. One P&G spokesman said they were dropped for "economy reasons," but the architect says P&G thought that they would further incite religious fundamentalists into more rumor spreading and boycotting.

In April 1985, the company announced it would remove the logo from its product packages in an attempt to squelch the Satanic association rumors. The symbol would be removed over the next several years as the packages were redesigned, but P&G would continue to use the seal on its letterhead and annual reports. On May 16, 1985, P&G filed suit against four individuals, accusing them of spreading malicious and untrue statements linking the firm with Satanism. More specifically, P&G accused them of libeling the firm's character by distributing literature that says P&G supported the church of Satan and that the P&G trademark is a symbol of Satanism. These individuals are also accused of encouraging others to stop buying Procter & Gamble products.

The company said it filed these suits against persons in Madison Heights, Virginia, Dunmore, Pennsylvania, and Wichita, Kansas. With these actions, it would seem that the company's problems with the logo would have been laid to rest. But as it has in the past, the specter appeared again in the spring of 1990. The P&G hotline was swamped with nearly 200 calls a day from consumers in several Southern states who asked if the company has really pledged its profits to the devil. Company operators attempted to dispel the callers' fears, P&G sleuths tried to trace the sources of the rumors, and a spokeswoman said, "We will take whatever steps are necessary to put this to rest." After a little over a month, the calls trickled back to the normal level.

## ANALYSIS QUESTIONS

1. What role do religious subcultures and subcultural symbolism play in the spread of the Satanism rumors? Does the symbol and what consumers see in it relate to their social environment?

2. Do the people who spread the rumors really believe that P&G is in league with Satan and that the firm's president actually admitted it on a nationwide television program?

3. P&G has been quite concerned about the rumors. What effect on the attitudes and beliefs of present and future buyers of P&G products might the rumors have?

4. The symbol on P&G's products is so small that most people do not even notice it. Why did P&G take so long to decide to drop it?

## REFERENCES

"P&G To Tout the Name Behind the Brands," *Wall Street Journal,* Dec. 19, 1990, p. B-1; "P&G Once Again Has Devil of a Time With Rumors About Moon, Stars Logo," *Wall Street Journal,* Mar. 26, 1990, p. B-3; "P&G's Worldly New Boss Wants a More Worldly Company," *Business Week,* Oct. 30, 1989, p. 40; "New Found Pep at P&G," *New York Times,* Feb. 3, 1985, p. 27; "Rumor Bedevils Procter & Gamble," *Washington Post,* Apr. 18, 1985, p. B-5; "Meanwhile, P&G Is Losing One of Its Best Customers," *Wall Street Journal,* May 1, 1985, p. 35; "P&G Earnings Dropped 27% In Its 3rd Period," *Wall Street Journal,* Apr. 25, 1985, p. 10; "P&G Sues, Alleges Four Libeled Firm With Devil Rumors," *Wall Street Journal,* May 17, 1985, p. 8; "Pressed by Its Rivals, Procter & Gamble Is Altering Its Ways," *Wall Street Journal,* May 20, 1985, p. 1; "P&G Makes an Architectural Statement," *Wall Street Journal,* Jun. 10, 1985, p. 20; "Procter & Gamble Fighting to Stay on Top," *Maine Sunday Telegram,* Aug. 11, 1985, p. 6C; "No Soap Opera: Procter & Gamble Makes a Play to Regain Some Lost Markets, *Savvy,* May 1985, p. 19; "Beat The Devil," *Forbes,* Dec. 3, 1984, p. 240; "Procter & Gamble Fights New Rumors of Link to Satanism," *Wall Street Journal,* Nov. 8, 1984, p. 18; "Devil Rumor Haunts P&G." *Wall Street Journal,* Oct. 25, 1984, p. 25; "Rumor Returns to Bedevil P&G," *Advertising Age,* Oct. 22, 1984, p. 1; "Coming Out in the Wash," *The Economist,* Oct. 1, 1983, p. 71; "Why Procter & Gamble is Playing It Even Tougher," *Business Week,* Jul. 18, 1983, p. 176; "Satanism: No Soap," *Across the Board,* Dec., 1982, p. 8; "Procter & Gamble and the Devil," *Public Relations Quarterly,* Fall, 1982, p. 16,"P&G Rumor Blitz Looks Like a Bomb," *Advertising Age,* Aug. 9, 1982, p. 1; "P&G Sues Over Satanism," *Advertising Age,* July 5, 1982, p. 1.

**PROCTER & GAMBLE**

**EXHIBIT 11-1**

**Evolution of the Corporate Symbol**

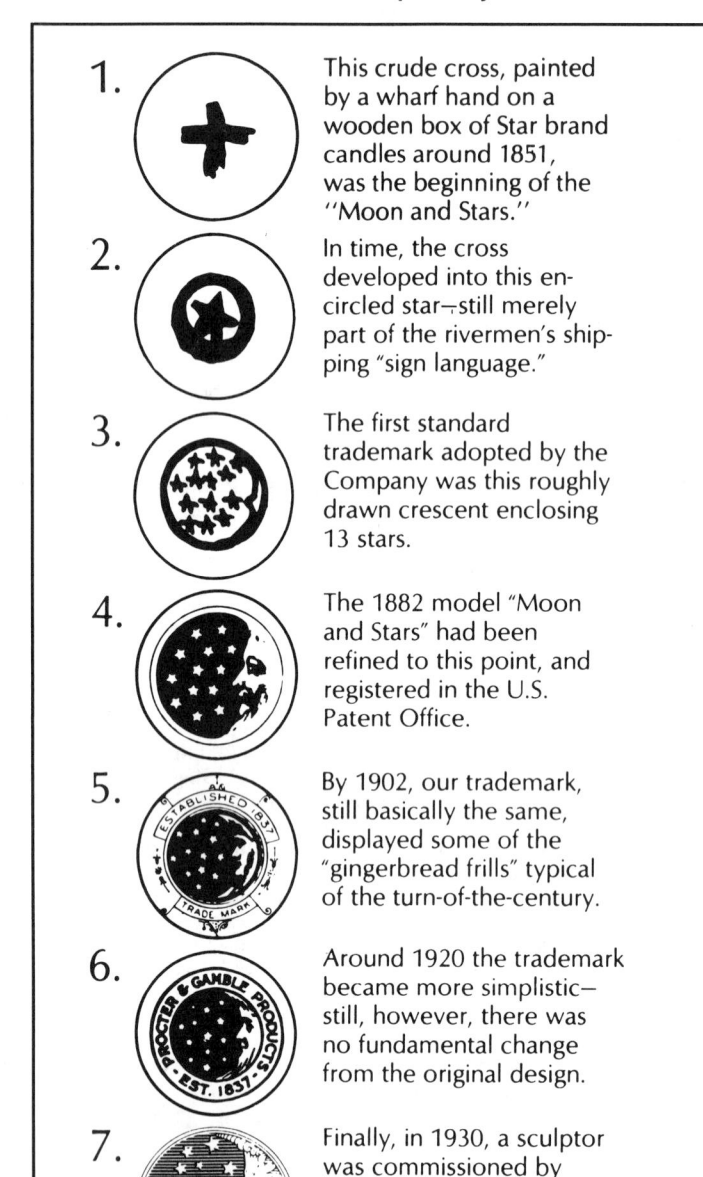

| | | |
|---|---|---|
| 1. | | This crude cross, painted by a wharf hand on a wooden box of Star brand candles around 1851, was the beginning of the "Moon and Stars." |
| 2. | | In time, the cross developed into this encircled star—still merely part of the rivermen's shipping "sign language." |
| 3. | | The first standard trademark adopted by the Company was this roughly drawn crescent enclosing 13 stars. |
| 4. | | The 1882 model "Moon and Stars" had been refined to this point, and registered in the U.S. Patent Office. |
| 5. | | By 1902, our trademark, still basically the same, displayed some of the "gingerbread frills" typical of the turn-of-the-century. |
| 6. | | Around 1920 the trademark became more simplistic—still, however, there was no fundamental change from the original design. |
| 7. | | Finally, in 1930, a sculptor was commissioned by P&G to design today's authorized version of the famous "Moon and Stars." |

*Source*: Used with permission of Procter & Gamble

**PROCTER & GAMBLE**

**EXHIBIT 11-2**

**Present Corporate Symbol**

*Source*: Used with permission of Procter & Gamble.

PROCTER & GAMBLE

EXHIBIT 11-3

The Corporate Symbol on Several Products

If you have questions or comments about Charmin, please call us toll-free. In the continental U.S., call 1-800-543-0480 (Ohio residents call 1-800-582-0490).
Made in U.S.A. by PROCTER & GAMBLE
Cincinnati, Ohio 45202   ©P&G
Made under one or more U.S. Patents: 3,994,771; and 4,191,609.

37000 60141  YELLOW

## CONVENIENT JUMBO ROLL

IMPORTANT FOR MICROWAVE OWNERS—Use NEW, specially formulated BOUNTY MICROWAVE for your microwave tasks. It's a new Bounty made just for you.
Made under one or more U.S. Patents:
3,414,459; 3,905,863; 3,974,025; 4,191,609; and Des. 239,137.
IF YOU HAVE QUESTIONS OR COMMENTS ABOUT BOUNTY, please call us toll-free.
In the continental U.S., call 1-800-543-0480 (Ohio residents call 1-800-582-0490).
Made in U.S.A. by
PROCTER & GAMBLE
Cincinnati, Ohio 45202   ©P&G

37000 63361

**Crest** HAS AN ADVANCED FORMULA WITH FLUORISTAT* WHICH HAS BEEN CLINICALLY PROVEN TO FIGHT CAVITIES EVEN BETTER THAN ORIGINAL CREST.

"Crest has been shown to be an effective decay-preventive dentifrice that can be of significant value when used in a conscientiously applied program of oral hygiene and regular professional care."
— Council on Dental Therapeutics–American Dental Association

INGREDIENTS: SODIUM FLUORIDE IN A DENTIFRICE BASE OF SORBITOL, WATER, HYDRATED SILICA, TRISODIUM PHOSPHATE, SODIUM LAURYL SULFATE, FLAVOR, SODIUM PHOSPHATE, XANTHAN GUM, CARBOMER 940, SODIUM SACCHARIN, TITANIUM DIOXIDE, AND FD&C BLUE NO. 1.

*Fluoristat is a trademark for a proven decay preventive composition (active ingredient: sodium fluoride)
If you have questions or comments about Crest, please call us toll free.
In the continental U.S., call 1-800-543-7270 (Ohio residents call 1-800-582-1891)

Made in U.S.A. by PROCTER & GAMBLE
Cincinnati, Ohio 45202  U.S. Pat. 4,254,101; 4,314,990

# CASE TWELVE

# MARY KAY COSMETICS

In late 1985, Martha Trescott was a housewife in Toledo, Ohio, with two small children in school. "In the beginning," Martha said, "I was just looking for something that would bring in a little extra money and would get me out of the house for a while." So she was delighted when she met her cousin Ellie from nearby Sandusky, Ohio, at the annual Trescott family picnic. Ellie had been with Mary Kay Cosmetics for several years and was now a sales director. "What she was doing fit right in with what I had in mind," Martha explained. "Ellie said all I had to do was give Mary Kay parties at my house a few times a month, and I enjoy doing things like that! She said she would teach me what I needed to know. I couldn't wait to get started."

Cousin Ellie explained in more detail what Martha had to do. The parties are usually held in the afternoon, but sometimes in the evening. They last about two hours and no more than five guests are invited. The hostess is the "beauty consultant" who gives a free facial to each guest and explains or demonstrates beauty tips at the same time. Afterward, she serves refreshments, then takes orders for the 45 products in the Mary Kay line. Ellie stressed that the guests need to be gently, but firmly, pushed into buying several of the products, not just one.

She went on to tell about the potential for moving up in the firm's sales group and about the chances for substantial earnings, and gave Martha a copy of the Mary Kay Marketing Plan (see Exhibit 12-1). She also stressed that each salesperson worked on commission and that the harder one worked, the higher the earnings would be, and she pointed out that each Mary Kay consultant is an independent contractor, not an employee. The company simply acts as a wholesale house from which the consultant buys at wholesale prices and sells at retail to her clients.

Ellie, herself, had started as a Mary Kay beauty consultant in Sandusky about three years ago. "After a year or so giving parties," she said, "I began to find others just like you, Martha, who wanted to earn extra money. After I recruited a few, I was promoted to sales director, where I am now." In addition to her own sales commissions, Ellie gets an additional 4 percent for each new consultant she recruits, another commission for training them, and 3 percent of the sales that they make. She is also required to wear the sales director's uniform, which consists of a gray suit, Hanes quicksilver panty hose, and a pink, strawberry, or (preferred) amethyst blouse, when she is working. "Right now," she confided, "I'm trying to meet a higher sales quota so I can earn my pink Cadillac. And this is the best time to try for it because everybody will know Mary Kay after they feature her on '60 Minutes' later this month."

Ellie drew a chart showing that there were more rungs up the Mary Kay success ladder above sales director, including division manager and national sales director. Exhibit 12–2 shows this hierarchy.

## MARY KAY'S COMPANY

Already a grandmother in 1963, Mary Katherine Ash bought the formula for her initial skin-care products for $500 from the granddaughter of a local Texas tanner. Then, with her son Richard Rogers, she began the company that is now among the top ten party-plan merchandisers in the United States. The firm started with only Mary Kay and her son as full-time employees and used nine Dallas women who were willing to work on straight commission selling the products. The company's underlying philosophy finds its roots in the fundamentalist Christian beliefs of its founder: "God first, family second, and career third."

Initially, the company shrewdly positioned itself in the skin-care end of the cosmetics market—and this comparatively narrow niche is one of its strengths. A Mary Kay consultant has only about 50 items to show to a customer, while Avon representatives deliver catalogs with about 250 items out of 650 in the total line. Thus, Mary Kay consultants are able to carry inventory and deliver a customer's items immediately, while Avon representatives have to take orders and deliver the merchandise later.

Another strength is the way in which Mary Kay's sales force management is compensated and motivated. Its seven national sales managers earn well over $75,000 and 150 division managers earn over $50,000. Some members of the commission group do even better. The 31 national sales directors earn an average of $90 to $100,000, the 1,500 senior sales managers get fixed compensation plus 4 percent of the retail sales of their units, while the 4,000 sales directors earn an average salary of $30,000 plus 9 to 13 percent of retail sales, a 3 percent sales bonus, and a rental car. The strategy of this type of operation is the "pyramid," where incentives in the form of build-up commissions and exotic prizes entice "consultants" not only to sell heavily but, vital to the entire scheme, to recruit constantly.

Of Mary Kay's three children only Richard Rogers is still with the firm, as its president. Mary Kay has been described as the "heart of Mary Kay cosmetics" but Richard is known as the "operational brains." Mary Kay has long since left the day-to-day affairs in Richard's hands. But she still works closely with the salespeople, who are vital to the firm's continued success, and is often found baking cookies for new management trainees or handing out rewards, such as pink Cadillacs, furs, jewels, and vacations at the company's annual inspirational sales meeting in Dallas.

She is also the "image" of the company, and the ideal, or envy, of other women who would like to mirror her success and life-style. She has taken her own passion for pink and parlayed it into a national symbol of her firm: the pink Cadillac. A typical photo of Mary Kay with the Cadillac is shown in Exhibit 12-3. She often wears a pink lace dress and lives in a 19,000 square-foot pink mansion in Dallas. In the $5 million structure which has five bedrooms, eleven bathrooms, a library, game room, cabana, three kitchens, and an Olympic-size swimming pool, she sees "just the right amount of room for a single woman who likes to entertain." On a recent shopping trip in France she bought enough antiques to fill an entire railroad boxcar; they were used to furnish the pink mansion.

## THE SUCCESS OF MARTHA TRESCOTT

"I just love Mary Kay," gushed cousin Ellie. "And I know you will too." Martha was a bit uneasy when Ellie told her she would have to buy her own "beauty showcase" kit of sample products, and probably a small inventory of popular items. "It helps to have the merchandise on hand," cautioned Ellie. "Otherwise you have to take an order and have the customer pay in advance. Some don't like to do that. Also, it means you have to deliver the order when it comes in." The basic showcase and inventory would cost about $750. The company suggests that new consultants start off with bank loans, since they do not usually have established credit. "The logic behind this," Ellie explained, "is that if consultants have to meet payments, they are forced to put the money back into the business and won't spend it right away."

To get the cash for her initial investment, Martha borrowed $750 on a note from a bank, cosigned by her husband, and she stocked her shelves. She spent the next several days learning how to give the facials, what kind of refreshments were best to serve, how to keep the conversation going, and how to sell, sell, sell. She was so anxious to begin that she stayed up late at night making lists of all her relatives and friends who might come to the parties themselves, and also bring others with them.

Soon she was hosting two parties a week. Her own enthusiasm for the products, and the expertise she acquired by constantly improving her technique for giving facials, seemed to motivate guests to spend lavishly. She was also rather surprised when several relatives, and other guests she did not know, asked about becoming Mary Kay consultants themselves. By the end of the following year, she had recruited almost enough novice consultants to qualify for her promotion to sales director. Her inventory had risen to over $1,500 and she had no problem getting credit. Also, her income had risen appreciably. She not only had income from her own sales but she got an additional percentage for training recruits, and a percentage of their sales. She kept in touch with what was happening in the company, and got new ideas for recruiting, training, and product promotion from the company "Newsline" publication, shown in Exhibit 12-4.

As a successful party-plan hostess, she also assumed the role of an opinion leader in her specialty area. Martha had worked hard to become an expert in giving facials and probably something of an actress as well. At the same time, she satisfied some needs of her own—to interest the guests in her product line and to make a profit by selling it. Because she is known either first- or second-hand to her customers, and because the brand she sells has a good reputation, risks are reduced. She also fulfills a social function by providing a party occasion as well as a buying opportunity.

In 1988, her income matched that of her husband. "If anyone asks why I've been so successful," Martha remarked, "it's because I wanted to make it. Just dangle a pink Cadillac in front of me!"

By late 1989, she had over 150 consultants working for her and was driving a pink Cadillac. But sales were becoming a little harder to make and recruiting was also more difficult. Martha knew that nearly half of those she recruited would last only a few months and would have to be replaced. But she was concerned that a few of her more steady and faithful salespeople were leaving, mostly to take full-time jobs. She knew that the success of her operation lay in constantly replenishing the sales force. The new recruits are enthusiastic at first, and their initial sales are high. This source accounted for nearly two-thirds of Martha's, as well as the company's, income. And the novices also bring in other recruits, bolstering the base of the pyramid. If recruiting slows, the new blood is lost and sales stagnate.

Another problem that was brought up by consultants with increasing frequency during 1989 was attendance at the parties. "I have to invite eight or ten now, and hope that four or five will show up. Sometimes, only one or two will come and even they don't buy." Others reported that sales were as brisk as ever. But Martha knew that a number of factors were involved in the party-plan business. First, of course, working women could not come to parties during the day and did not want to give up precious time in the evenings or on weekends. Second, these same working women are the pool from which new recruits came, and they are now opting for the security of full-time salaried jobs. Third, many women are now earning comfortable incomes and prefer to shop for more expensive beauty products at department stores and salons. And because they have less time, they may buy their makeup where they do the rest of their shopping—at the supermarket. She also read in a "Newsline" that the direct-selling approach that Mary Kay and others were using depended upon networks of relationships—women selling to their extended family, friends, and neighbors. This type of selling does best in ordinary neighborhoods; small towns; and in urban working-class, or ethnic areas.

In spite of these problems, Martha's group was performing reasonably well but sales were just about holding their own. She had also seen data showing that door-to-door (including party-plan) sales were about 11 percent of total retail makeup sales in 1990—the same percentage as in 1980. Exhibit 12-5 shows the retail sales breakdown for 2 of 4 recent years.

But recruiting spurted in late 1990 and early 1991 as the result of the recession, expanding the base and bringing in new orders. Martha expanded her direct-mail advertising to attract customers who were reluctant to attend parties. These circulars advertised free "color consulting" by appointment, listed sale-priced Mary Kay products, and solicited applications for positions as beauty consultants. By the spring of 1991, she had earned her second pink Cadillac.

## THE FUTURE OF MARY KAY

Although many sales directors like Martha continue to do well, some experts wonder if Mary Kay, as a party-plan retailer, has any place to go. If social trends and the economy continue in their present direction, the firm will eventually run out of recruits. As recently as two years ago, nearly 120,000 Mary Kay salespeople were either fired from the company or left for other reasons. Of those remaining, only about 60,000 were really productive.

In an attempt to revitalize the recruiting effort, Mary Kay devoted all of its advertising and promotion to recruiting and more than quadrupled the budget for it. And, financial rewards for salespeople who bring in new recruits were also increased substantially, while all hiring at the corporate level was frozen.

In addition to expanding the product line somewhat, Richard has moved the firm's products into markets in Canada, Australia, Argentina, and Guatemala, but thus far some of these have been less than successful.

Mary Kay's earnings peaked in the first quarter of 1983 at $12 million but dropped to less than half of that by the third quarter. Since then there has been a steady decline. In 1979, its common shares sold for about $5.00, but in May 1981 they peaked at $66, and company president Richard Rogers announced a two for one split. In 1985, they have sold for $13, with a low of $8. See Exhibit 12-6 for earnings from 1980 through 1985. In 1985, the company became a closely held private corporation and stopped publishing financial information. Analysts in the industry, however, estimate 1990 revenues at $420 million. In 1989, Mary Kay expressed direct and public interest in acquiring Avon Products, Inc. Avon, a giant in the direct selling and cosmetics business, reported sales of over $3 billion in 1990. Two weeks earlier, the Amway Corp., another diversified direct merchandiser, offered slightly over $2.1 billion for Avon. Avon flatly rejected both bids and remains a separate company.

Skin-care products have accounted for nearly half of Mary Kay's earnings, with makeup the next largest item at 25 percent. Mary Kay, herself, is enthusiastic about plans to further expand the line. "We have only 4 percent of the total retail cosmetics market," she says. "The way I see it, 96 percent of the people in the United States are using the wrong product." Exhibit 12–7 shows the outlets in which cosmetics are sold.

## CASE ANALYSIS QUESTIONS

1. How are "situational factors" involved in the party-plan concept and the recruiting process?
2. What do Exhibits 12-5 and 12-6 suggest to you about Mary Kay's lower sales and earnings in recent years?
3. What shifts in life-styles or social patterns have made "party selling" more difficult today than it was in the past?
4. Mary Kay depends upon the party-plan and a constant influx of new recruits to communicate product information and to sell. Can you think of methods the firm can use to communicate to working women?

## REFERENCES

"Mary Kay Executive is Rebuffed by Avon," *New York Times,* May 31, 1989, p. D-4; "Avon Products Inc. Spurns Mary Kay's Takeover Overture," *Wall Street Journal,* May 31, 1989, p. C-15; "Mary Kay Cosmetics May Make Avon Bid," *New York Times,* May 26, 1989, p. D-4; "Big Names Are Opening Doors for Avon," *Business Week,* June 1, 1987, p. 96; "News Release," *Mary Kay Cosmetics,* December 4, 1985, announcing the firm will be privately held after Dec. 4th.; Cosmetics Makers See a Glowing Market for Men's Skin Conditioners and Creams," *Wall Street Journal,* Dec. 30, 1985, p. 15; "Direct Selling Firms Scramble to Boost Morale, Productivity," *Wall Street Journal,*Oct. 3, 1985, p. 33; "How Cosmetics Makers are Touching Up Their Strategies," *Business Week,* Sept. 23, 1985, p. 66; Pantry Pride, If Buys Revlon, Might Sell Health Care Lines, Analysts Say," *Wall Street Journal,* Aug. 16, 1985, p. 37; "Mary Kay's $5 Million Mansion Shows She's In The Pink," *Dallas Morning News,* August 5, 1985, p. 18; "Mary Kay Ash, The Embattled Cosmetics Magnate Still Holds the Line on What She Believes," *Family Weekly,* Aug. 6, 1985, p. 11; "Avon Products, Market's One-Time Darling Appears to Show Hint of Its Former Blush," *Wall Street Journal,* June 21, 1985, p. 47; "The Party at Mary Kay Isn't Quite So Lively, as Recruiting Falls Off," *Wall Street Journal,* Oct. 28, 1983, p. C-6; "Mary Kay Cosmetics Posts 29% Profit Drop For The Third Quarter," *Wall Street Journal,* Oct. 26, 1983; "Mary Kay, Jafra, Show Dramatic Growth," *Advertising Age,* August 23, 1982, p. 22. Also Company publications and reports such as *Newsline, Annual Reports,* etc. (thru 1985 to time of privatizing).

## MARY KAY COSMETICS
### EXHIBIT 12-1
#### The Mary Kay Marketing Plan

When Mary Kay and Richard Rogers founded the Company, they developed a special marketing plan, including the best features and avoiding the mistakes which Mary Kay has seen in her twenty years with direct sales companies. They made sure that every salesperson's opportunity is as big as her ambition and her ability.

Beauty Consultants are the wholesale purchasers of Mary Kay products and, operating independently of corporate management, derive their profits from retail sales of Mary Kay products to the ultimate consumers. Beauty Consultants may consult with Sales Directors concerning that Mary Kay businesses.

Each sales Director began as a Beauty Consultant, and gained the title of Sales Director in the Mary Kay independent sales organization by demonstrating her ability to sell and to build a successful sales unit of her own. A Sales Director makes available: meetings, training, motivation and suggestions for Beauty Consultants within her sales units who wish to share the benefits of her experience. She receives additional incentive compensation from the Company for her sales leadership activities in the form of a percentage of her total units sales.

*Marketing Built on Retail Sales.* The entire marketing structure is based upon and intended to foster retail sales to ultimate consumers, with commissions being earned only on products sold at retail.

*All Products are Purchased Directly From the Company.* All products are purchased by everyone (Sales Directors and Beauty Consultants) directly from the Company based on the *same* discount schedule. There is only one wholesale sale (from Company to Consultant) and one retail sale (from Consultant to customer). Our products do not pass through several levels of distributors. Every Consultant is recruited to sell her own products at retail, rather than to others at wholesale.

*Mary Kay Does Not Sell Franchises or Distributorships. You Decide to Advance Yourself on the Basis of Proven Ability.* In some companies there are several levels of distributors and a "distributorship" at any level can be purchased by buying a required amount of product, or by paying prescribed fees. "Managers" can thus buy their way in, whether or not they know anything about the product, or how to manage a business. In Mary Kay, you know your Sales Director first proved her abilities as a Consultant. She is your "business consultant," has been in your place, and knows what to do to help you. And you can decide to become a Sales Director, too, by proving your own ability.

*There are No Territories to Limit Where You May Sell or Recruit.* Many companies sell franchise rights within a limited geographic area and many assign territories. Mary Kay feels this is unnecessary. You can recruit and sell merchandise in any of the 50 states, U.S. Territories, or Puerto Rico—on trips or when you visit relatives.

This means that you may hold beauty shows (which we also call skin care classes) and take orders wherever you happen to be. Because your business is your own, your hours are yours also.

*Your Beauty Showcase is the Beginning of a Rewarding Career.* Beginning

(continued)

your Mary Kay career starts with a beauty showcase and does not require the purchase of any additional amount of product. Many new Consultants find it both convenient and profitable to order a modest inventory of merchandise at the outset of their careers. This enables them to obtain the most favorable discount and to better serve their initial retail customers.

From time to time, Mary Kay Cosmetics offers special incentives to new Consultants in connection with initial orders of merchandise. These offers may result in special discounts and may even enable new Consultants to earn their showcases. This inventory purchase is entirely at the discretion of the individual Consultant. No compensation is earned by anyone on a new Consultant's beauty showcase purchase, i.e., "for introducing a new Beauty Consultant." Advancement cannot be "brought" by an "investment": it must be earned. Original and unused products are repurchased by the Company from terminating Beauty Consultants and destroyed.

### Avenues of Income on the Mary Kay Ladder of Success

The Mary Kay marketing plan provides substantial earning opportunities and benefits for each Beauty Consultant through the following avenues of income.

*Beauty Shows.* When Beauty Consultants teach skin care to five or six guests in someone's home, they receive a generous profit for the products they sell. Beauty shows provide a continuous source of profit for their business.

*Facials.* Consultants also provide individualized skin care classes for their customers. Complimentary facials provide another opportunity to introduce Mary Kay products and earn a profit while doing so.

*Dovetailing.* Occasionally, Consultants are unable to hold a previously booked beauty show. When they ask another Consultant to hold or dovetail it, they are still able to earn a percentage of the profit from sales made at that show.

*Advancement to Sales Directorship.* Proven leadership, recruiting and sales ability lead to advancement as a Mary Kay Sales Director. Mary Kay Directors not only receive income from the above-mentioned sources, but an additional Director's commission from the Company for educating, motivating and inspiring their unit members to success by providing them with the necessary training. They also share their business knowledge and experience. Mary Kay Sales Directors may also receive unit and recruiting bonuses, additional Company-sponsored insurance benefits and Seminar awards including the popular pink Cadillacs and Regals.

*Company Promotions and Unit Contests.* When Consultants achieve certain sales and recruiting goals, they earn valuable contest prizes from the Company and their sales unit.

*Self-Employment Benefits Program.* Mary Kay Consultants who are active with the Company are able to enjoy self-employment benefits programs designed to aid them in meeting their Health, Dental/Optional Group Life and Product Replacement Insurance needs.

*The Ultimate Achievements in Mary Kay.* The climb up the Mary Kay ladder of success to Senior, Future National and National Sales Directorship represents significant management, leadership and teaching experience. These top Directors

(continued)

enjoy even more income earning opportunities. Company-sponsored benefits and a special sense of accomplishment in having helped so many others to achieve success in their Mary Kay careers.

*Reorders.* Beauty Consultants provide their customers with dependable, personalized service. This gives them a solid base of recorder customers and a continuous source of profit.

*Recruiting Commissions and "VIP Car".* As they share their Mary Kay opportunity with others, Consultants develop their careers and build their businesses. When they provide their new recruits with career guidance, they receive 4%, 8% or 12% recruiting commissions from the Company on all wholesale orders placed by these recruits. The amount of the check depends upon the number of active recruits and the amount of their monthly purchases. Recruiting commissions can become a sizeable contribution to their income as well as lead to use of a "VIP Car."

Each year, hundreds of Sales Directors earn over $30,000 in commissions, and we have more women earning over $50,000 a year than any other company. Our National Sales Directors average approximately $150,000 a year.

*Special Help in Developing Self-Confidence.* The typical first reaction to a recruiting proposal to become a Mary Kay Consultant is: "Me in sales? Oh, I've never sold anything in my life!"

While this remark is made frequently, Beauty Consultants consistently prove that it's a false fear particularly since they begin learning *how to teach skin care* almost immediately.

Mary Kay Cosmetics is eager to contribute to their career growth and reminds them that they're "in business for themselves, but not by themselves," with these supplementary aids:

- Good, reliable products
- Proven market acceptance
- Advertising and public relations support
- Publications
- Career-building aids
- Training materials
- Incentives for productivity
- Inspirational and motivational resources

Thus, the Mary Kay career opportunity is only limited to the ambitions, determination and willingness to work which each Consultant demonstrates. Consistent efforts, positive attitude and the desire to help others succeed, are the keys to a profitable and rewarding career as a Mary Kay Beauty Consultant.

**138** MARY KAY COSMETICS

**MARY KAY COSMETICS**
**EXHIBIT 12-2**
**Sales Hierarchy**

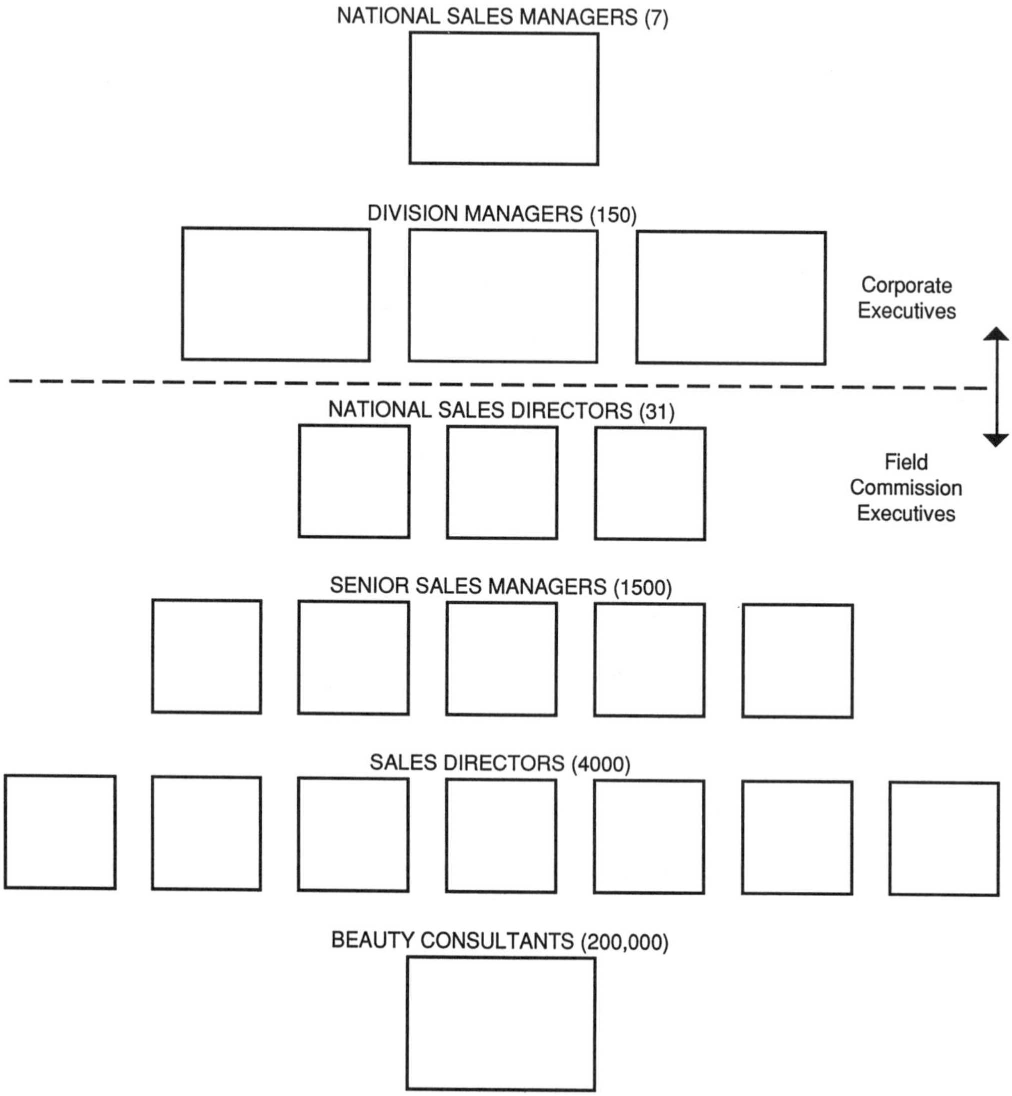

NATIONAL SALES MANAGERS (7)

DIVISION MANAGERS (150)

Corporate Executives

- - - - - - - - - - - - - - - - - - - - - - - - - - - - - - - - - - - -

NATIONAL SALES DIRECTORS (31)

Field Commission Executives

SENIOR SALES MANAGERS (1500)

SALES DIRECTORS (4000)

BEAUTY CONSULTANTS (200,000)

**MARY KAY COSMETICS**
**EXHIBIT 12-3**
**Mary Kay Ash, Company Founder**

*Source*: Reproduced by courtesy of Mary Kay Cosmetics, Inc.

**MARY KAY COSMETICS**

**EXHIBIT 12-4**

**Newsline**

# MARY KAY COSMETICS, INC.
# newsline

- Advertising and P.R. Notes, pages 4 & 5
- Mary Kay Milestones, page 6
- Business Briefings, pages 7 & 8

## Growing Profits Cast a Glow on Mary Kay Cosmetics, Inc.

"Industry analysts say the biggest problem they have with Mary Kay Cosmetics is that they can't find much bad to say about the company." **Dallas Morning News,** February 13, 1983

### For The Incomparable Mary Kay, Skin Is Not To Be Treated Lightly.

"Scientific rather than commercial, "Skin Deep" (at the Museum of Science & Industry in Chicago) is a guide to how the human skin functions and how to care for it."

"Her (Mary Kay's) company has bankrolled 1,500 square feet of museum space because she thinks the public needs information about skin, the human body's largest organ." **Chicago Sun Times,** December 21, 1982

### The Industry's Hottest Segment...

at the moment is skin-care products, with Dallas-based Mary Kay Cosmetics, Inc. the growth leader. **TIME, October 11, 1982**

### New Vogue: Company Culture

"Management thinkers now acknowledge that organizations have distinct identities and tones, often acquired from their chief executive — Mary Kay Cosmetics' cheerful nurturing of employees ... are repeatedly assured by the founder, Mary Kay Ash, that 'you can do it.'"
**The New York Times, January 7, 1983**

### Study Shows Mary Kay Ranks Tops Among Career Women

In a recent survey conducted by *SELF* magazine, Mary Kay was shown to have the greatest rate of increase in customer loyalty in all product categories; placed number one in customer loyalty in the facial foundation category and placed second in customer brand loyalty in both the facial moisturizer and brush-on blushers categories.
**SELF magazine survey, 1983**

### newsline

is published by **Mary Kay Cosmetics, Inc.** for use by its independent **Beauty Consultants and Sales Directors.** Betheny L. Reid, Editor and Coordinator of Public Relations.

*Source*: Reproduced by courtesy of Mary Kay Cosmetics, Inc.

## MARY KAY COSMETICS
### EXHIBIT 12-5
### Retail Sales Breakdown by Sales Source
### (in billions)

| Sales Source | Year | Amount | Percent |
|---|---|---|---|
| Drug and Department Stores | 1 | 1980 $1.8 | 72% |
| | 4 | 1984 $2.38 | 66% |
| Mass Merchandisers and Food Stores | 1 | 1980 $ .42 | 17% |
| | 4 | 1984 $ .828 | 23% |
| Door-to-Door | 1 | 1980 $ .275 | 11% |
| | 4 | 1984 $ .396 | 11% |
| Total sales | 1 | 1980 $2.5 | |
| | 4 | 1984 $3.6 | |

## MARY KAY COSMETICS
### EXHIBIT 12-6
### Selected Sales and Income Data, (in thousands)

| | Year 1 | Year 2 | Year 3 | Year 4 | Year 5 | Year 6 |
|---|---|---|---|---|---|---|
| Net Sales | $166,938 | $235,196 | $304,275 | $323,758 | $277,500 | $289,200 |
| Cost of Sales | 52,484 | 71,100 | 87,807 | 88,960 | 79,867 | 85,344 |
| Selling, G&A Exp. | 86,998 | 120,880 | 154,104 | 168,757 | 156,202 | 161,050 |
| Operating Income | 27,456 | 43,316 | 62,364 | 66,041 | 41,431 | 42,806 |
| Net Income | 15,135 | 24,155 | 35,372 | 36,654 | 41,431 | 42,806 |

**MARY KAY COSMETICS**

**EXHIBIT 12-7**

**Retail Sales Breakdown by Sales Source**

WHERE MAKEUP IS SOLD

Total Retail Sales

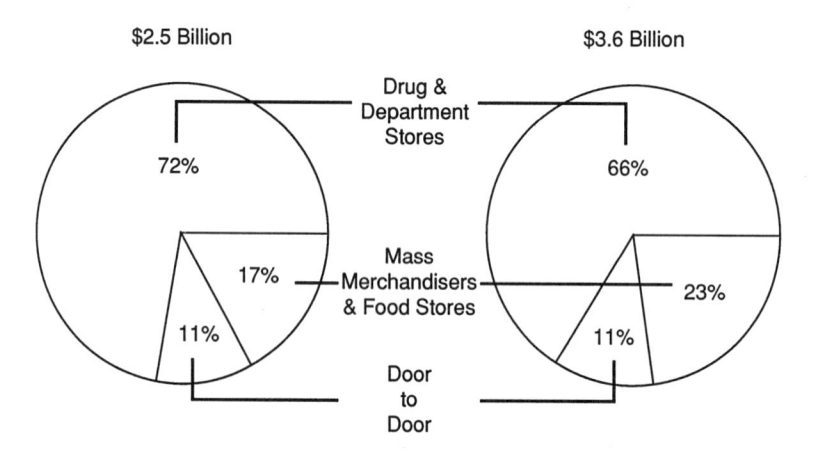

$2.5 Billion — Drug & Department Stores: 72%, Mass Merchandisers & Food Stores: 17%, Door to Door: 11%

$3.6 Billion — Drug & Department Stores: 66%, Mass Merchandisers & Food Stores: 23%, Door to Door: 11%

Data Maybelline Co.

# CASE THIRTEEN

# THE PEARL TRAVEL SERVICE

It was after closing time on a dark winter afternoon. In the small office at the rear of her storefront travel agency, Pearl Kaufman was pondering an article she had just read in *The Wall Street Journal:*

> Most travel agents see strength in both vacation and business travel, especially the latter. In Boston, Corporate bookings are 20% stronger than they were a year ago, while vacation bookings are 10% stronger.... But travelers are bargain conscious, forcing agents to work harder than usual. "It's much more competitive and dog-eat-dog out there," says a travel spokesman in San Francisco. "Many corporate clients insist on discount fares," notes a Portland, Maine, agent. A Chicago booker says that more business travelers achieve savings by arranging trips well in advance—40 days to 2 months. To keep business, more agents are forced to split commissions with corporate clients.

She thought back over the four years since she started the business and the hopes she had for quick success and expansion. She also wondered why some of the record numbers of travelers managed to avoid using her firm's services. Although the agency had been moderately profitable, business had leveled off, and for the past two years the increase in earnings had hardly exceeded the inflation rate. "Maybe I should just go back to Freedom Travel, where I can work regular hours and make a better living than I do now," she mused. Idly, she picked up her four-year income statement and glanced over it, although she knew every figure by heart (Exhibit 13-1).

## HISTORY OF THE AGENCY

After graduating from an Illinois community college, Pearl was hired as a trainee by Freedom Travel, a midwest chain with over 75 offices in major and some smaller cities. After an intensive three-month training program, she was assigned as an assistant to tour directors on several U.S. and foreign tours. There she learned the practical side of the business: how to make the dozens of arrangements needed for tours, how to assure that accommodations and services were satisfactory, and how to handle the sometimes difficult personalities in the tour group. After several of these tours, she settled into one of Freedom's offices in a medium-sized Indiana city.

Pearl was intelligent and hard working, and in two years when the manager was transferred to a larger office, she moved into that job. But she never lost sight of her long-term objective—to have her own agency. About a year after her promotion, Freedom decided to close the office and consolidate it with one in a nearby city. Although she was offered the assistant manager's job in the larger agency, Pearl saw this as the chance she had been waiting for. Quickly, she arranged to sublet the location, bought the furniture and equipment from Freedom at a sacrifice price, and hired the two assistants who had worked for her. It was business as usual when the sign Pearl Travel Service replaced Freedom's above the store window.

## THE EARLY YEARS

During the first year, Pearl's net income increased 10 percent over the amount she had received from Freedom, and she was able to give her employees small raises. But commissions, her main source of income, had not increased much. Expecting that most of her business would come from regular customers telling others about her services, Pearl used only token, reminder advertising in local newspapers. But in the second year, she began running weekend ads on special tours in the travel section of the Sunday paper. Bookings increased and so did commission income, which was up 30 percent over the previous year. The third year was disappointing, with commission income rising less than one-fourth of the increase of the previous year. Last year, Pearl noted sadly, it was up only 7 percent, about equal to the increase of year 3 over year 2.

## TODAY'S PROBLEMS

Pearl wondered, as she looked over the income statements, what she might do to increase her customer base. Her main competitor was a regional chain with an office in the downtown area, while hers was in a large suburban shopping center. Also, the chain could buy discount tickets in bulk, which added appreciably to its profitability. It also offered rides to the airport and free gifts based on the amount of bookings during the year. But the chain tended to be rather inflexible and some of Pearl's customers who had tried it returned to her, complaining they did not get much personal attention.

Pearl also noted that advertising increases of $3,000 in year 3 and nearly $4,000 in year 4 were not bringing in much more business. In her third year, she had continued to advertise the same number of tours but offered a different mixture from earlier years, using the format shown in Exhibit 13-2. Most of the $3,000 increase in advertising expenditures for year 3, however, went into ads and radio commercials aimed at people who were not aware that travel agents normally did not charge commissions to make travel or hotel reservations. She still used this theme, but she was not sure how effective the ads were in attracting new business. She also wondered if these ads were helping her competitors as much as they did her. The ads were similar to those shown in Exhibit 13-3.

She knew that most of her commission income came from domestic travel reservations (with a commission rate of about 10%), overseas travel (8% commission), hotel reservations (10% commission), and tours (10% commission). The breakdown of customer type was:

a. Corporate travel and hotel reservations (33%)
b. Individual travel and hotel reservations (30%)
c. Tour reservations (26%)
d. Miscellaneous other (11%)

This customer mix had stayed about the same since Pearl took over the agency, although the percentage of tour reservations had risen 10 percent since she began advertising. Tours were more work, but they were also more expensive than individual reservations so commissions were higher.

She was concerned particularly about the corporate part of the business. Because only travel agents could get commissions, it was industry practice for agencies to set up "branches" in the offices of their corporate customers. These branches were actually the company's travel department, and they handled reservations, ticketing, and other arrangements. The travel agency then refunded part of its commission, usually 3 percent, to the client firm to help defray the salaries and operating expenses of the "branch." Pearl refunded 5 percent because Freedom had allowed that amount before she took over.

## COMMUNICATION AND ADVERTISING

Pearl was concerned about how she could identify and reach those in her area who were likely to be consumers of travel services. She knew that her present clients were older—age 55 or more. They used both tours and individual reservations and were a steady year-round business. But in the last year or so more younger customers seemed to be traveling in off seasons, as well as in the busy summer months. She had heard that her competitors—the chain and two other independents—seemed to be doing well. She also knew that once clients used her services they were satisfied and likely to come back. They recommended her to their friends, but that method was not generating enough new business. Something else had to be done, and some new type of advertising was probably the answer.

She remembered from her experience with the Freedom agency that some type of celebrity might be useful in attracting attention to ads. But she also recalled that the source used in the ad, celebrity or not, had to have credibility in the mind of consumers. The problem was that most celebrities in the area would charge a heavy fee for permission to use their photograph in an advertisement. Many others would not associate themselves with advertising at all. About a year ago, though, her advertising agency had suggested a well-known and well-liked TV weather reporter whose photo could be used in an ad for $1,500, but she wasn't sure this was the right type of person—one who might simulate an opinion leader.

Almost all the other businesses in her shopping mall used the yellow pages extensively, with separate, freestanding advertisements or at least a boldface type listing. The Freedom agency, however, had always used a plain single line, and a district manager once told her that people did not use yellow pages much to find travel agencies.

Pearl was still not sure whether she should continue to advertise both individual tours and the advantages of using travel agents. If she could decide on a single goal, she could allocate a large part of her rather meager budget to it.

## CASE ANALYSIS QUESTIONS

**1.** What type of advertising was Pearl's ad that told consumers they paid no commission for travel agency services? What is the problem with this kind of ad? Should Pearl continue to use it?

**2.** Why didn't the Freedom management use yellow page advertising?

**3.** Do you think the weather reporter would be enough of a celebrity for consumers to notice the ad? Would such a spokesperson be a credible source?

**4.** How should Pearl redesign her advertising/communication plan?

## REFERENCES

"Keeping Up With Today's Travel Trends," *Compass Readings,* March 1991, p. 42; "U.S. Travel Agencies Going Global," *Washington Post,* Dec. 29, 1989, p. F-3; "Giving People What They Don't Want," *Wall Street Journal,* Nov. 30, 1989, p. B-1; "Travel Industry Gets More Businesslike," in "People Patterns," *Washington Post,* July 10, 1989, p. B-1; "Start to Upstart in Less Than a Year, *Sales and Marketing Management,* Jan. 14, 1985, p. 51; "Freebie Bookers," *Fortune,* Nov. 11, 1985, p. 101; "Travel Agencies Change Tactics to Keep Clients," *Wall Street Journal,* Sept. 27, 1985, p. 31, "High Ticket Travel Takes Off," *Newsweek,* Dec. 17, 1984, p. 97, "Travel Agents Experimenting With Set Fees," *Washington Post,* June 11, 1986, p. 33; "Airline Confusion Has Travel Agents Flying Blind," *Business Week,* Oct. 17, 1983, p. 43; "Taking Out the In-Plants," *Fortune,* Sept. 19, 1983, p. 169; "Charting a Course for New Market Realities," *Advertising Age,* Apr. 25, 1983, p. M-9; "Carriers Support Travel Agencies," *Aviation Week & Space Technology,* Jan. 10, 1983.

## PEARL TRAVEL AGENCY
### EXHIBIT 13-1
### Income Statements, Years One through Four

|  | Year 1 | Year 2 | Year 3 | Year 4 |
|---|---|---|---|---|
| Commission Income | $157,810 | $201,880 | $217,770 | $233,100 |
| Less Expenses: | | | | |
|   Corporate refunds | 22,010 | 36,204 | 37,155 | 39,112 |
|   Salaries | 54,352 | 65,191 | 72,751 | 77,565 |
|   Rent and utilities | 37,341 | 41,753 | 46,200 | 50,123 |
|   Advertising | 5,666 | 9,430 | 12,414 | 16,751 |
|   Administration and tax | 6,349 | 9,017 | 11,653 | 15,307 |
|   Total Expenses | 125,718 | 161,595 | 180,173 | 198,858 |
| Net Income | 32,092 | 40,285 | 37,597 | 34,242 |

THE PEARL TRAVEL SERVICE
EXHIBIT 13-2

## PUT YOURSELF IN THIS PICTURE...

### With PEARL TRAVEL SAFARIS

Visit exotic Kenya with four game parks and majestic Kilimanjaro Mountain! See animals in their natural habitat! Explore the contrasts of Nairobi! 10 glorious days, $2350 - 3195 including airfare from Chicago. Experienced leaders, small groups.

Safaris leave Jan. 15, Feb. 10, and Feb. 25. For information and free brochure: CALL PEARL!

**PEARL TRAVEL SERVICE**
202 West Friel St.

**375-2349**

THE PEARL TRAVEL SERVICE

EXHIBIT 13-3

# Train, Plane, Boat, Hotel, Theme Park . . .

Let your LOCAL TRAVEL AGENT make reservations for you . . FREE.

There is no extra cost to you when Pearl Travel makes normal reservations for you! And we can find times to fit your schedule, special fares to fit your budget, and hotels to fit your style!

We can book individual travel, fly-drive tours, all inclusive plans for groups, and special tours for senior citizens.

Call PEARL TRAVEL SERVICE Today!

**PEARL TRAVEL SERVICE
202 West Friel Street
375-2349**

YOUR LOCALLY OWNED TRAVEL AGENT

# CASE 14

# THE PALACE WARSAW

As he gazed out his office window onto the gray, damp Warsaw street, George Larsen wondered if the Palace Warsaw Hotel would ever become a financial success. He had just finished a meeting with Stanislaw Balowicz, the head of a local Cultural Society, who had delivered complaints from the organization. They claimed that the hotel was not representing the country's heritage with proper decor and food. Mr. Larsen explained that the job of the hotel and its staff was to provide "a world-class hotel experience that Westerners are used to, and we know from experience the kind of surroundings and food the travelers want." He did, however, agree to make some additions to the menu, including Polish dishes that fit in with standard offerings.

Not many Poles stay at the Palace. With top room rates close to $200, nearly 60 percent of the guests come from the United States (35%), Britain, West Germany, and Japan. Today, Mr. Larsen knew that the Palace was the only Western-style hotel in Warsaw, and he realized how important it was to keep both service and other amenities at a very high level. Establishing a reputation was vital because there was little doubt that other Western chains were actively negotiating their own joint-venture agreements.

## PALACE WARSAW—THE BEGINNING

As the cold war drew to a close in 1989, U.S. travel to Eastern Europe increased severalfold as the political climate became more favorable. A Pan American

World Airways spokesperson said that traffic to Poland, Romania, and Yugoslavia was up 25 percent over 1988. Travel agents booked 40 percent more trips to Hungary during the same period. In 1990 and early 1991, bookings declined drastically because of the Persian Gulf war. But they were up again by mid-1991.

But hotel accommodations in the Soviet Union and adjoining Eastern European countries fall far short of those needed to serve the burgeoning demand. Early in 1990, one large Chicago travel agency advised its clients that many Moscow and Leningrad hotels were booked solid for the summer. And Budapest hotels were sold out in the spring and fall, according to the Ibusz Hungarian Travel Co. Another agency noted that the hotels in the more popular Eastern countries are full even in the off-seasons.

Whether or not space is available, the state-run hotels in former Communist countries are well known for inefficient and grudging service, as well as minimum accommodations. On top of that, they have very few facilities for Western travelers who expect such amenities as shops, pools, and night clubs. A U.S. travel publication observed that "East Germany is no Disneyland. They will have to provide more things for visitors to do."

In 1986, long before the lifting of the Iron Curtain, the atmosphere in Poland was grim. The economy was on the brink of collapse, the Solidarity Union was banned, and the Communists held firm control of the government. But a new law had just been passed that permitted joint business ventures between the Polish government and Western companies. Most prospective partners, however, thought the terms of such ventures were much too restrictive, and therefore risky, particularly in the long run.

In Stockholm, however, the outlook was not as gloomy. There, a major Swedish commercial bank with considerable experience working with Eastern European countries, had close ties with the Palace Hotel Corp. in the United States. The bank persuaded Palace that there were long-term advantages to be realized in Poland and that there would be heavy demand for a Western-style hotel in Warsaw. The director of Palace's Foreign Enterprises Division thought so too. "It should be a good place to do business. As the political situation stablizes, more people will be coming to Poland. All of our research indicates there will be much more east-west trade and traffic."

The Swedes also had their eyes on an ideal site for a new hotel. In 1978, a Polish state agency began to build a high-rise structure in the central area of Warsaw. The framework was soon erected, but shortly afterward construction was halted and the skeleton sat unfinished for eight years. A Swedish construction firm proposed to use the framework for a hotel to be operated by the Palace Hotel Corp., with financing provided by a Western bank. Construction began soon afterward.

In October 1989, Poland was shedding the Communist yoke. Among the first arrivals were Western government officials to make arrangements for economic aid and to otherwise help the new government. They were followed by busi-

**THE PALACE WARSAW**

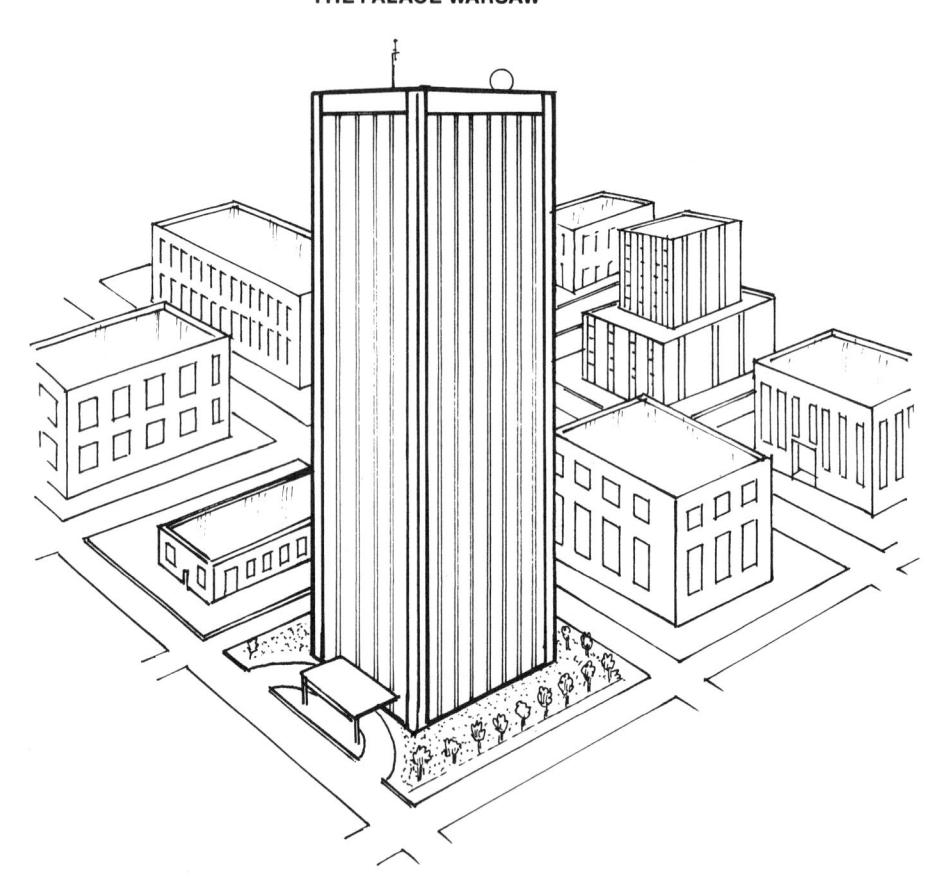

ness people who saw opportunities for selling goods and establishing connections, as the country moved toward a market economy.

In November, before the official opening of the Palace, advance guests included a number of top U.S. government officials, together with business executives and government delegations from Western European countries. When the Palace celebrated its grand opening in December, it was among the first hotels in Eastern Europe to be managed directly by a Western chain. The hotel looms into the Warsaw sky, a sparkling glass rectangle overshadowing the nearby Polish Palace of Science and Culture, as well as other gray hotels managed by the government tourist bureau.

## MORE THAN A LANDMARK

The Palace Warsaw, however, is more than a landmark or a symbol of Western-style commerce. It represents Poland's first taste of a consumer culture where the primary goal is to serve customers and anticipate their needs. For Western guests, the hotel matches, or even exceeds, the standards back home. For Warsaw's people, it is a bizarre tourist attraction, ideally located across from the railroad station, and connected to it by an underground passage. Travelers say they can easily spot where city maintenance of the tunnel ends and the Palace's begins by the change in the degree of cleanliness.

Hundreds of Poles flock to the hotel each day to walk on the glowing marble floors and, if there is room, to sit in comfortable chairs on the mezzanine. There, in the afternoon, they may listen to schmaltzy music played by a string trio. There are 11 separate food and beverage service operations in the hotel, which serve an average of 4,500 meals a day. Some of the restaurants are very popular and reservations must be made far in advance.

## STAFFING AND STOCKING THE HOTEL

After construction was well under way, Mr. Larsen and other executives were faced with the problems of staffing the hotel, as well as finding supplies, furniture, and other items needed to provide Western-style service and surroundings for the guests. Recruiting personnel proved to be the least difficult. Initially, they planned to hire on the basis of previous hotel experience, but after some consultation with personnel managers of Western European firms that had been in Warsaw for some time, they decided not to hire anyone who had worked in a Polish state hotel, or who had any other hotel or hospitality training, and to be selective about hiring those who had worked in any state organization. Because such organizations were not profit motivated, there was no incentive to provide the type of service Western guests expected.

The company initially hired 30 native Poles to be managers of the various hotel functions. Since none of them had any hotel or food service experience, they were all sent to the United States for an 18-month training course at Palace hotels. There, they were assigned to a number of different tasks involving Palace procedures, handling of guests, and supervision of others.

Over 5,000 responses were received to the Palace's hiring announcement to fill 1,000 jobs. The personnel director said the hotel was looking for "cheerful, younger people who have a big smile and are willing to work, but we would rather they had not worked in other jobs before and, perhaps, learned bad habits. Because many of our guests will be from the United States, Britain or Canada, they will have to speak English."

## LOOKING FOR WORK

One afternoon, Pawel Wisniewski and Loda Podelko strolled through the ornate lobby of the Palace Warsaw. "This looks as though it would be a nice place to work," Loda ventured. "A lot of the staff seems to be around our age. And they say that the waiters get as much as $50 a month, and tips as well. That's what my uncle makes, and he's a doctor at the State Hospital." Pawel was looking at all the different jobs there seemed to be, just in the lobby itself. "Yes," he replied, "We could be baggage carriers or stand out in front and get taxis. Maybe we could even work up to be a desk clerk. My father said they earn $100 a month! I'll bet the English course we took in high school will help." Loda wasn't quite as enthusiastic. "I don't know about that," she said. "My oldest brother applied here last month but was turned down because he had worked in the government for five years."

As they looked around for a likely person to ask about getting work, Pawel exclaimed, "Loda! There's Stefan Maszyk who graduated with us last month." Dressed in his bellman's uniform, Stefan seemed glad to see them but kept glancing around the lobby. "They don't like it if I stop to talk with people," he said. "But if you're looking for a job, I'll ask Wieslaw in the back office. You remember him from English class. He's very smart and is in training for desk clerk, then he will move up to be an assistant manager."

Weislaw greeted them cordially, and they chatted about other school mates. "Stefan is only one of several working here now," he said. When Loda told him why they were there, he handed them a set of application forms and volunteered some tips on what to do if they were called for an interview. "I listen sometimes when the interviewers talk with each other, and they say if you make intelligent conversation, you could be slated for manager training later on. If you smile a lot and have an outgoing personality, you may end up with one of the good jobs at the front desk. If you are more ordinary, you may carry bags, bus in the restaurant, or clean rooms. Even in those jobs, if you show a lot of promise and work hard, they will move you up."

It was more than two months before Loda was called for an interview, and she went to the hotel with some misgivings. She wasn't sure if she could make intelligent conversation, if she should come on heavily, or just smile a lot. She waited with several other applicants who talked about how anxious they were to work for Americans in such a fine hotel.

Her name was finally called by a pleasant woman, who seemed to be a Scandinavian. She introduced herself as Mrs. Lindstrom and seemed pleased that Loda had just graduated from high school. Then she described at length the hotel's concept of hospitality—always being cheerful and tending to the guest's wants. Loda listened carefully, but she found it difficult to relate to the notion of "service," or strict cleanliness, since she had never experienced anything but grubby stores and slovenly service in Polish establishments. After some discussion of Loda's home and background, Mrs. Lindstrom thanked her and said they would call her if there were a suitable opening.

## HOSPITALITY TRAINING

Loda was thrilled several days later when she was offered the job of assistant housekeeper on the fifth floor. She began her training course the following week, along with about a dozen other trainees. The course was designed to cover all aspects of the Palace operation, and specifically what the housekeeping staff was supposed to do. The morning lectures covered most of this general information. Then the group was taken to one of the hotel rooms where the training staff demonstrated in detail how to clean, make up, and resupply items in the rooms. This staff was recruited from Palace hotels in the United States and Western Europe, and they were meticulous in their instruction, as well as in explaining how to deal with guests' special requests or complaints.

The group was then taken to another room where one trainee was asked to clean; one to make up the room; and another to resupply soap, towels, and other items. A fourth one then inspected the room and pointed out any inadequacies. This exercise continued until even the instructor found nothing wrong. Loda was delighted with the light, airy, and luxurious rooms, as well as the helpful instructors and the other pleasant trainees. She was eager to start work when the course ended and considered herself lucky to have a job there. "This is way ahead of a grubby store or a dirty factory where I would have ended up," she said happily to herself.

## SUPPLYING THE RESTAURANTS

When McDonalds of Canada planned for its first Moscow restaurant, its most difficult problems were obtaining enough quality beef, potatoes, lettuce, and other ingredients for the items on the menu. State-run factories and farms could furnish neither quantity nor consistent quality. So McDonalds was forced to build its own factory to supply some of the goods and to go to the United States and other European countries for the rest.

At the Palace Warsaw, one of the chefs planted an herb garden in his backyard, and the hotel operates its own facilities for canning and freezing vegetables so only the best quality are served year-round. Much of the other produce is grown locally from Dutch seeds that the Palace bought and distributed to the collective farms. Still, the executive chef scours the markets, farms, and other sources to get enough supplies to run the restaurants. In a capitalist economy, salespeople and farmers would wait in line to see him and take orders.

Fresh, quality meat was another problem. The best cuts are imported from the United States. Others come from local suppliers, but deliveries are uncertain. If an order is placed for, say 100 kilograms of lamb or pork, the delivery may be 200 or 50 kg, but the Palace needs all it can get. Imported items have to be paid for in hard currency such as dollars, pounds, or yen, which must come directly from Western guests.

## MORE PRIVATE ENTERPRISE

In 1988, after having discouraged private business and workshops for decades, the Polish government began to actively promote them by easing rules. The earlier joint-venture legislation was made less restrictive and more appealing to Western investors. As a result, Polish entrepreneurs began to flourish, and more than 1.5 million of them were operating more than 600,000 businesses.

## THE FUTURE OF THE PALACE

Mr. Larsen reviewed the Palace's latest operating data with little pleasure. The occupancy rate for the past three months was about 51 percent, compared to an objective of 65 percent. He knew the Palace had an overwhelming advantage in accommodations, restaurants, and service. But Polish hotels, with their connections to the state travel agency, were much less expensive. Also, the agency enables them to sell prepaid foreign exchange and room vouchers for their hotels only, as well as government gasoline vouchers. As a private venture, the Palace can't provide these services. And even though the Palace's foreign guests must pay for their rooms with hard currency, they may use Polish zlotys in the hotel restaurant and for other services. Zlotys have no value outside Poland, so the Palace cannot use them to pay for imported goods.

"At least," thought Mr. Larsen, "the work force is shaping up well, and it looks as though government restrictions are easing a little. Also, a few more private suppliers are beginning to come in with better quality products and dependable delivery schedules." Out the window, the sky was still murky, and shabby passers-by moved slowly down the gritty street. "Maybe," he said to himself, "we'll make it after all."

On the fifth floor, Loda and her partner, Krystyna, were taking a last look at the room they had just finished. Giving one last fluff to the pillows, Loda exclaimed, "I can't believe I've been working here over three months! At first I thought I'd never get everything perfect, but now it seems easy." "I know," Krystyna replied, "and I don't think I ever had enough money to buy something pretty to wear! Let's go shopping after work." Chatting happily, they moved to the next room.

## ONE YEAR LATER

Mr. Larsen worried needlessly. After a year of operation, the hotel not only turned a profit, but it also received the highest "guest satisfaction scores" of any Palace hotel. And there were plenty of guests who made more reservations there than at any of Palace's other international hotels. The corporate management was pleasantly surprised, too. An executive said, "We thought it would be a good location, but we weren't prepared for the rousing success."

## CASE ANALYSIS QUESTIONS

**1.** Why does Mr. Larsen balk at using Polish decor in the hotel public rooms and serving Polish cuisine in the dining rooms? Few Poles stay there, but large numbers apparently eat there.

**2.** When U.S. firms do business in other countries, they are usually advised to learn and abide by the customs and practices of the country. Why, then, does Palace send its managers to train in the United States and have U.S. employees train the Polish staff? Is this a "reverse" of the consumer learning process?

**3.** One definition of culture is "the sum total of learned beliefs, values, and customs . . . " Considering this, what aspects of her culture did Loda have to revise when she went to work at the Palace Warsaw? What was her attitude toward the new aspects?

**4.** Despite the important advantages that Polish state hotels have, and the many problems in supplying the Palace Warsaw, the hotel was able to out perform most of the Palace Corp.'s other worldwide hotels. How do you explain this?

## REFERENCES

"Once Complacent Hotel Industry Is Forced to Learn How to Market," *Wall St. Journal,* Nov. 9, 1985, p. B-17.; "For a Jump-Start, Poland Tries a Jolt of Capitalism," *Business Week,* Aug. 8, 1988, p. 38; "Tourists Will Find Hotels Scarce in the Eastern Bloc," *Wall St. Journal,* Dec. 11, 1989, p. B-1; "Marriott's Polish Pursuit," *Washington Post,* Jan. 8, 1990, p. 1; "Poles Find the Freeing of the Economy Lifts Supplies—and Prices," *Wall St. Journal,* Feb. 21, 1990, p. 1; "Shock Treatment for East Europe," *Washington Post,* Feb. 18, 1990, p. 1; "New York's Newest Hotels are Built for Business," *Business Week,* Apr. 23, 1990, p. 130; "Warsaw Hotel's Success Even Surprises Marriott," *Marketing News,* Dec. 10, 1990, p. 18.

## CASE FIFTEEN

# THE WHEELS AND BOARDS OF FORTUNE

During the past ten years or so, the attitude of the U.S. public toward gambling has rotated almost 180 degrees. Except in a few isolated locations such as Las Vegas, casino-type board and wheel games were concealed in hidden rooms or behind boarded-up storefronts. Numbers games were surreptitiously played on street corners or out of bottom desk drawers in offices. We might say that gambling "products" were specialty goods, painstakingly sought out by would-be consumers.

Widespread social disapproval of gambling was based on the popular perception that it was a vice, similar to alcoholism, that deprived families of their livelihood and drove people into financial gutters. This feeling was intensified by the perception that most organized gambling was under direct control of the Mafia. Thus, the games were not only crooked, but gamblers with unpaid debts were dealt with violently.

Today, most types of gambling are widely accepted as standard products, and consumers "purchase" them in the same manner as they do other goods. Gambling first took on an aura of legitimacy when state lotteries appeared on the scene, and people could gamble without guilt. When respectable religious groups, charities, and leisure-oriented corporations entered the business, there was no longer a place for the undercover mob or numbers game. During the past several years, Virginia voters approved a state lottery as well as horse racing. South Dakota authorized video slot machines in bars, and in nine southern states, consumers play MegaBingo simultaneously from huge video screens in halls. The numbers are drawn in Tulsa, Oklahoma, and beamed by satellite to other locations. In

Princeton, Maine, the Passamaquoddy Indian Tribe packs the hall with weekly Bingo games offering substantial prizes. Most games such as this are staged by professional, legitimate promoters who run the entire operation and pay a percentage of revenue, or a fixed fee, to the sponsors. The Passamaquoddy Tribe nets about 14 percent.

Lotteries, horse race betting, bingo, other charitable games and even continued illegal gambling account for only about one-third of all U.S. betting dollars. The remaining two-thirds come from casino slots and board games. This is why casino managements are vitally concerned with market research and the identification of consumer segments that produce the highest yields. To illustrate, let us look at Atlantic City, New Jersey, as an example of the second Fun City in the United States.

## GAMBLERS BY THE BUSLOAD

Josie Anderson waited for the Atlantic City bus in a suburban shopping center north of Washington DC. The sun was just coming through the early morning haze and promised another hot, humid August day. It was her day off from the supermarket where she worked, and she looked forward to a lazy day at the beach, and perhaps a pull or two at the slot machines. It was Josie's fourth trip to Atlantic City since June. Not only was it a kind of adventure, but the total cost fit well within her meager entertainment budget.

The round-trip fare for the rather long ride was only $25.00, and she also received a $12.50 chit for quarters, a $5.00 voucher toward lunch, and another $5.00 voucher she could cash in on her next trip. Today she had one of those from the last time she was there. The bus pulled up to the stop; Josie hopped on and promptly went to sleep. Her routine when she arrived in Atlantic City was always the same. She first picked up her quarters and played the slots until they were gone. Usually this took no more than five or ten minutes, but today she was lucky and hit several heavy payoffs. She set aside $25.00 of her quarters, then played for about 15 minutes until the remaining ones were gone. Josie always put at least $5.00 into the machines because the casino was paying for most of her trip, and she felt guilty if she didn't put at least some of it back.

By then it was shortly after noon, and she had a sandwich at the casino's outdoor cafe, paying with the $5.00 voucher and $3.50 of her own money. Afterward, she strolled along the beach for a while, then changed into her bathing suit in a locker room. She found a pleasant spot, spread her beach towel on the sand, and spent the rest of the day in the sun reading and dozing. After an early dinner at the casino cafeteria ($3.97), she boarded the 7 P.M. bus back to Washington. On the way back, she listened to the other riders discuss their wins and losses. Most of them seem to have spent most of the day on the slot floors. Among them were a few who claimed to be winners, some who broke even, and many who said they lost a hundred dollars or more. Regardless of which group they were in, most seemed to be tired, but happy, after a long day.

## ON THE BAORDWALK

It was late afternoon when Ethel and Ed Morrison wheeled their mid-sized recreation vehicle into a hookup lot in Atlantic City. On this Tuesday in late October, there was plenty of room and they were quickly connected to all the service lines. Since they planned to stay several days, they were in no hurry to get to the casinos. Anyway, the main reason for this visit was to see the fabulous Taj Mahal and, incidentally for them, to try their luck at the slots. Sometimes, Ed would sit in a few low-dollar blackjack games but not for long.

This was the fourth time they had been to Atlantic City since they had retired. Ed, who is 68, turned his small plumbing business over to his son two years ago, and shortly afterward, Ethel left her job as an office manager. The Morrisons were comfortably off financially, with income from Social Security, a Keogh Plan Ed had established, and his share of profits from the plumbing business.

For them Atlantic City was a reasonable distance from their home in lower New York state, and they thought of a visit there as a form of entertainment—something different to do. Yes, it would be nice to win a fortune, but they really considered the modest amount they set aside for gambling as a reasonable price for the fun they had. It was a substitute for what some of their friends spent for theater tickets, major sports events, and overseas vacations.

After dinner in their RV, they strolled down the strip to the Taj Mahal. Awed by its size and the ornate Arabian Nights motif, they explored all the public areas. Finally, they ended their tour at a large slot floor. Ethel started with $30.00 in quarters and Ed carried his $100 in silver dollars to the "97% Payoff" slot section across the floor. It was about 11 P.M. when Ed appeared at her machine clutching a small cardboard pail full of silver dollars. "Let's go home! If I stay any longer, I'll just put them back in." Ethel pumped the last four quarters of her second $30.00 into the machine and turned away sadly. "I guess it just wasn't my night," she complained as they walked over to change the dollars into bills. Ed was more cheerful. "We're certainly nowhere near our $200 loss limit for today," he said. "We might even come out ahead on this trip."

## THE HIGH ROLLERS

George and Ruth Ferris, along with Ruth's sister Doris and her friend Patrick, drove their new Infiniti to Atlantic City from Paoli, Pennsylvania, for the weekend. George and Ruth own an automobile dealership, and Doris is a partner in the

Paoli Bowling Alley, where Patrick works. As they pulled up to the entrance of a luxury hotel, the doorman welcomed them by name, suitably impressing Doris and Patrick. While the doorman parked the car, their bags were whisked into the lobby. "You're all registered, Mr. Ferris," said the desk clerk. "Here's the key, and your bags are on their way up." A few minutes later, they were settling into their two-bedroom suite on the 14th floor.

The Ferrises came to Atlantic City about once every month or two, usually bringing another couple with them, and stayed two or three days. They confined their play to high-stakes board games such as blackjack, bacarat, and roulette. Both George and Ruth were rather heavy gamblers and would sometimes wager several thousand dollars on one hand. This was the first visit for Doris and Patrick so they looked forward to trying some of the boards, as well as slots. Since they were among the hotel casino's group of regular and valued customers, there was no charge for the Ferrises' hotel suite.

After a seven-course dinner (compliments of the management), they headed for the tables. All four were plentifully supplied with chips and silver dollars, courtesy of George. While Doris and Patrick drifted toward the slot floor to start, George and Ruth found table seats and began to play in earnest with their beginning stakes of $2,000 each in chips.

## THREE CONSUMER SEGMENTS

Josie is a "bus" customer, and casinos work hard to bring such customers in. For Josie and some other nongamblers, the trip is almost a free day's outing. Most of the other bus riders, however, not only fill up the casino floors during the day, but pump sizable amounts into the slots—up to $150 each. The new Taj Mahal, alone, had visits from more then 120,000 bus customers a month during its first summer. The casinos normally pay the bus company $3.00 to $5.00 over the fare each customer pays. The riders are dropped at the sponsoring casino, where they tend to do most of their gambling. Later in the day, they may visit other casinos and hotels, but by then most have either spent their limit or decided to quit.

The Morrisons are people whom casino managements call "bread and butter" (B&B) customers. Mostly retired, they tend to be regular and frequent visitors. Most of them come every few weeks, more often than Ed and Ethel. Since they drive themselves, they stay longer than the "bus" customers. About half come in their own RVs, but the rest drive cars and stay in hotels, taking advantage of low midweek rates. B&Bs are usually more profitable for the casinos than the one-day visitors. Most of them live within a few hours, but usually no more than a day's drive from Atlantic City, so the radius of attraction for this segment is limited. With no major airport close by, almost all of Atlantic City's customers come by car or bus.

Although a significant proportion of these "middle-range" gamblers have characteristics similar to those of the Morrisons, others are so diverse that they are difficult for casinos to target.

The Ferrises are "high rollers"—the "cream of the crop" segment who constitute 20 to 25 percent of the market. Casinos vie for their business by offering free luxury hotel rooms, around-the-clock service, and other amenities. Managers and employees always greet them by name, "Mr. and Mrs. Ferris! We're certainly glad to see you back." Investing a few hundred dollars in perks for the high rollers nets substantial profits for the casinos. These customers often come in groups of four or more and are not as limited to a one-day driving radius as the B&Bs. Most of them have their own businesses and gamble with some of their extra income.

## IMPORTANCE OF IDENTIFYING CONSUMERS

Beginning in 1989, both revenues and visitors declined at Atlantic City for the first time since 1978, so the characteristics of various types of customers are of vital concern to casino operators there. And it is even more important to know which segment of gamblers is not coming. One industry expert noted that the 1990 summer gaming table income declined by about 55 percent. Almost all of that would have been in chips bought by credit card. Overall, the heavy betters normally use credit to buy chips while lower-level gamblers, such as the Morrisons, pay cash. In Atlantic City, the small, but consistent gamblers are still coming, but the high rollers are not betting as much and tend to come less often. Exhibits 15–1 and 15–2 show revenues and numbers of visitors from 1978 through 1990.

## THE FUTURE

Some small revenue gains in early 1990 suggested that the decline may just be a pause for adjustment. The opening of the gaudy Trump Taj Mahal in April 1990, at a cost of $1.1 billion, brought a pall of uneasiness to Atlantic City. Some casino owners wondered if the market could grow enough to absorb this new operation. If not, the Taj's customers would have to come out of existing establishments. Exhibit 15–3 shows how the Taj Mahal appeared to affect revenues of other casinos. A view of the new Taj Mahal is shown in Exhibit 15–4.

Industry analysts estimated flat growth for Atlantic City in 1990, and also a fall in gambling revenues for 1991. Las Vegas will also be affected by the downturn. Its overall growth was about 7 percent in 1990, but is expected to be only 4 to 6 percent in 1991.

Atlantic City casinos recognize that Las Vegas is the traditional all-out gambling mecca in the United States and that their location is a far-off second. Nevertheless, they are located in the midst of one of the most densely populated areas in the country. Attracting the right segment of consumers and attracting them frequently and in large numbers are the challenges faced by Atlantic City.

## CASE ANALYSIS QUESTIONS

1. What motives seem to apply to the three segments of gambling consumers? To what social class does each of the groups belong?

2. What degree of involvement in the casino gambling product do the customers have? Explain.

3. Would you expect regular consumers of lottery and bingo products to also be regular consumers of casino gambling? Why or why not?

4. Would you use the same advertising and communication themes to attract all consumers to Atlantic City casinos, or a different one for each segment? What theme(s) would you use?

## REFERENCES

"Trump Castle's 1990 Results Show Cash Flow Slump," *Wall Street Journal,* Mar. 15, 1991; "The Tables Have Turned on Gambling," *New York Times,* December 9, 1990, p. 3-1; "Casino Gaming Giant, Ever the High Roller, Now Bets Its Future," *Wall Street Journal,* Oct. 9, 1990, p. 1; "Laughlin, Nev., Casinos Fed By Meat-and-Potatoes Diet," *Wall Street Journal,* Sept. 24, 1990, p. B-1; "Atlantic City Casinos Slide Into the Red," *Wall Street Journal,* August 16, 1990, p. B-1; "Player's Club Sees a Good Bet in Niche Left by Casinos," *Wall Street Journal,* May 10, 1990, p. B-2; "Trump's Taj—Open At Last With a Scary Appetite," *New York Times,* April 8, 1990, p. F-5; "United Gaming," *Fortune,* March 12, 1990, p. 90; "America's Gambling Fever," *Business Week,* Apr. 24, 1989, p.112; "Bingo! Are Indian Tribes Hitting the Jackpot?" *Business Week,* Apr. 24, 1989, p. 115.

**WHEELS AND BOARDS OF FORTUNE**

**EXHIBIT 15-1**

**Gambling Revenues—Atlantic City, 1978-90**

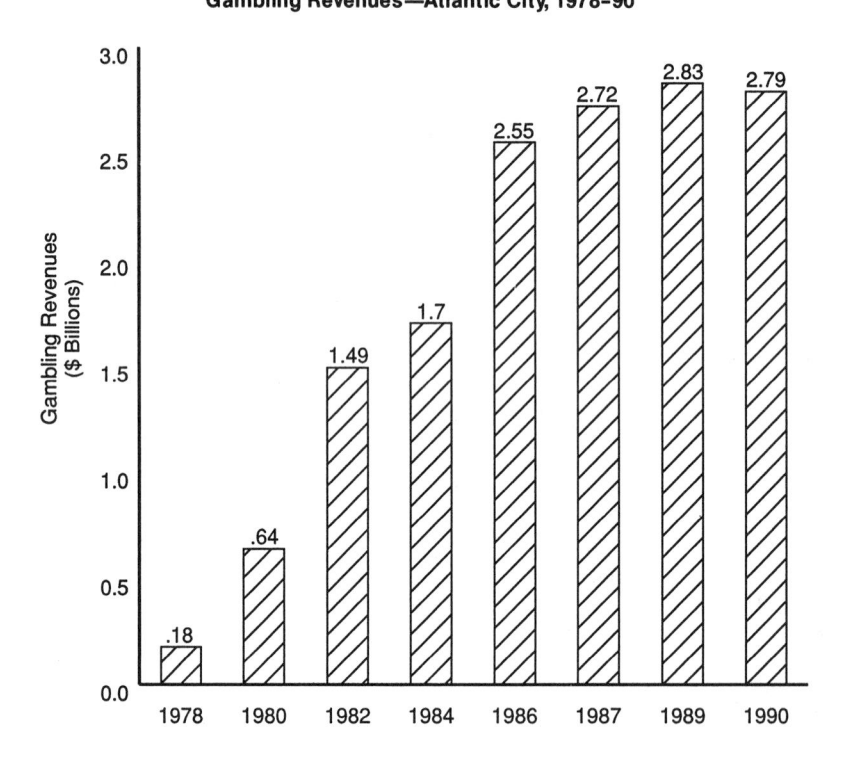

| Year | Gambling Revenues ($ Billions) |
|---|---|
| 1978 | .18 |
| 1980 | .64 |
| 1982 | 1.49 |
| 1984 | 1.7 |
| 1986 | 2.55 |
| 1987 | 2.72 |
| 1989 | 2.83 |
| 1990 | 2.79 |

## WHEELS AND BOARDS OF FORTUNE
### EXHIBIT 15-2
### Atlantic City Visitors, 1978-90

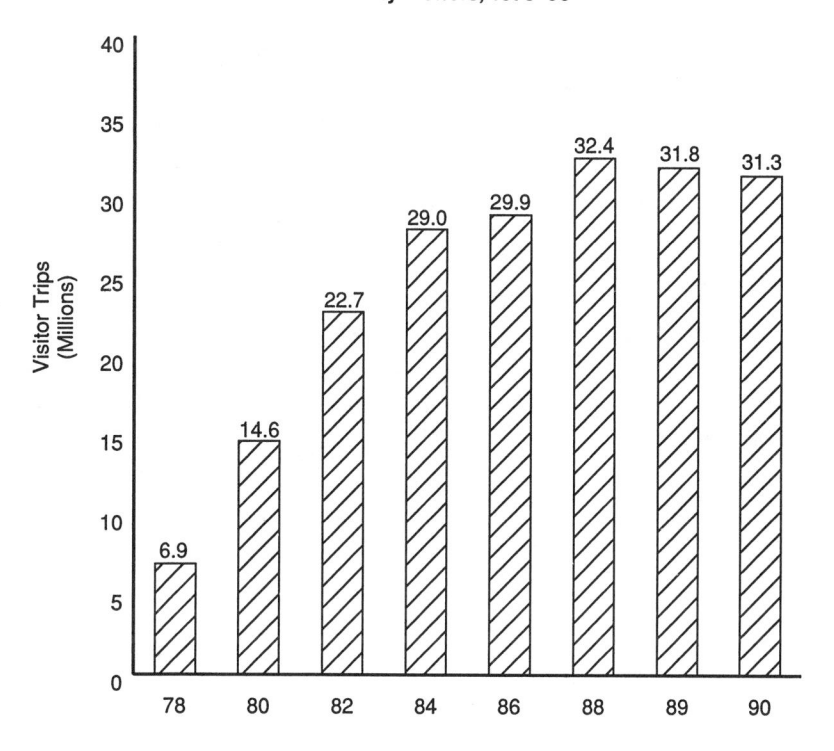

| Year | Visitor Trips (Millions) |
|------|--------------------------|
| 78   | 6.9                      |
| 80   | 14.6                     |
| 82   | 22.7                     |
| 84   | 29.0                     |
| 86   | 29.9                     |
| 88   | 32.4                     |
| 89   | 31.8                     |
| 90   | 31.3                     |

## WHEELS AND BOARDS OF FORTUNE
### EXHIBIT 15-3
### Revenues: Selected Atlantic City Casinos, 1989-90
### (through November, $ millions)

|                    | 1989 | 1990 |
|--------------------|------|------|
| Trump Castle       | 240  | 215  |
| Trump Plaza        | 280  | 258  |
| Caesars            | 275  | 268  |
| Harrah's Marina    | 265  | 257  |
| Trop-World         | 260  | 255  |
| Bally's Park Place | 259  | 246  |
| Showboat           | 237  | 227  |
| Sands              | 210  | 223  |
| Resorts            | 217  | 190  |

**WHEELS AND BOARDS OF FORTUNE**
**EXHIBIT 15-4**

# CASE SIXTEEN

# THE OLD SPAGHETTI MILL

> The scene is a suburban home on a Friday evening. It is a little after 5:00 P.M. Jane, age eight, and Jim, age ten, are sprawled in front of the television set in the family room. They hear Mom's car in the driveway and a moment later she walks in. "What a day! I must have shown this woman a dozen houses and she wants to see a dozen more tomorrow. Let's eat out." "Yeah," the kids shout simultaneously, "McDonalds!" "I don't care where," said Mom, "as long as it isn't here. Let's see where Dad wants to go when he gets home." A little while later, Dad walks in. "We're going out to McDonalds!" cries Jim. "OK with me," says Dad, "but how about trying the Spaghetti Mill over in Appledale? Jim Johnson told me about it the other day. He and Joanne should know; they go to a lot of restaurants, and they said lots of people take their kids there."

## BACKGROUND

The Old Spaghetti Mill is a large, limited-menu restaurant with table service and a bar. It is located along a well-traveled state road about eight miles from the downtown section of a large eastern city. Although this road is the most direct route from a freeway exit to the city's northwestern suburbs, it is also the most congested, passing through business districts and shopping areas of varying sizes and densities. The restaurant is near a crossroad where several other east-west and north-south roads converge in what had been a small country center known as Appledale some 20 years before. Although its country nature disappeared, the name remained and now Appledale contains a number of stores, restaurants, and service businesses. It also hosts a large neighborhood shopping center with 40 stores, anchored by a major supermarket and a K-Mart. Even though Appledale cannot be called run-down, neither can it be considered a modern or well-kept area. Nevertheless, since it forms a hub to several access roads leading to northern and eastern suburbs, it is a busy commercial area.

The Spaghetti Mill is owned by Tri-State Restaurants, Inc., which, in turn, is controlled by Ray Osborne and several members of his family. The corporation owns 12 restaurants in this and two adjacent states, but there is no pattern or theme to them. There are three in a large seacoast city: a pancake house, a seafood "grotto," and a standard "sit-down" featuring American specialities. In addition to the Spaghetti Mill, another pancake house, a steak–roast beef restaurant, and a Mexican "Hacienda" are located in the metropolitan area surrounding Appledale. The other five are in larger cities in the two nearby states.

The "Mill," as it is known locally, is a large, one-story building that had once housed a W. T. Grant store. There is a spacious parking lot in front, with easy access to Appledale Road. Inside, there is a medium-sized lobby with coat racks, rest rooms, and a hostess station. Off the lobby is an open section, with a service bar in the rear and a small "family" area with a few tables. Since the Mill does not take reservations, patrons can wait in the bar on busy nights until their names are called. An intimate discotheque can also be accessed from the right side of the lobby. A plan of the complex is shown in Exhibit 16–1.

The large dining room seats 280 at a total of 74 tables, with the following size distribution:

```
2 person   20
4 person   42
6 person   12
```

There is little demand for large parties at the Mill, but when they are scheduled, tables are set up at the far end of the dining room and are isolated by a movable partition that extends from floor to ceiling. The Mill's menu is shown in Exhibit 16-2.

## TARGET MARKET

The Spaghetti Mill's initial strategy was to attract younger consumers, roughly in the 21–34 age group, who would eat a late dinner and then move on to the discotheque for the rest of the evening. Thus, most of the dinner business is parties of two or four. Often, couples who came for dinner and dancing became acquainted with each other at the discotheque and made up parties of four and even six when they next came to the Mill. The hostess has come to know many of these "regulars" and estimates that most of them come in about once every two or three weeks.

> It was a little after 6:00 P.M. when Mom, Dad, and the kids got to the Spaghetti Mill. The lobby was a little crowded, but the hostess promised them a table in about ten minutes. They noticed the calls for other patrons came rather quickly, and it seemed they waited no time at all until they were called and seated. Dad was a little surprised at the rather limited menu, but he was very pleased with the prices. When he asked the kids what they wanted, Jane cried, "Spaghetti and meatballs." "I want hamburger steak," said Jim. "Would you kids like a soda or something while we're waiting?" asked Dad. "Okay, two Cokes and two dry martinis," he ordered from the waiter. "And we'll have a large carafe of red wine with dinner."

During the past several months, the manager noticed that the early dinner period, between about 5:00 P.M. and 6:30 P.M., was attracting more and more customers. Until about eight or ten months ago, there were seldom more than eight or ten parties seated during that time. She also noticed that there seemed to be more children—as many as one-third of all the diners, and that the number of three- and four-person groups had risen considerably. After about 7:00 P.M., though, the customers were more likely to be younger couples, older married couples, and groups of four or more adults.

The manager, Maggie Thurston, discussed this change in the mix of customers with Ray Osborne, Tri-State's president and CEO, when he dropped in for lunch one day. He visited about once a week since his offices were only a quarter of a mile down the road. "And another thing," she said, "liquor, wine, and beer sales have nearly doubled in the past six months, and most of it seems to be in the dining room. Disco sales are up only a little." She showed Mr. Osborne the data which she had tabulated from the dinner checks for the past week. Both food and liquor were included, with the latter broken down into three time periods: 5:00 to 7:00, 7:00 to 9:00 and after 9:00. The 5:00 to 7:00 period data are shown in Exhibit 16-3. He was quite interested in her figures, and they discussed the situation for a while. They wondered why this new group of customers suddenly materialized. Because of its relatively low prices, the Mill had done little advertising. Except for the large sign on Appledale Road, the only advertising had been periodic "50 cents off" coupons in local suburban newspapers to stimulate weekday sales. But this promotion had not been very successful, and the new customers were coming in on weekends when the coupons were not valid.

## A NEW MARKET SEGMENT?

Before he left, Mr. Osborne asked Ms. Thurston for a few additional numbers, then took all the data back to his office. There he made some additional calculations, which are shown in Exhibit 16-4 and 16-5. He was somewhat surprised to note that Ms. Thurston's tabulations showed that cocktails and mixed drinks far surpassed sales of wine and beer, and he noted the relatively high number of drinks per person in the 5:00 to 7:00 P.M. period. He was also amazed to see the large number of diners served during that time and the high proportion of low-priced pasta dishes that were sold in comparison to the relatively stable sales of steak, even on weekends. Even the inexpensive chopped steak dinner was a comparatively slow seller.

Mr. Osborne was quite pleased with the performance of the Mill, since it had been his idea from the beginning. He found the location and designed both the exterior and interior himself, the latter with some help from his sister-in-law who was a commercial decorator. In the short space of three years—not long for a restaurant—the Mill was a financial success, and most of it had come in the past year.

But there was more involved in his recent detailed interest in the Mill's sales and its customer mix. After all, the company had analysts and accountants on its staff to do that. For some time he had been considering revising Tri-State's hodgepodge pattern of restaurants and concentrating on a single theme that offered something unique and that could be used in other geographical areas—perhaps even franchised! Tri-State was prepared to open another restaurant somewhere in its territory but had not yet decided what type it would be. So the Mill's recent success made it a likely prototype for a group of future restaurants.

But Mr. Osborne was a little uneasy about going ahead on the basis of the operational and financial data he now had, favorable though they were. The Mill had moved from showing sluggish, plodding improvement to being an overnight success. It was clear that there had been a major change in the demographic makeup of the Mill's customers, but it was not clear why this change had occurred. He wanted more information on this before he went any further with his plans.

Mr. Osborne was no stranger to marketing research. He had used it several times in the past when he needed to know what type of restaurant would be most likely to succeed in a particular area or location. What he needed to know now he would probably find out by using focus groups rather than by conducting personal interview surveys, mainly because the information he needed would probably have to be extracted from consumers. Before he contacted the market research consultants, he got together with Maggie Thurston and Tri-State's marketing vice-president. After explaining the situation to them, he asked them to help in making a list of things they needed to know. They came up with a list of five topics to be explored in the focus interviews:

1. How did the new customers find out about the Mill? Did they ask an opinion leader? Did it just come up in conversations? Did they see the sign or the ads?
2. Which member of the household made the suggestion or decision to go out to dinner? Which member suggested the Spaghetti Mill?

3. What motivated that family member to suggest the Mill? Why did they want to go there?
4. What features of the Mill did family members enjoy most, or think were most important (e.g., informality, price, selection, quantity, service, parking, location, etc.)?
5. Where does the family usually go out to dinner together? Why do they like it?

## SELECTION OF GROUPS

Mr. Osborne contacted Tri-State's research firm and set up a meeting for the following day. It was confirmed that focus groups were the way to go and the process of planning for them was begun—whom they would include, and how they would be selected. Obviously they would need to be members of the new customer group who had actually dined at the Mill. The research director suggested that two groups be set up. One would include individual adults from different family groups. This would enable discussion to be conducted without interaction from other family members. The second would be made up of the members of three or four families who ate at the Mill, including any children over the age of ten. This group would provide interaction within the family group, and discussion with other families as well. There would be two sets of each group.

People leaving the restaurant would be offered the opportunity to be a member of the groups, which would meet twice at a nearby location for one and a half hours each time. For each meeting, individuals would receive a $15 dinner certificate, and a free carafe of wine. Families would receive a $30 certificate. The panel members were lined up during the following week, and the focus groups were conducted by experienced group leaders the next two weeks after that. Mr. Osborne and several of his executives watched the first two groups through one-way mirrors.

## RESEARCH FINDINGS

While the final report from the marketing research organization was a lengthy one, and included a detailed analysis of the discussions, the findings were consolidated as follows:

### Individual Adults

In the two individual sessions, there was a total of 12 males and 14 females, all within the ages of 26–38; median 34, mode 33. All lived in households with one or more children. The males got information about the Mill from friends or officemates, in about even proportions by asking for recommendations from someone they considered might have the knowledge, or the Mill came up in conversations about where to take the kids. While females also got information from similar sources, more of them said they heard about it on radio or saw an ad on TV. In the discussion, two even described the ad (the one they described was from an Italian restaurant on the other side of the city). About half of the group said they passed by the Mill about twice a week or more. Most females believed the Mill was suggested by the male adult, but many of the males thought it came from the children or the female. But the initial suggestion, or plan, to go out to dinner apparently came equally from the male and female. During the discussion, it was brought out that mostly the decision was made on the spur of the moment, after one or the other (or both) had had a hard day. There was a good deal of give-and-take in the discussion about motivating factors for choosing this restaurant. Initially, the consensus was because the atmosphere was informal—a good place to take the kids (socially acceptable), then it changed to a cheap place with average food, the helpings were large, and it filled the kids up. Later, sparked by an off-chance remark, there was general agreement (after a somewhat heated discussion between the males and females) that it was one of the few restaurants where the entire family could have a sit-down, served dinner, where the parents could get a drink, as well.

After this, it was easier to discuss the Mill's most important attributes. With some minor disagreement, they ended up as: (1) you can get a drink there, (2) it's cheap and reasonably good, and (3) it's informal enough to take the kids.

While the group mentioned a number of different restaurants where they normally went with the family, many of these were rather formal and expensive (socially acceptable). The concept here is that people often first bring out socially acceptable points (there may be more than one) then move on to the real points or motives. After some members questioned these choices, it became apparent that most families went to fast-food outlets, with McDonalds, Pizza Hut, and Roy Rogers leading the list. These, they said, were where the kids wanted to go, but they could eat at the Spaghetti Mill for about the same price (for food) as at the fast-food outlets.

*Family Groups*

There were two groups. The first consisted of three families: Two of these were male-female, two children each; the third was male, two children. The second group was three male-female, each with one child. Thus, the two groups were composed of 6 adult males, 5 adult females, 5 female children, 4 male children. The two groups reacted very similarly to the suggestions of the leader. Five of the males and four of the females (all of whom were employed outside the home) said they got information by asking at work, in conversations at work, or at social occasions, and three said they also noticed the restaurant and its sign while driving by. The last female said she heard about the Mill during social conversations and saw an ad. In the discussion, several males and females said they saw TV ads, but the children were sure *they* had never seen such an ad, even late at night. Those children who had heard of the Mill did so from friends at school or in the neighborhood. Less than half of them had heard of it before they went there. As with the other group, all but two of the males thought the Mill was suggested by the female or one of the children, while the children thought it had come from the adult male. The decision to go out for a family dinner was initiated by the male most of the time if it was planned in advance. Mostly, if the decision was made after the working adult(s) got home, or before any cooking was begun, it was initiated by the adult female. This is the way almost all decisions to go to the Mill were made. Motivation did not emerge as clearly with this group as with the other, but the kids maintained that they most often wanted to go to one of the regular fast-food outlets for hamburgers or pizza. They explained: "Mom or Dad always wants to go to the Spaghetti Mill. Sometimes one does, and the other doesn't, but we seem to end up there anyway." Another said: "When we all go out together, it's always the Mill. I get tired of it. We get better spaghetti at home." The parents rationalized, "We don't have to dress up, they have big servings, it's cheap, and you can get a drink if you want one."

Although the group didn't actually rank the attributes, they emerged somewhat in this order: (1) the food is good and reasonably priced; (2) they let you take your time, no rushing; and (3) it's close to home, no parking hassle, and they don't seem to mind the kids. The families also went to the standard fast-food restaurants, but the kids felt that most of those visits were when either one or the other parent had to work late or was out of town. There was much more discussion of schedules by children in families where both parents, or the single parent, worked than there was in the adult group, even though the proportion of working parents was about the same.

> The time is 7:25 P.M. Mom, Dad, and the kids are leaving the Mill. The kids are full; Mom and Dad are relaxed. "And all of this for four people for a little over $30. Hard to believe!" chuckled Dad. "We'll have to come back here."

## CASE ANALYSIS QUESTIONS

1. When the decision to go out to eat is made on the "spur of the moment," is it autonomic? Syncratic? Dominated by the male or female adult? Children? What part did opinion leaders play in the decision?

2. What factors did the focus groups bring out that might be difficult to get from questionnaires? Were the two groups consistent?

3. It is clear from this case that a great deal of the information about the Spaghetti Mill is diffused by interpersonal communication, or word-of-mouth. What does this case suggest that the Mill might do in terms of product and promotion to help this information-sharing process along?

## REFERENCE

Empirical data collected by author. Restaurant name disguised.

## THE OLD SPAGHETTI MILL

**EXHIBIT 16-1**

**Restaurant Floor Plan**

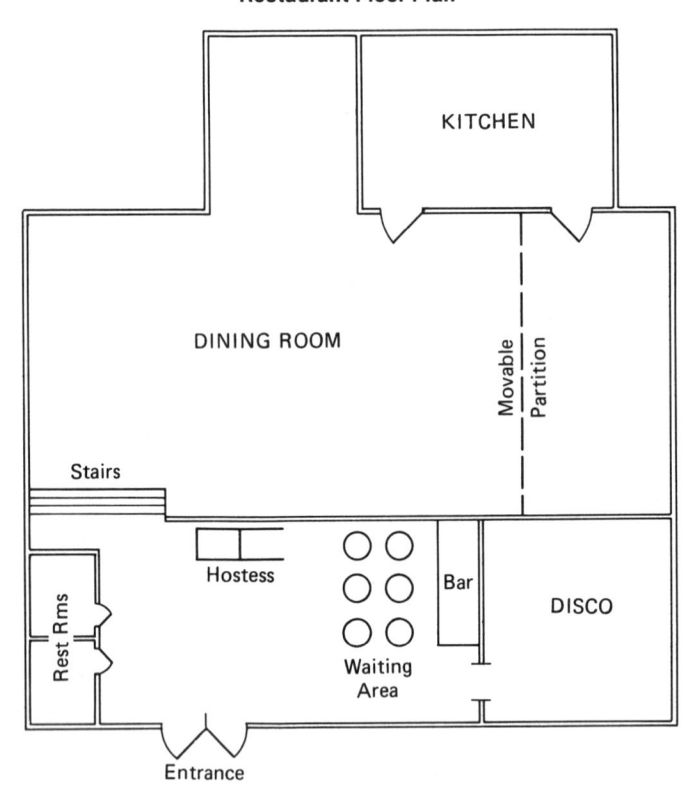

**THE OLD SPAGHETTI MILL**
**EXHIBIT 16-2**
**Dinner Menu**

---

| | | | |
|---|---|---|---|
| **Appetizers** | Antipasto (for 2) | | $3.50 |
| | Shrimp Cocktail | | $5.00 |
| | Soup du Jour | Bowl $.95 | Cup $.70 |
| **Dinners** | *Pasta* | | |
| | Spaghetti with Sauce (1) | | $6.95 |
| |   Meat Sauce | | |
| |   Meatballs | | |
| |   Clam Sauce | | |
| |   Mushroon Sauce | | |
| |   Onion & Gartlic Sauce | | |
| |     Extra Sauce $1.00 | | |
| | Ravioli | | $7.50 |
| | Canneloni | | $7.75 |
| | Fettucini Alfredo | | $7.95 |
| |   Children's portion $1.00 less | | |
| | *Beef* | | |
| | Sizzling 12 oz. Prime T-Bone | | $12.95 |
| | Sizzling 10 oz. Sirloin | | $10.95 |
| | Chopped Steak w/mushroom sauce | | $7.95 |
| | All dinners served with salad bar, bread and butter. Steak main dishes also include potato or spaghetti. | | |
| | Salad Bar only | | $3.50 |
| **Desserts** | Ice Cream | | $1.50 |
| | French Pastry Tray | | $2.00 |
| | Tortelloni or Spumoni | | $2.50 |
| **Beverages** | Coffee  Tea  Milk  Soft Drinks | | |
| | House vintage wine Carafe: | | |
| |   Small $4.50    Large $7.50 | | |
| | Beer: Domestic | | $1.50 |
| |   Imported | | $3.00 |
| | Cocktails    Mixed Drinks | | |
| | NO SUBSTITUTIONS PLEASE | | |

## THE OLD SPAGHETTI MILL

### EXHIBIT 16-3

### Number of Menu Items Sold in Six-Day Period (Closed Mondays)
### (From Tabulation of Dinner Dining Room Checks) 5 to 7 P.M.

| Description | Tues. | Wed. | Thurs. | Fri. | Sat. | Sun. |
|---|---|---|---|---|---|---|
| No. Customers | 178 | 204 | 246 | 489 | 513 | 326 |
| **Pasta Items** | | | | | | |
| ($6.95–$7.95) | 129 | 147 | 169 | 371 | 378 | 235 |
| **Beef Items** | | | | | | |
| T-Bone ($12.95) | 20 | 29 | 28 | 43 | 46 | 35 |
| Sirloin ($10.95) | 15 | 10 | 24 | 45 | 51 | 27 |
| Chopped Steak | 11 | 14 | 19 | 20 | 16 | 20 |
| Total | 46 | 53 | 71 | 108 | 113 | 82 |
| Salad Bar Only | 3 | 4 | 6 | 10 | 22 | 9 |
| **Beverage[a] Servings** | | | | | | |
| Beer | 46 | 37 | 46 | 89 | 133 | 74 |
| Wine | 14 | 41 | 33 | 85 | 152 | 71 |
| Cocktails or Mixed Drinks | 51 | 63 | 78 | 151 | 194 | 86 |
| Total | 111 | 141 | 157 | 325 | 479 | 231 |

[a] Beer is counted by the bottle or glass. Wine is sold by the glass or carafe but is counted only by the glass; carafes are converted to glass equivalents.

## THE OLD SPAGHETTI MILL

### EXHIBIT 16-4

### Number of Adults without Children Served Beverages
### by Time Period for Six Days–Dinner Only

| Description | Tues. | Wed. | Thurs. | Fri. | Sat. | Sun. |
|---|---|---|---|---|---|---|
| No. of Adults Served | 86 | 121 | 145 | 277 | 345 | 196 |
| Time Periods | | | | | | |
| 5 to 7 P.M. | 24 | 35 | 59 | 137 | 165 | 64 |
| 7 to 9 P.M. | 32 | 51 | 55 | 84 | 107 | 77 |
| After 9 P.M. | 30 | 35 | 31 | 56 | 73 | 55 |

## THE OLD SPAGHETTI MILL
### EXHIBIT 16-5
### Types of Beverages Served by Time Period for Six Days—Dinner Only

| Time Periods | Tues. M | Tues. W | Tues. B | Wed. M | Wed. W | Wed. B | Thurs. M | Thurs. W | Thurs. B | Fri. M | Fri. W | Fri. B | Sat. M | Sat. W | Sat. B | Sun. M | Sun. W | Sun. B |
|---|---|---|---|---|---|---|---|---|---|---|---|---|---|---|---|---|---|---|
| 5 to 7 P.M. | 8 | 6 | 10 | 4 | 17 | 14 | 18 | 23 | 18 | 61 | 27 | 49 | 52 | 67 | 46 | 17 | 34 | 13 |
| 7 to 9 P.M. | 20 | 3 | 9 | 24 | 7 | 10 | 29 | 12 | 14 | 38 | 22 | 24 | 31 | 54 | 22 | 26 | 20 | 31 |
| After 9 P.M. | 15 | 4 | 11 | 23 | 1 | 11 | 17 | 5 | 9 | 30 | 18 | 8 | 27 | 19 | 27 | 19 | 11 | 25 |

M = Cocktails or Mixed Drinks
W = Wine
B = Beer

# CASE SEVENTEEN

# RIVERSIDE SAVINGS BANK

In March 1991, John Fraser, chairman of the board of directors of the Riverside Savings Bank, was discussing the future of the bank with its board members. "It appears that we at the bank have some problems. Even though we are on the edge of a fast-growing metropolitan area and we still rank number five among similar institutions, we have had some decline in the growth of savings deposits. Rather than wait any longer for a trend to show clearly, I wonder if we shouldn't take a closer look at our market. Perhaps we need to serve it in different ways."

Actually, in response to the growing population in Seneca County, Riverside had already made a number of major changes in the past five years. While the main office was located in an older section of Seneca City, the county seat, three branch offices had opened since 1985. The nearest branch, a walk-in facility, was established in the Seneca Shopping Center, which had opened in 1983. The other two branches were both walk-in and drive-in and were located in relatively new (1983 and 1986) shopping centers on access roads that run from a nearby thruway to the towns of Harrison and Woodford-Toland. Exhibit 17–1 shows the location of the main bank and of the three branch offices. This expansion reflected the expanding population and changing character of the previously rural farming area.

## EARLY HISTORY

The Riverside was established as a savings and loan association in 1926 by several Seneca City businessmen and attorneys to provide a source of long-term loans for farmers and home buyers, as well as a repository for their savings. As differentiated from a "commercial" bank, Riverside could accept savings deposits, make home mortgage and certain other loans, but could not offer checking accounts or services that were the exclusive prerogative of the commercial banks. Nonetheless, it prospered over the years. By 1980, over 4,000 loans were outstanding for a total of over $100 million, and the total of the savings accounts was $65 million. See Exhibits 17-2 and 17-3 for a balance sheet and recent operating statements.

In 1975, the bank constructed a large, substantial building in the downtown area of Seneca City. Riverside's lobby was a comfortable, shabby-genteel kind of place where customers liked to stop by and chat for a while after attending to bank business, or just when they went by. Until the mid- to late 1970s, most of these customers were Seneca County farmers, business people from Seneca City and its neighboring towns, and local people, mostly blue-collar workers in several small manufacturing and service businesses. Others were white-collar salespeople in local stores, as well as office and clerical county employees. The bank officers often came out of their offices and spent a few minutes discussing the weather, crops, and business conditions with these visitors.

Riverside had spent very little on advertising or sales promotion. There was some reminder advertising in the Seneca City newspaper, which served all towns and rural areas in the county, together with a few spot announcements on the local radio station. Most of the advertising stressed the virtues of saving and called attention to the interest rate paid by savings and loan associations (which was one-quarter point higher than that offered by commercial banks). In the spring of each year, the bank offered a choice of small electrical appliances to each new customer who deposited over $200 a savings account.

## CHANGING CONDITIONS

Several new conditions challenged Riverside to rethink its approach. During 1982, changes in the banking laws brought about a turning point in Riverside's somewhat market-oriented but generally conservative strategy. For the first time, savings and loan associations were permitted to offer NOW checking accounts, business loans, auto loans, and a number of other services that placed them in direct competition with commercial banks. One of Riverside's first moves was to assure that its new position was firmly established in the minds of consumers by changing its name to the Riverside Savings Bank.

Except for the three towns shown in Exhibit 17-1, the county was still largely rural, but shopping areas, fast-food franchises, and service businesses were proliferating along the access roads that led to the interstate thruways. One of these, Biggers Avenue, was a commercial "strip" from the thruway to the Seneca City town line. Several large housing developments had grown up behind the strip, on both sides. The houses, both the single-detached dwelling and the townhouse variety, were designed mainly for medium- to lower-income families who were unable to find adequate housing in the state capital of Jefferson City, about 20 miles away. So, although the latest population figures showed Seneca City to have about 100,000 inhabitants, practically all the recent growth was in the newer housing areas near the thruway. The downtown sections of Seneca City, Harrison, and Woodford-Toland were all but deserted.

## THE NEW MARKET

When he asked about the market, Mr. Fraser was referring directly to this new, large group of "bedroom" residents. Most of this group worked in Jefferson City and commuted the 20 miles each way on the thruway. By living this rather long commuting distance away from the city, people were able to buy a single-family home or town house for from $20,000 to $30,000 less than they would pay for a comparable dwelling in or near Jefferson City. These commuters were state employees, clerical or lower-level managerial workers, or owners-managers of small businesses, primarily in the lower-middle class. A second, smaller group of new residents was composed of employees of a rapidly expanding plant near Seneca that made electronic controls for the automobile industry. The bank had received most of this market information from builders, real estate agents, and from the few mortgage loans Riverside had made to new residents. Most of these residents, however, had obtained their loans from Jefferson City banks. From discussions with local business people, Mr. Fraser found that many of the new residents still kept their checking accounts in the city.

As the discussion continued in the board room, Roger Chapman, the bank's president, commented on plans announced the previous week by the Central Bank and Trust Co. Central was a full-service commercial bank with its main office in Jefferson City. It was planning to build a large, multistory office building almost directly across the access road from Riverside's Seneca Shopping Center branch. "Most of the traffic in and out of this immediate area uses that road," Chapman said. "I understand that Central is putting one of its branches on the main floor and placing three, large, illuminated signs on the top floor. With that kind of exposure, they sure have the potential of hurting us in the long run."

Both Chapman and Fraser were local men in their early sixties. Although they devoted a considerable amount of time to the bank's activities, they also ran a law practice and a Chevrolet agency, respectively. As is usually the case in this type of financial institution, the bank officers are investors, and a full-time executive vice-president or chief operating officer is hired to run the organization. Frank Lindstrom was Riverside's executive vice-president. He joined the bank as an assistant cashier in 1979 after receiving his bachelor's degree in business administration from a local university. Five years later, he earned an MBA through evening courses, majoring in finance and marketing. With innate intelligence and hard work, he moved up rapidly and, three years ago, was selected to be Riverside's third chief operating executive.

## PLANNING DISCUSSION

"It seems to me," said Mr. Lindstrom, "that we need to develop an overall strategy for the next five years. The Jefferson City PMSA [Primary Metropolitan Statistical Area] is crawling steadily toward us and soon we'll be just another suburban town. Two things are very clear. First, we have a market that is vastly different from the one we have served since we opened in 1926. Our newer residents have different life-styles, they are in different social classes, and they participate in different kinds of activities. Second, we are not attracting that market. Maybe the reason we aren't is that we have an old-fashioned image, or because we haven't told them enough about us. The point is, we don't know, and we need to find out more about these potential customers: who they are, what their needs are, and why they continue to bank away from what is now their home. We also need to know who does the banking and who makes the decision about where to bank. We need to be more aggressive in making mortgage loans to this market. Now that we are a full-service bank, we can offer everything the commercials do, and if customers have their mortgage with us, they will use our other services as well. Third, we want to be sure we don't make so many changes to get this new market that we alienate our old one. But before we do anything, I think we should form a committee to get the basic information together and to make suggestions as to what we should do."

After some further discussion, the board elected Mr. Lindstrom, George Kulak (the comptroller), and Flo LaFrance, manager of the Woodford-Toland branch, to serve as a three-person committee. They were instructed to make recommendations to the board by August 1.

The group met several times in the following months and gathered a considerable amount of information about the Seneca County area, including the most logical direction of expansion, new road plans, plans for new shopping centers, firm and tentative plans for home building, prospective industrial locations, and area zoning. Their findings indicated that most of the shopping and residential expansion in Harrison and Woodford-Toland would take place along the Route 295 thruway, in the semi-open area between the two towns. In Seneca City itself, expansion would be mostly to the north and northwest since the land east and northeast was somewhat wet and undesirable for building. The automotive electronic components plant (see Exhibit 17–1) on the north side of route 295 was scheduled for expansion in 1991, to half again its present size. The total work force would increase from 800 to 1,200 at that time. There were also plans underway by a group from Jefferson City to build a shopping center on the road between the plant and Seneca City. But construction was delayed indefinitely since backers were having trouble securing the needed loans.

When it came to discussions about customers and their characteristics, the committee gathered some general demographic data for the new residents from county records. They were able to compare these data with those of Riverside's present customers from bank files. The comparative data are shown in Exhibit 17-4. They were also able to extract information on the various ways both groups saved from mortgage applications, but there were only 177 of these from new residents. Mr. Lindstrom also did some research in recent marketing journals and college-level texts. He thought the following statistics might have some bearing on Riverside's strategic planning:

> Recently, women have played more influential roles in male-dominated areas, such as financial services.
> There is more joint decision making in middle-class families than in upper- or lower-class ones. Wives who are working, and those having more liberated views, are more active in family financial decisions.
> Families look to peers in the same social class for purchase information on goods and services.
> Families in life cycle stage 3 are not as financially secure as those in the "newlywed" stage, mainly because they may be buying a home. In stage 4, however, their salaries are rising. They begin saving for children's education and start making financial plans.

Before reporting to the board, the committee thought it should review the information it had collected, together with what it knew about potential competition.

## CASE ANALYSIS QUESTIONS

1. What are the major differences in personal and social characteristics between Riverside's present customers and the new residents? How might these differences influence saving and banking habits, including why newcomers still bank in Jefferson City?
2. Are there any factors other than those mentioned in the case (e.g., life cycle stages) that might influence banking habits?
3. What do you think has caused the problems Riverside has today? What strategies should it pursue to attract the new market? Will this market be profitable in the near future?
4. What advertising and promotion appeals should Riverside use to reach the new market?

## REFERENCE

Data and situation adapted from research conducted by author. Names disguised.

# RIVERSIDE SAVINGS BANK
## EXHIBIT 17-1
### Seneca County

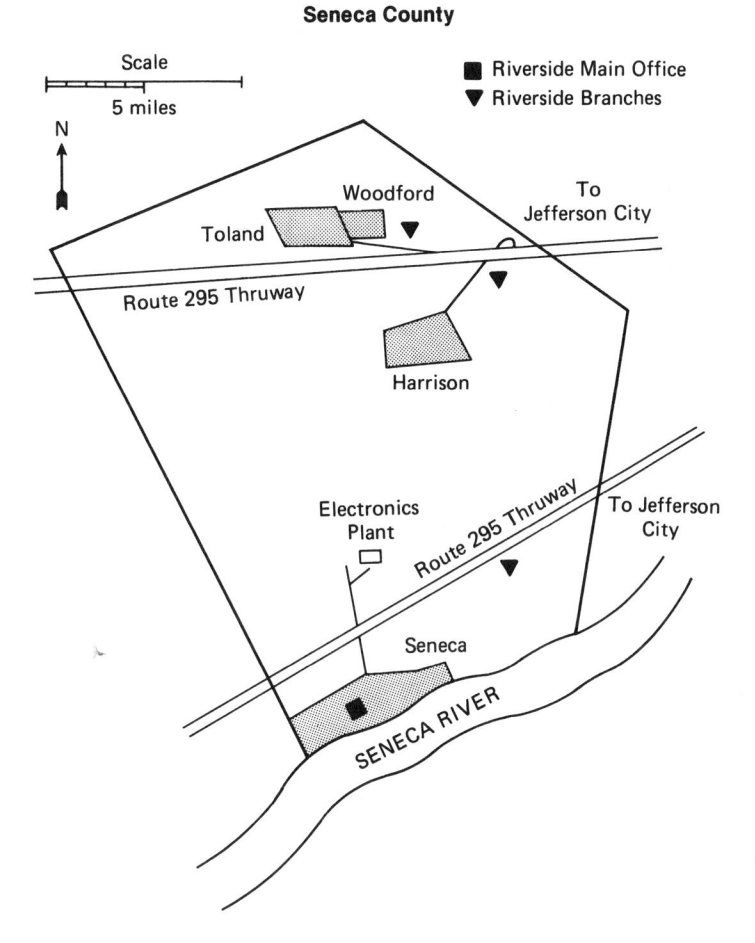

## RIVERSIDE SAVINGS BANK

### EXHIBIT 17-2

### Balance Sheet Assets, December 31, 1990 ($ millions)

| Assets | |
|---|---:|
| Mortgage Loans Outstanding | $120,558 |
| Insured Mortgages and MB Securities | 15,757 |
| Home Improvement Loans | 1,383 |
| Loans on Savings Accounts | 1,008 |
| Loans on Mobile Homes | 821 |
| Other Consumer Loans | 1,923 |
| Cash and Investments—liquid | 17,544 |
| Other Investments | 3,647 |
| Federal Home Loan Bank Stock | 1,475 |
| Investment in Service Corporations | 1,401 |
| Other Assets | 8,397 |
| Total | $176,511 |

## RIVERSIDE SAVINGS BANK

### EXHIBIT 17-3

### Operating Statements 1988, 1989, and 1990 ($ millions)

| | 1988 | 1989 | 1990 |
|---|---:|---:|---:|
| Operating Income | $14,297 | $16,613 | $18,319 |
| Operating Expenses | 2,017 | 2,287 | 2,619 |
| Net Operating Income | 12,280 | 14,324 | 15,700 |
| Interest on Savings Deposits | 10,601 | 13,788 | 15,000 |
| Interest on Borrowed Funds | 1,477 | 2,347 | 2,983 |
| Net Income before Taxes | 304 | (1,568) | (1,502) |
| Net Income after Taxes | 199 | (1,181) | (1,066) |

## RIVERSIDE SAVINGS BANK
## EXHIBIT 17-4
### Demographic Data: Present Customers and New Residents

| Category | Present Customers | New Residents |
|---|---|---|
| **Savings Method** | | |
| Savings Accounts | 79.4% | 61.2% |
| Money Market Funds | 21.3 | 14.4 |
| Savings Certificates | 39.0 | 19.8 |
| Common Stocks | 8.3 | 21.7 |
| Mutual Funds | 15.9 | 3.8 |
| U.S.Treasury Bills/Bonds | 5.3 | 6.6 |
| Corporate/Tax-Exempt Bonds | 4.9 | 3.2 |
| **Age** | | |
| 18–25 | 4.3 | 14.7 |
| 26–34 | 10.1 | 30.1 |
| 35–44 | 22.5 | 37.3 |
| 45–54 | 29.6 | 11.5 |
| 55–64 | 16.3 | 4.0 |
| 65+ | 17.2 | 2.4 |
| **Education** | | |
| High School or Less | 39.2 | 21.5 |
| 2 years of College | 28.4 | 27.3 |
| College Graduate | 21.7 | 35.8 |
| Graduate Degree | 10.7 | 15.4 |
| **Income** | | |
| Under $15,000 | 10.7 | 9.3 |
| $15–24,000 | 16.0 | 19.6 |
| $25–34,000 | 21.5 | 26.4 |
| $35–44,000 | 27.1 | 16.2 |
| $45–54,000 | 10.3 | 16.9 |
| Over $54,000 | 15.4 | 11.6 |
| **Occupation** | | |
| Artisan/Technical/Service | 18.3 | 10.1 |
| Clerical/Retail Sales | 12.7 | 27.3 |
| Manufacturing | 27.1 | 12.2 |
| Gov't/Managerial | 12.5 | 28.6 |
| Home | 15.4 | 4.2 |
| Retired | 9.8 | 1.1 |
| Other | 4.2 | 16.5 |
| **Female Adult Members Employed** | 23.7 | 41.3 |

# CASE EIGHTEEN

# HATTON AND MAYER GENTLEMEN'S WEAR

Ernest Hatton and his partner, Sid Mayer, turned out the lights, then tried the lock as they closed the front door to their store. Just as they walked out into the mall, an older man rushed up. It appeared as though he wore a dinner jacket over an undershirt. "Are you closed?" he panted. "Just turned out the lights," Sid replied. "Open in the morning, 9:30." "But I've just got to get a dress shirt. I ripped mine down the front putting it on," the man exclaimed, "and I've got to make a speech at nine o'clock!" "We'll fix you up," said Sid, unlocking the door. "You go ahead, Ernest. See you tomorrow. What size?" he asked, turning to the customer, "15, 35, for studs, if you have one," the older man replied.

While Sid was getting the shirt, the customer introduced himself. "I'm Jeff Henderson," he said. "I certainly appreciate you taking the time to help me out: I should have looked at that old shirt earlier." He went on to explain that he was president of the area council of senior citizen's clubs and that he was the speaker at the annual banquet downtown at the Copley Plaza Hotel that evening. As he walked with Sid to the cash register, he went on to say, "I used to own Henderson Wholesalers down in Quincy before I retired three years ago. I've been in here once or twice before, and I sure won't forget your helping me out in a pinch." He paid and rushed out.

## BACKGROUND

Hatton and Mayer was not really founded, but sort of materialized over the years in Boston's north end. Sid's father Sam had started a tailoring business in 1921, and because he was active in local politics, he was soon fitting many of Boston's officials. But his high quality and workmanship brought him more business than he could handle. The number of garments he could make by hand was limited, and thus, so was his income. He had hired several helpers, but their work was never up to his standards and they didn't last long.

"I guess I'll never be anything but a poor tailor," he confided to his friend Byron Hatton, who owned the dry goods store next door. "I sell my suits and coats for good prices, but I just can't make enough of them."

"Maybe you should put in a good line of clothes for customers who would be satisfied with a well-tailored, ready-made suit, and with your alterations it would be the next best thing to handmade," Byron suggested in a half-joking manner. But Sam was thoughtful. "I could do that," he said slowly, "but there isn't enough room in my store for a tailoring room and a retail showroom. I'd have to move." Byron was becoming a little excited. "We could put our stores together, go into partnership!" he shouted.

This was the beginning, in 1930, of Hatton and Mayer, Men's Clothiers. Even in the depression years, the business prospered and after World War II, it moved to a prestige location on Boylston Street not far from the Boston Common. It became "the" place where boys were outfitted for prep school and college, and where business and professional men "on their way up" bought their clothes. As the movement of the middle classes to the suburbs became apparent, H & M opened a branch in a new suburban shopping center in the early 1970s.

The oldest sons of the two families had been schoolmates through high school and were close friends. Both worked in the store Saturdays and during summer vacations. But they went to separate colleges and when they graduated, Sid got a job at City Hall and Ernest worked for an industrial abrasives firm in Worcester, about 40 miles east. They saw each other from time to time, but it appeared to the families as though they were drifting apart. So no one could have been more surprised than Byron and Sam when they both appeared for Sunday dinner at the Mayers and announced they wanted to go into the business.

Byron retired in 1979 and Sam in 1981. By 1985, the "boys" had closed the downtown store, since the area was declining, and established their main store in a prestige suburban shopping mall. They also had two branches in similar malls, and one in Portland, Maine. Their market remained essentially the same as it had been in the 1930s, but their (unwritten) objective was "To be an alternative to Brooks Brothers since it had become a regional chain." (Brooks Brothers was an upscale, status men's and women's clothing store in the eastern United States.) If that was the real objective, it had been a successful one since Hatton and Mayer became a well-known status business, respected for quality and personal attention to detail. The business was also quite profitable. Although H & M followed the slight changes that characterized men's fashions, such as wide versus narrow lapels and double- or single-breasted suits, they avoided being blatantly trendy.

## BREAD UPON THE WATERS

Sid had forgotten about the dress-shirt incident when, about ten days later, a well-dressed older couple came into the store during the mid-afternoon slack period. The man wanted to look at raincoats and since most of their salespeople took a break at this time, Sid waited on him. "Jeff Henderson sent me here," the man said as he tried on an expensive coat. "He told me one of your people helped him out the other evening and that you had some good-looking clothes. We usually go to Holloways [a department store]." He tried on another coat. "It looks like Jeff was right about your merchandise," he said, as he called his wife, to get her approval. When she looked it over and nodded, he ordered, "Wrap it up."

Some of the salespeople began to drift back as the couple was leaving. One of them mentioned to Sid, "Seems to me I've seen a few more older customers than usual the last couple of weeks." Thinking it over, Sid thought so too, although he hadn't really noticed it at the time, so he asked Ernest. "Yes, there do seem to be a few more than usual," Ernest said, "and some of them must be new because I don't recognize them." Although the older customers did not exactly stand out, most of H & M's clientele were young to middle-aged business and professional men, most of whom were from the baby-boom generation. They could be described as "achievers" who were moving up in their occupations, and often asked Sid's or Ernest's advice about clothes. The partners, who were in their fifties, joked about being a "father figure" for many men in that group.

## A NEW MARKET SEGMENT?

There were, of course, a number of older men who had bought at H & M since their younger days, and Ernest and Sid knew almost all of them by name. But this abrupt change in the mix of their customers alerted the partners that a little investigation might be in order. They had not thought much about the potential of catering to an older clientele, although they had read some articles about the increasing affluence of that group. But as they discussed it over lunch the next day, they had a number of questions about whether or not they should actively go after the segment.

Sid suggested that since Jeff Henderson was indirectly responsible for their problem, it might be a good idea to contact him to see if he could provide answers to some of their questions. As the head of what seemed to be a large and influential organization, he should have some idea of what the general needs and desires of its members were.

Mr. Henderson seem delighted to receive a luncheon invitation and after they had finished the meal, listened carefully to Ernest as he explained what they were looking for. He replied;

> I have to admit that I'm quite surprised at how comprehensive your questions are, but I wonder if you shouldn't try to delve a little deeper into the motives these consumers might have to buy your kind of clothing. Apparently the market you cater to now is looking for status, mildly trendy, business and professional clothing that says "I have arrived." I suspect that many of your new "older" customers are retired and may be interested in clothes that are more personally flattering, that make them look younger. Also, you said more older couples are coming in. Do you notice that women are more influential in these situations, while your present customers tend to make their own choices? I can give you some rather simple answers to some or all the questions, but the kind of decision you need to make will take more than that.

He went on to suggest that the best way to proceed would be to gather population and income trend information. "The Census Bureau makes projections on these, by age, geographic area, and many other breakdowns," he pointed out. He also suggested that there was a wealth of additional data and other information to be found in academic research literature. "Our organization doesn't keep this on file," he said, "but we go to the library whenever we need to get anything specific. You can find most of the articles in the Business Periodicals Index there. But suppose I do this—I'm going to the library tomorrow on another matter. I'll collect some basic data for you and give you a list of some characteristics of this market that have been researched. If you need more information, you can take it from there. But you will have to make a few observations yourself about how these newer customers behave and what motivates them."

## MR. HENDERSON'S INFORMATION

True to his word, Mr. Henderson breezed into the store about three o'clock the following Friday. He was armed with a bundle of papers and a sheaf of his own handwritten notes. As he, Ernest, and Sid settled down in a small conference room, he said, "I'll start out by talking about people over 50, since it is considered 'mid-life' and most companies selling consumer goods aren't interested in anyone over that age." He went on to point out that the U.S. government defines "senior citizens" as those over 65 years of age, although the medical profession fixes 75 as the age when we start becoming increasingly frail. A New York advertising agency survey also identified a group called "extended middle age" from 60 to 75. This group no longer has the work responsibilities of the fifties middle age and does not yet have the infirmities of old age. Ninety percent of them show no decline in mental powers, and only 17 percent of those over 65 are unable to carry on major activities because of ill health. This should be a new demographic market for those who have ignored all buyers over 50.

## AGE AND MARKET SIZE AND INCOME

"This whole market segment is growing rapidly," Mr. Henderson said and brought out a chart, Exhibit 18–1. He explained that the real growth in the over-55 population will begin in 1990, increasing about 1 percent by 2000. But in the next ten years, the growth will be 6.2 percent, and 4.7 percent in the following ten, bringing this segment to nearly one-third of the U.S. population by 2020.

He went on to explain that, since 1982, the poverty rate for the elderly has been well below that for the general population (Exhibit 18–2). Although the income for persons over 65 drops considerably from the 45-64 levels, by this age, children are through school, mortgages are paid off, and many discounts and other benefits become available in the form of "imputed" income (see Exhibit 18–3). Also, financial assets of over-65 households average over $57,000 as shown in Exhibit 18-4. Exhibit 18–5 indicates substantial growth in total incomes of over-50 households (up 55%), with a 58 percent rise in the proportion of households with incomes over $25,000.

Mr. Henderson said that although many of the members of the senior citizen clubs in his council were not affluent, they were not living in poverty either. "Most of them are comfortable. They live in their own homes or apartments and drive cars. I guess about 10 to 15 percent of our membership might be considered affluent." He held up Exhibit 18–6, showing the income of one generation beginning in stage 2 of the family life cycle in 1940 and ending in stage 5. Although income drops at age 65, the 55–65 years have the highest income of any stage in the cycle, by far.

## BETTER EDUCATED

Mr. Henderson suggested that each succeeding generation of the older segment has a higher level of education, which, in turn, brings increasing affluence and more market potential. For households headed by persons in the 30–35 age group today, about 30 percent have college degrees but for those 65 to 70, the proportion is only 12 percent. Most of those, however, are in the higher-income segment of the older population. As more educated consumers enter the over 50, or over 65 group, they are likely to demand more products, services, and attention than do the mid-lifers or the elderly of today.

## INDIVIDUAL CHARACTERISTICS

"I jotted down some findings of several academic studies that might have some bearing on your questions. These are life-style and personality characteristics that might help with your decision," Mr. Henderson said. He briefly described them, cautioning Sid and Ernest that these results apply to the majority in the studies and not necessarily to all other consumers:

- The elderly are less likely to complain to the management of stores and companies from which they have received poor goods or services.
- They generally do not feel old and do not like to be reminded they are old. Many, even those in their early seventies, look and act younger. They are also very active in the market.
- They have a considerable amount of leisure time, and many of them devote at least some of it to politics. They are a major force in several states and areas and apply continuing pressure for increased benefits.
- They "learn" and react to advertising messages in the same way as other age groups, but at not quite the same pace. Newspapers ads get better results than fast-moving television ones.
- They replace fewer household appliances than do younger consumers, but they spend more on travel and clothing.
- A large proportion (60%) of the retired population started drawing benefits before the age of 65, and about one-third of married women stopped work about three years before starting to draw Social Security benefits.
- Many firms offer discounts to the elderly. Even though many take advantage of the lower prices, others resent being asked if they are eligible for them. Mr. Henderson noted that in some areas the telephone company places a special symbol in the yellow pages for firms that offer senior-citizen discounts. He also had a summary (Exhibit 18-7) of special discounts and services offered by airlines and by Sears Roebuck's new "Mature Outlook" organization.

## ANSWERING THE QUESTIONS

"I hope this is enough information to lead you to the right decision about the market potential of older consumers. I noticed in some of the articles I read that we are called a "subculture" because many of us are no longer in the mainstream. But I think you will find there is more of a market than most business people think there is, and it is bound to increase steadily in the next ten to 20 years. I suspect that the people I sent to your store have started you thinking about it. Good luck."

With this last statement, he waved and left the store. Sid and Ernest looked at each other thoughtfully, picked up the papers Mr. Henderson had left, and began trying to answer the questions that the three of them raised. "What we are talking about is formulating a strategy that will let us serve two markets, yet will not alienate either one," said Ernest, "and that may not be very easy to do."

## CASE ANALYSIS QUESTIONS

1. Are there enough affluent older customers in this market today? What is its future potential? Will it increase in size? What factors are important here?
2. Are the tastes of this market, in general, similar to or different from H & M's present market segment? Do they need separate lines? Do they need to employ older salespeople for this market?
3. Should H & M open a separate store for "seniors" (or whatever term would be acceptable)? Or should they simply add them to the segment already served by the present stores? What would be the problems associated with these proposals, if any?

## REFERENCES

U.S. Government, Bureau of the Census, (1991), *Statistical Abstract, 1990,* Washington, D.C., U.S. Government Printing Office; "American Association of Retired Persons Report on Older Consumer Behavior," Washington, AARP, June 7, 1990; "Special Needs of the Elderly," *Marketing Needs,* Feb. 5, 1990, p. 9; "Graying Market May Not Be So Golden," *Wall Street Journal,* Dec. 27, 1990, p. B-1; "CBS Gears Fall Lineup to Older Viewers," *Wall Street Journals,* Sep. 27, 1989, p. B-1; "Forget the Rocking Chairs," *Business Week,* Sep. 25, 1989, p. 145, "Shedding Light on Mystique of Aging, Women," *Washington Post,* Feb. 19, 1989, p. A-21; "Going After the Gray Dollars," *New York Times,* Feb. 5, 1989, p. K-1; "Senior Citizen? No Way!" *New York Times,* Jan. 22, 1989, p. D-18; "Riding the Silver Streak," *Arthur Anderson Retailing Issues Letter,* Sept. 1989. "Determinant Behavior Characteristics of Older Consumers," *Journal of Consumer Affairs,* July, 1988, p. 136; "Marketers Err By Treating Elderly as Uniform Group," *Wall Street Journal,* Oct. 31, 1988, p. B-1; "Targeting the Elderly Makes Sense—Sort of," *Wall Street Journal,* Oct. 14, 1988, p. B-1; "Discounts Galore for the 50-Plus Crowd," *New York Times,* Sep. 11, 1988, p. D-22, "Among the Elderly, Togetherness is Selling," *New York Times,* Aug. 28, 1988, p. D-25; "The Booming Business of Aging," *Washington Post,* Apr. 22, 1988, p. B-5; "Difficulty in Caring for the 'Oldest Old'," *Wall Street Journal,* Mar. 28, 1988, p. 33; "Retirees Shun Sun Belt and Most Other Moves," *Wall Street Journal,* Mar. 8, 1988, p. 37; "Older People's Lobby Gets a Message Across to All the Candidates," *Wall Street Journal,* Mar. 8, 1988, p. 1; "Older Consumers Adopt Baby-Boomer Buying Behavior," *Marketing News,* Feb. 15, 1988, p. 8; "Delivering What Makeup Only Promises: Drugs That Can Truly Keep You Looking Young," *Business Week,* Feb. 8, 1988, p. 63; "Ethicist Draws Fire With Proposal for Limiting Health Care to Aged," *Wall Street Journal,* Jan. 22, 1988, p. 29.

**EXHIBIT 18-1  U.S. Aged Distribution, 1980-2020**

FOR IMMEDIATE RELEASE

CONTACT:  Kendra Silverman          Marty Gordon
          Hilton Hotels Corp.        Burson-Marsteller
          (213) 205-4017             (213) 386-8776

## HILTON'S SENIOR HHONORS PROGRAM

### Description

Discount travel program for individuals age 60-plus at more than 330 hotels in the United States and around the world with complimentary membership for spouses, special services and HHonors bonus points for use toward exciting rewards

### Membership Benefits

| | |
|---|---|
| Worldwide Room Discounts | From 25 to 50 percent off Hilton's current daily rate (varies by location); applies to either single or double occupancy |
| | Applicable to extra room for parents, children or grandchildren traveling with member |
| Dinner Discounts | 20 percent discount on dinner for two at more than 260 participating Hilton restaurants in the United States and Canada |
| Other Benefits | • Members-only toll free reservations service<br>• Pre-registration<br>• HHonors check-in and late check-out (where available)<br>• Complimentary daily newspaper in the United States<br>• Free use of health and recreational facilities (where available) |
| Guarantees | • Rates are Hilton's lowest published for that hotel<br>• Rates are lower than hotel's AARP member rates<br>• Full refund of membership fees for new members who decide against using the program within 30 days of enrollment |
| Participating Locations | Available at more than 250 U.S. Hilton hotels and more than 80 international Hilton and Conrad hotels in 39 countries |
| Membership Fees | • Annual Domestic membership: $35<br>• Annual Worldwide membership: $50<br>• Lifetime Worldwide membership: $200<br>• No fee for spouse membership |
| Advisory Board | Panel of senior marketing and travel experts who assisted with the development of the program |

Membership applications are available through travel advisers or by calling Hilton Reservations (1-800-445-8667 Ext. 901).

**HATTON AND MAYER**

**EXHIBIT 18-2   Percentage of Population Living in Poverty 1978-88**

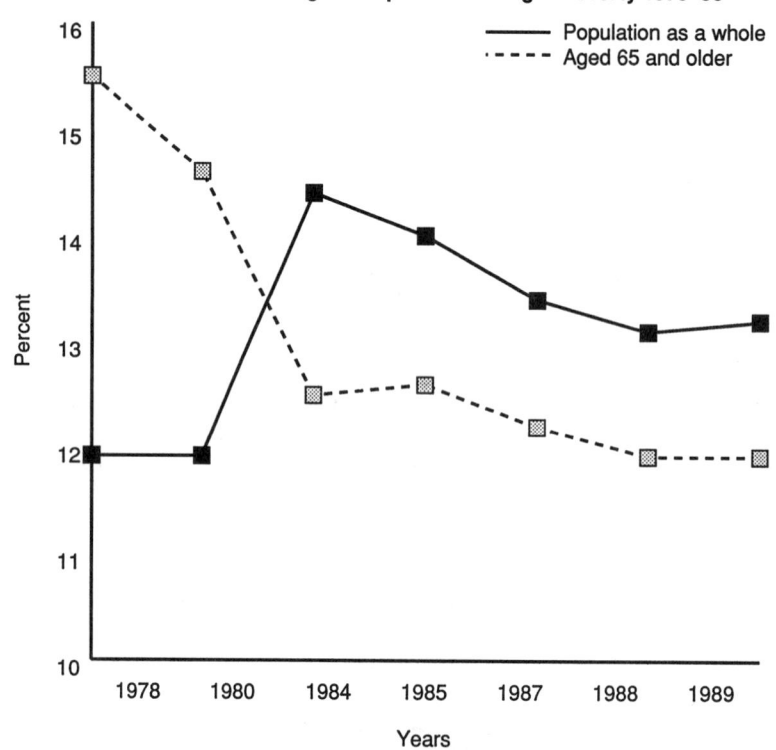

—— Population as a whole
- - - - Aged 65 and older

**HATTON AND MAYER**

**EXHIBIT 18-3   Household Income 1990**

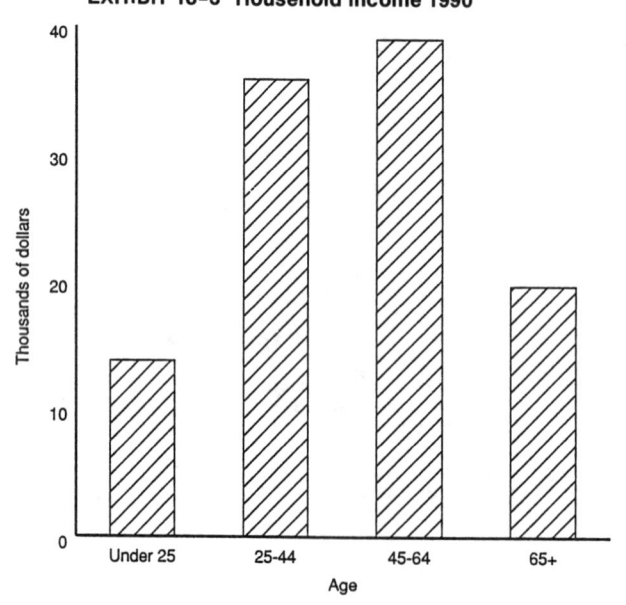

**HATTON AND MAYER**

**EXHIBIT 18-4**

**Financial Assets of Head of Household by Age, 1989**

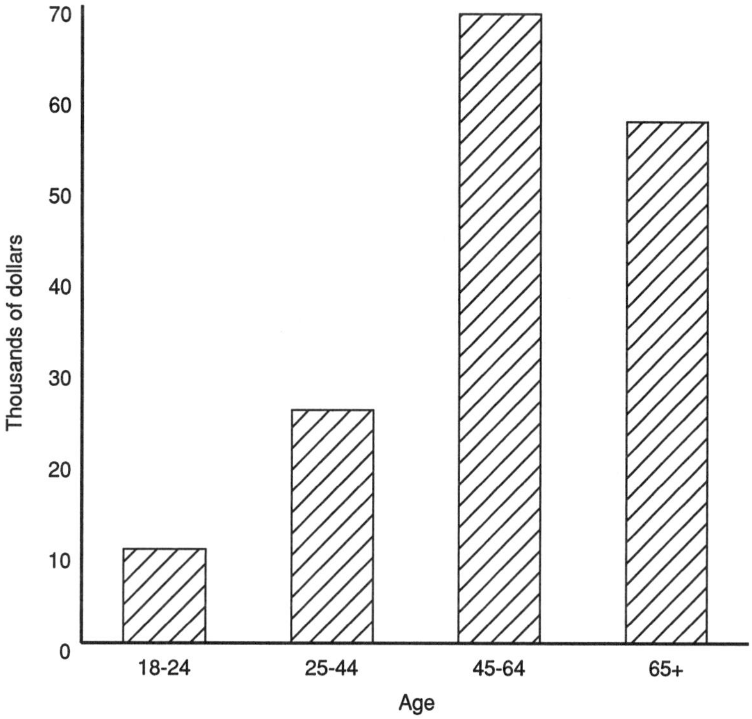


**HATTON AND MAYER**

**EXHIBIT 18-5**

**Household and Income Growth, over 50 Population, 1985-2000**

| *Household or Income* | *Percent Growth* |
|---|---|
| Total number of Households | +23% |
| Total Household Income | +55% |
| Mean Annual Household Income | +27% |
| Households with Incomes over $25,000 | +58% |

**HATTON AND MAYER**

**EXHIBIT 18-6**

**Income of One Generation Through the Life-Cycle**

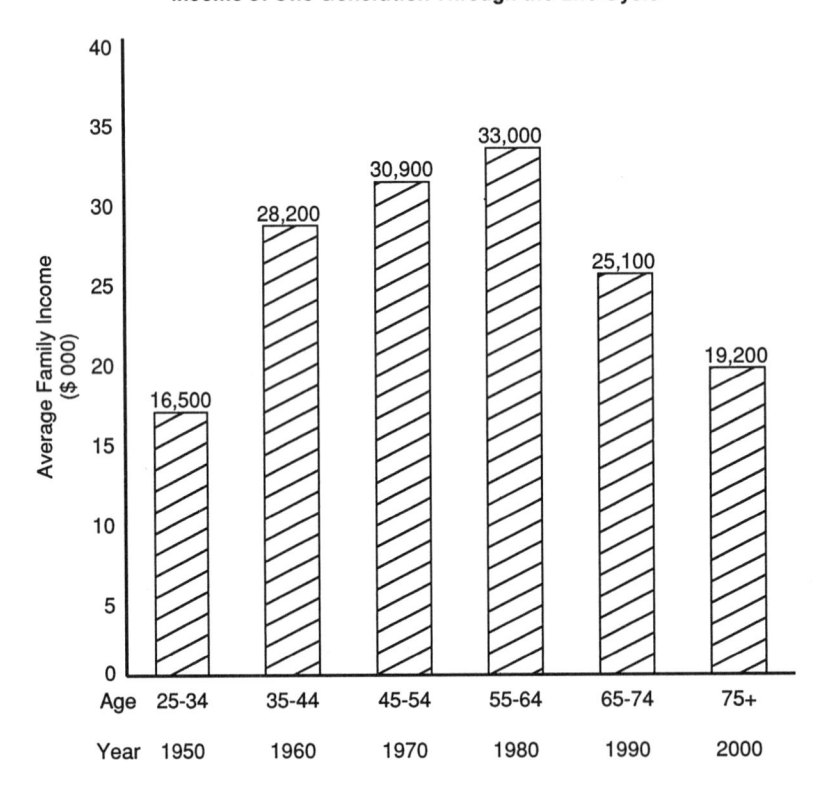

| Age | 25-34 | 35-44 | 45-54 | 55-64 | 65-74 | 75+ |
|---|---|---|---|---|---|---|
| Year | 1950 | 1960 | 1970 | 1980 | 1990 | 2000 |
| Average Family Income ($000) | 16,500 | 28,200 | 30,900 | 33,000 | 25,100 | 19,200 |

**HATTON AND MAYER**

**EXHIBIT 18-7**

**Recent Benefit Offerings to Older Consumers**

---

Sears Roebuck has a "Mature Outlook" membership organization for people over 50. For an annual membership fee, the organization offers a combination of benefits, information, and discounts especially tailored to the needs of older persons, such as:

> Mail Order pharmacy service, same day service at "lowest possible" prices, and same-day processing,
> Coupon savers book for up to 30 percent discounts on some Sears items,
> Auto service coupons for discounts at Sears Automotive Centers,
> Savings on Vacation Tours, bus travel and groceries.

Most airlines offer discounts to older travelers, and special discounts and fees for travel packages, off-season travel and other benefits, for payment of an initial, one-time fee. Hilton and other hotels, as well as car rental firms also offer special discounts and membership plans. One such offer is shown below [see page 198].

## Now that you have the time...
## Hilton brings you the savings!

**Save up to 50% at Hilton.**
Hilton Senior HHonors gives people 60 and over a way to travel in style...for less!

Senior HHonors members enjoy room rate discounts of up to 50%. That makes the Senior HHonors room rate at some Hilton hotels as low as $45 per night.

Members are guaranteed our *lowest* published rates—even lower than the special rates sometimes made available to AARP members.

And you can enjoy these savings and other membership privileges for as little as $35 a year!

**Select from over 330 Hiltons worldwide.**
Members receive discounts at over 250 Hilton hotels in the U.S....and more than 80 throughout the rest of the world! Including such exciting hotels and resorts as the Las Vegas Hilton, Hilton Hawaiian Village, the Scottsdale Hilton Resort & Spa, and London's Hilton on Park Lane.

**Enjoy these additional savings and privileges.**
As a Senior HHonors member you'll also enjoy a 20% dinner discount at over 260 participating Hilton restaurants in the U.S. and Canada...free membership for your spouse...and the same low Senior HHonors room rate for your children or grandchildren anytime they travel with you.

**Money-back guarantee.**
If you do not use your Hilton Senior HHonors membership within 30 days, your membership fee is fully refundable.

**Choose the membership that's right for you.**
- $35 Annual Domestic membership entitles you to savings at more than 250 participating Hilton hotels in the U.S.
- $50 Annual Worldwide membership entitles you to savings at more than 80 international Hilton and Conrad hotels, as well as more than 250 participating Hilton hotels in the U.S.
- $200 Lifetime Worldwide membership entitles you to enjoy savings at all participating Senior HHonors hotels worldwide for a one-time fee.

To enroll in the Senior HHonors program, or to request more information, please call:
**1-800-445-8667, ext. 901**
or complete and mail the coupon below.

The information we send you will include a complete listing of participating Senior HHonors hotels and rates, and will be mailed within 7 days after we receive your request.

---

YES! I would like to receive more information about the Hilton Senior HHonors program. Please send me an information package and application.
**For faster service, call 1-800-445-8667, ext. 901**

Name (please print clearly)

Address

City            State            ZIP Code

Reservations are required and may not always be available at participating hotels. Offer cannot be combined with other certificates, coupons, discounts, packages or promotional offers. Rates do not apply to group meetings or conventions and do not include taxes. Rates are subject to change without notice. Other restrictions apply.

MAIL TO: HILTON SENIOR HHONORS
Hilton Hotels Corporation
P.O. Box 645
Addison, TX 75001-9977

**HILTON Senior HHonors**

# CASE NINETEEN

# TOYS R US

Most of us think of toys as things we give to children at Christmas or other occasions, and over 60 percent of all toys are bought during the holiday season. Most of the rest are given on birthdays. Psychologists suggest that Christmas toy giving helps to restore the special social bond between parents and children. Toys also remind family members of the "togetherness" they wish to preserve. Because today's society prizes individualistic achievement in school and business, people are often rewarded for subordinating their marriages, children, families, communities, and churches in favor of work and success. Toys, therefore, represent a bulwark against the forces of modern society that threaten to tear families apart.

**TOYS AND US**

On the other hand, toy giving at the holiday season does not imply that givers spend any time with the children upon whom they have bestowed the gifts. Paradoxically, one purpose of the toys is to keep children occupied without making demands on the parents' time.

Toys, therefore, become a means to accustom children to solitary play and solitary striving for achievement. Video games typify the latter goal and intensify the image of the lone individual against powerful cartoon characters. The concentration and fantasy developed in video games and other toys tend to foster resentment of interruptions or interference, and the children become unsociable.

Younger children, particularly, are heavy influencers of toy purchases, motivated by television commercials. Later, they often make their own buying decisions for video games, and they influence the purchase of other kinds of toys. Television, itself, is another toy for lonely and unoccupied children. According to one estimate, 98 percent of all U.S. homes have television sets, and children from two to five years watch it some 28 hours a week. Those aged six to eleven watch about 26 hours, but many of them are also heavy players of video games.

According to one expert, on the other hand, parents want to "socialize" children and improve their overall development. When parents implicitly say to children, "We give you these toys in order to bond you to us, now go play with them by yourselves," they are conveying an important message about contemporary civilization. In addition to bonding, parents also use toys for a seemingly contradictory purpose—to shape the children into solitary, self-sufficient individuals, but in school, playing with toys is emphasized to encourage cooperation with others.

## TOYS R US

Whether or not the most successful toy retailer in the world understands the cultural philosophy just described, Toys R Us certainly acts as though it does. Chairman and founder Charles Lazarus realized quite early in the game that the parent-child toy-related bonding isn't restricted to the holiday season.

He started in the business in 1948 by opening a children's furniture store in the back of his father's bicycle repair shop in Washington, DC. Fortunately, he was just in time for the post–World War II baby boom. "I wanted to get married and have kids," he said, "and there must be a lot of others like me." He also wondered if there might not be a year-round market for toys just waiting to be activated. "Children break toys," he observed. "They have birthdays. And, of course, there are doting grandparents who buy toys at all seasons." So he opened a new store, Baby Furniture and Toy Super-Market, and five years later, he expanded into the first Toys R Us store in Washington, DC. Today, he describes his market somewhat differently: "People marry later and have fewer children. There will be more only children with older parents who will shower the child with loads of toys. Grandparents wait longer and have fewer grandchildren. Divorced parents wallowing in guilt buy toys for weekend visits, the start of school, and numerous other standard occasions."

Charles Lazarus had an entirely different approach to retailing from that of his competitors, particularly in buying and pricing merchandise. Most retailers base their selling price on the wholesale price they pay. But Lazarus would first decide if a product could be sold in large quantities. If it could, he would then decide the price *he had to pay for it* in order to sell that many.

This is one reason why Toys R Us has created a low-price image for itself. Back in 1977, a new electronic game called "Simon" was a popular "hot" item. It was in short supply, so some stores charged as much as $30.00 for it. Toys R Us, however, charged less than $20.00 because Mr. Lazarus thought that shoppers would believe everything in the store must be as good a bargain. And they apparently have.

## COMPUTER TRACKING

Charles Lazarus knows precisely what his customers are buying, and a major key to his company's success is an automated system that transmits cash register information for every item consumers buy to the company headquarters computer. So management is able to keep up-to-date on sales. The computers also spot trends in the popularity of individual toys long before competitors do, and reorders are placed automatically. In 1981, when the product-tracking system indicated that the early electronics games might be bottoming out, Toys R Us began to slash prices, selling some of the hand-held models well below cost. "Once an item stiffs out," says Mr. Lazarus, "we keep marking it down until it blows out."

The system also uses a sophisticated Universal Product Scanning code which is affixed to each item in the stores. This code not only reduces transaction time at the cash register, but also provides more reliable sales information by reducing key-punch errors and prevents store losses due to label switching. And training time for cashiers is cut to a minimum. In the future, the company plans to scan refunds and returns as well.

Like many K-Marts, Toys R Us stores are located away from malls and busy shopping centers so customers won't be distracted by other stores nearby. Also, customers don't want to carry bulky toy boxes into malls while they do other shopping. So the strategy is to make a trip to Toys R Us a special one so the car won't be far away. The store's merchandise arrangement encourages impulse buying, and disposable diapers and baby food are also available—both at rock bottom prices. Mr. Lazarus maintains, "People with new babies are the most important customers we have. They will be with us for 12 to 15 years!" Each of the 46,000 square-foot, warehouse-type stores carries no less than 18,000 items. The stores are basically self-service operations and, although they run occasional ads, they never have sales.

In addition to baby supplies, Toys R Us carries some nontoy items such as paper party products, of which the biggest seller is hats. "Hats make the birthday party," Charles Lazarus exclaims, "and parents will spend at least $30.00 on birthday party products."

## NINTENDO RULES THE CHANNEL

Like the proverbial 500-pound gorilla, Mr. Lazarus is accustomed to getting what he wants. But he met his match during early dealings with Nintendo of America, whose video games have kept toy sales edging upward in the past several years. His pleas and threats to increase shipments fell on deaf ears, since Nintendo's policy was to keep supply below demand. It is fearful of having its products wind up in landfills as did the first generation video games. Eventually, however, even Nintendo couldn't ignore Toys R Us and its tremendous retail potential.

In the 1980s, Lazarus saw Toys R Us setting financial records while the toy business overall was struggling. Sales were flattening out and many of the industry's leading manufacturers were losing money. One of the reasons was that there have been no real "hot" fads to replace the Cabbage Patch dolls or Teddy Ruxpin bears. So consumer dollars spent on Nintendo games and systems had to come out of the hides of traditional toy manufacturers. When there are no "hit" toys that kids *must* have, shoppers don't know what to buy. So they flock to the store with the huge selection, Toys R Us.

## NEW OPPORTUNITIES

Ever alert for new opportunities, Charles Lazarus foresaw the increasing specialization in clothing markets, especially those for children. "What better combination of diversification and line-extension tie-ins could we have than a Kids R Us children's chain," he said. So, in July 1983, the first store was opened in Paramus, New Jersey, where the company headquarters are located.

Unfortunately, both retailers and manufacturers of children's wear were not overjoyed at this assault on their established markets. Department and specialty store operators blanched at the thought of the Toys R Us–type of competition in children's clothing. So they pressured name-brand vendors to refuse to supply the new chain. But name brands were a "must" to the Kids stores just as they were to Toys R Us, and the promise of similar large and consistent orders soon brought the producers around.

Kids R Us began showing a profit in 1988, with earnings around $7 million. Sales approached $400 million from the 165 stores in 1990, with earnings close to $13 million. Name-brand manufacturers are now actively soliciting orders from the chain, which has a reputation for quick response to customers' needs, innovative merchandise displays, a high level of service, and a wide assortment of styles and sizes. In the fall of 1990, however, the stores reported disappointing back-to-school sales, as did other large children's apparel chains. Analysts were predicting that the slump would move into the Christmas season. By the winter of 1990–91, several new chains, or kids' store extensions of other mass merchandisers, were being discontinued, or scaled back, leaving more of the market to Mr. Lazarus.

## THE FOREIGN ADVENTURE

Since 1984, Toys R Us has aggressively expanded into lucrative foreign markets. Chairman Charles Lazarus states the company strategy for locating these stores as "anywhere the customer is becoming more like the American consumer." One of these places is apparently Hong Kong where a typical Toys R Us store was opened in the Ocean Terminal Shopping Center just before Christmas 1986.

> Sam Teng, his wife, and their two children threaded their way through narrow corridors, down stairs, and around corners to the new toy store. Finally, pushing and shoving, with their hands holding tightly onto the children, the Tengs entered Toys R Us. Mai-Ling Teng spied a line of shopping carts at a nearby wall. Tugging to pull one out, she found they were securely fastened together with a stout rope. "Too many people! No room for carts in the aisles," an employee explained. "You have to carry what you buy."
> Following the flow of the crowd, they went past shelf after shelf of every imaginable toy, doll, game, and electronic device. Wide-eyed, the Teng children pointed here and there: "One of those! the Bike! the Nintendo!" they shouted. Sam looked closely at several toys they had bought last year. "Look, Mai-Ling," he said, "half the price we paid at the neighborhood store for the same doll!"
> Over an hour later, the family was exhausted. "What a selection," marveled Sam, as he dragged the new bicycle carton (some assembly required) to the cash register, "I didn't know there were this many toys in the world."

Over 40,000 customers jammed the store on weekends, each carrying out several of the 18,000 stock items. Eighty percent of the toys are the same as those sold in U.S. stores, and the rest depend upon local tastes and customs. The Hong Kong store is only one of the 50-odd megastores that Toys R Us has opened overseas in the past several years.

## THE CHALLENGE OF THE JAPANESE MARKET

The announcement that Toys R Us planned to open stores in Japan in 1991 had important implications for both the Japanese toy industry and U.S. toy makers who still export mostly traditional low-tech products. The new chain will trigger intense competition for market share, and the multiple and complex levels of Japanese distribution, with its traditional, near-medieval structure, may be threatened. Through its usual procedure of buying huge quantities from manufacturers at a discount, then retailing at rock bottom prices, Toys R Us bypasses wholesalers completely. The size of the Japanese toy market and Toys R Us foreign sales volume are shown in Exhibits 19-1 and 19-2.

Retailers in Japan are also worried. "When Toys R Us comes in, Japanese toy stores will be badly hurt," said a retailer who operates eight shops in Niigata City where one of the new stores will be opened. At stake is the $5.5 billion Japanese toy market, and locating the stores will bring the first real test of Japan's Large Scale Retail Store Law. The law provides that retailers who want to open stores with more than 500 square meters (5,400 square feet) of floor space have to get prior approval from other retailers in the area.

In past years when large stores tried to move in, local retailers simply stalled, often for as long as ten years. The law doesn't specify how long local stores have to present complaints to a hearing authority, but even large Japanese retailers have problems. With such opposition, many foreign companies have given up trying to crack the market.

The Retail Store Law and other distribution problems inhibited U.S. firms from trading and expanding in the Japanese market. The complex system of merchandise distribution requires that retailers not only establish close working relationships with multiple layers of distributors, but also comply with a myriad of odd local laws as well. U.S. and Japanese negotiators have wrestled for several years with the structural problems that impede commerce. A major U.S. objective is convincing the Japanese government to relax its rules of entry for foreign businesses. And trade tensions between the two countries were placing increased pressure on Japan to modernize its medieval distribution system.

In a report titled, "Vision of the Japanese Distribution System in the 1990s," the Ministry of International Trade and Industry indicated there was a need for less restrictive policies that favored local retailers. If these new rules are established, the time to obtain local consent for the entry of new stores could be reduced from the present average of ten years to as short as two years. Some localities, however, have passed their own laws giving even greater protection to smaller retailers. At the forefront, urging fast and decisive action by the U.S. Trade Mission were representatives of Toys R Us, which was poised to enter the market as soon as the gates were opened.

Japan has long fostered a producer-oriented political system. Its distribution layers and protection laws for small farmers were originally designed to help feed the country after World War II and to help establish full employment.

Today, however, Japanese consumers themselves are increasingly discontented with the high cost of almost all consumer products. Everyday household staples cost at least 40 percent more than they would in the United States. Even optical and electronics goods, Japan's manufactured specialties, are more expensive. A $380 camera in New York costs $539 in Tokyo, and Japanese beer is 44 percent higher there. In fact, fully one-third of Japanese exports are more expensive at home.

As they learn more about the cost of protectionist impediments in their retail system from media reports of trade negotiations, Japanese consumers appear to be shifting their opinions. In the spring of 1990, a three-hour special on the national television channel explained how revamping the present economic structure could bring more goods at lower prices to them. Nearly all of the 700 viewers who phoned in their opinions after the program favored a change in the national policy. At about the same time, other polls yielded similar results. Nearly half of 10,000 voters who were polled, and 52 percent of respondents to a business magazine survey thought they would benefit if Japan's markets were opened.

These developments led Toys R Us executives to be "very optimistic" about opening Japanese stores in 1991.

With over 50 stores in Singapore, Canada, Britain, Kuala Lumpur, and France, Toys R Us has built its operations one country at a time, from the ground up, instead of acquiring existing firms. But in Japan, what *The Washington Post* described as "the most fearsome combination of monsters since Godzilla and the Thing laid waste to Tokyo," Toys R Us has entered into a cooperative venture with McDonalds of Japan: The two have joined forces to open toy stores. McDonald's franchisee, Fujita and Co., Ltd., is half-owned by the parent company and has 675 stores in Japan. Thus, the team will have the advantage of McDonald's ability to locate affordable land, combined with the retailing know-how of Toys R Us.

Fujita will hold a 20 percent stake in the toy business and will be able to open outlets in the stores, and Toys R Us will keep the remaining 80 percent. This arrangement will assure Toys R Us of control of the enterprise. It also avoids the need for licensing, the route used by most other U.S. businesses in Japan. Many experts agree that licensing makes it difficult to control what happens to your product.

## CASE ANALYSIS QUESTIONS

1. Do you think Mr. Lazarus understands directly, or instinctively, the cultural aspects of toy buying and giving described in the first part of this case? Explain.

2. What general perceptions do consumers seem to have about Toys R Us? How does the firm go about "creating" these perceptions?

3. Eighty percent of toys stocked in stores in other countries are the same as those in U.S. stores. Considering that cultures in many of these countries differ widely from each other, and from U.S. culture, how do you account for the success of the foreign stores?

4. Toys R Us stores have a unique set of attributes that consumers seem to like, such as a wide assortment, separate locations, and so on. Can the Kids R Us chain succeed in the same way? Why or why not?

## REFERENCES

"Toys R Us, Inc. Forecast for 1992" *Wall Street Journal,* Apr. 9, 1991, p. B-1; "As Toymakers Unwrap New Products, They Hope Video Games Are Peaking," *Wall Street Journal,* Feb. 11, 1991, p. B-1; "War Toy Makers Mobilize as Sales Rise," *Wall Street Journal,* Feb. 9, 1991, p. B-1; "Toy Makers Are Attacking Video Games With New Dolls, Cars and Movie Tie-Ins, *Wall Street Journal,* Feb. 15, 1990, p. B-1; "New Toys On The Block," *Washington Post,* Feb. 18, 1990, p. F-1; "Toys R Us and McDonalds Take on Japanese Toy Market," *Washington Post,* Sept. 27, 1989, p. B-1; "Who Says You Can't Break Into Japan?" *Business Week,* Oct. 16, 1989, p. 49; "Japan's Silent Majority Starts to Mumble," *Business Week,* Apr. 23, 1990, p. 52; "Is Japan Cracking? Hardly," *Business Week,* April 16, 1990, p. 22; "Retailers Scramble for Game Boy; Other Nintendo Products Pace Holiday Toy Parade," *Discount Store News,* Jan. 8, 1990 p. 62; "Superelf Plans for Xma$" *Fortune,* Sep. 11, 1989, p. 151; "Toy Industry Sailing on Troubled Waters," *Marketing News,*

Feb. 29, 1988, p. 23; "Will Toys "B" Great?" *Forbes*, Feb. 22, 1988, p. 37; "POS Technology: Scanners R Us," *Chain Stores Age Executive*, Mar. 1988, p. 95; "Retailers of the Year: Kids R Us Is Growing Up," *Chain Store Age Executive*, Oct., 1988, p. 53; "How Toys R Us Controls the Game Board," *Business Week*, Dec. 19, 1988, p. 58; "Toys R Us Goes Overseas—and Finds that Toys R Them, Too," *Business Week*, Jan. 26, 1987, p. 71; "Toymakers Could Wake Up With Coal Filled Stockings," *Business Week*, Oct. 12, 1987, p. 131; "Goo Goo Chic, A Day in the Life of an Upscale Baby," *Business Week*, Apr. 22, 1985, p. 62; "Greenman Bros. is No Babe in Toyland," *Business Week*, Aug. 26, 1985, p. 75; "Can Anyone Compete With Toys R Us?" *Fortune*, October 28, 1985, p. 71; "Founder Lazarus Is A Reason Toys R Us Dominates Industry," *Wall Street Journal*, Nov. 21, 1985, p. 1; "Ambivalence in Toyland," Brian Sutton-Smith, *Natural History*, Dec. 1985, p. 6; "Where the Dollars R" *Fortune*, June 1, 1981, p. 45.

**TOYS R US**

**EXHIBIT 19-1**

**Toys R Us Foreign Sales**

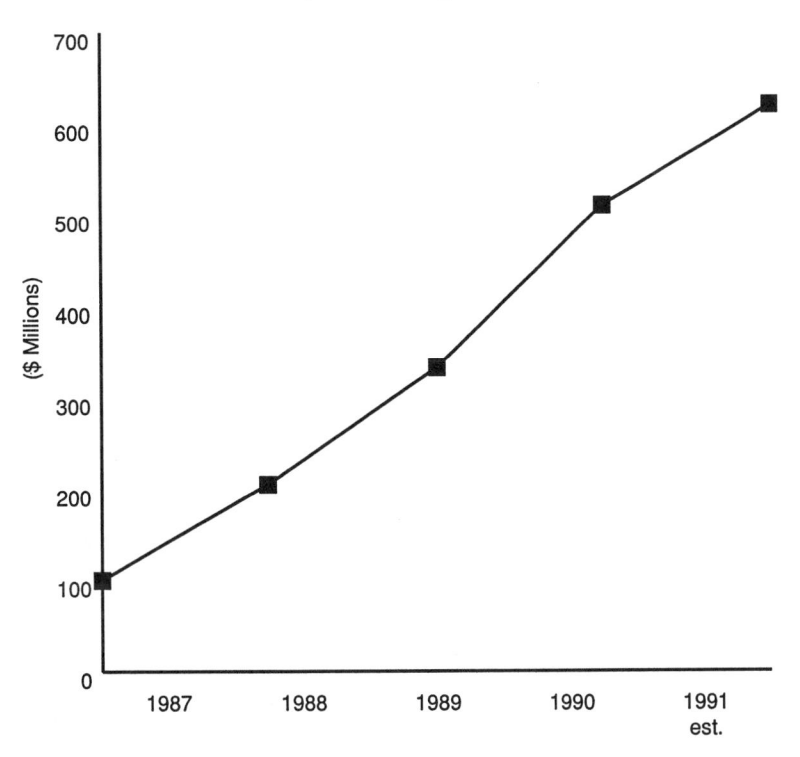

**TOYS R US**

**EXHIBIT 19-2**

**Total Toy Sales in Japan**

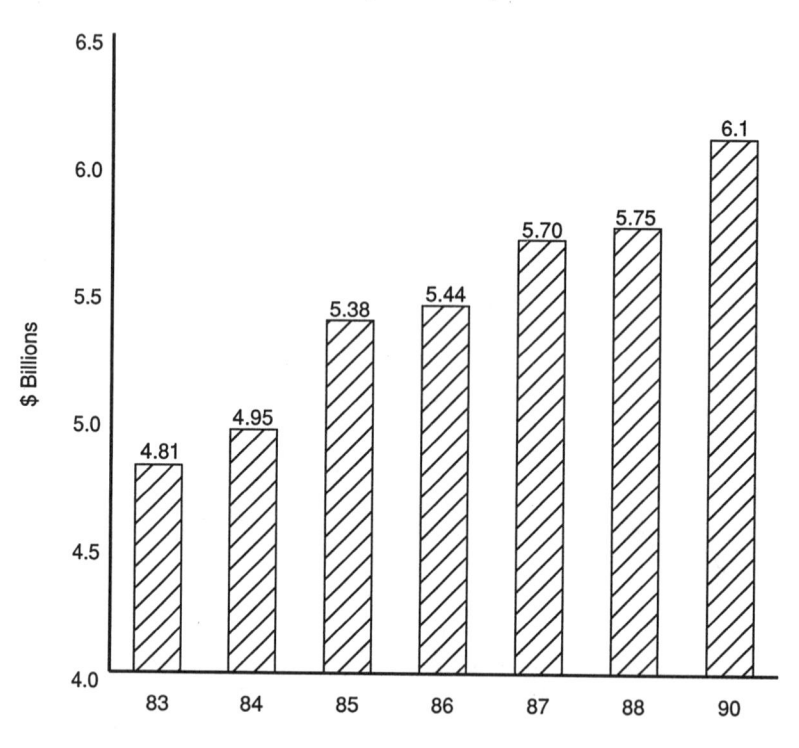

| Year | $ Billions |
|---|---|
| 83 | 4.81 |
| 84 | 4.95 |
| 85 | 5.38 |
| 86 | 5.44 |
| 87 | 5.70 |
| 88 | 5.75 |
| 90 | 6.1 |

## CASE TWENTY

# THE POLAROID CORPORATION

The Polaroid Corporation has been called one of the most successful single-product companies in the United States. It began nearly half a century ago when W. Averill Harriman, a political figure in the Roosevelt administration; James P. Warburg, a financier; and several others provided Edwin Land with $375,000 to form a research company. The new Polaroid Co. was to find a means of polarizing light. But Land was not seeking this technology for use in cameras or photography, but as the basis for new automobile headlight lenses that would reduce glare while still providing normal illumination. Unfortunately, the auto producers were not too interested in the lens. But World War II did create a demand for optic lenses that Land's company was able to produce in quantity and profitably.

After the war, the flow of lens orders dried up and, along with other highly specialized military contractors, the company was on the verge of bankruptcy. But, in the nick of time, Edwin Land announced he had discovered a near-magic process that would permit a camera to take a picture, develop it inside the camera, and turn out a photo print all in a matter of a few minutes. Sold first in 1948, the camera was advertised as an "instant" device, and it became an instant success, due mainly to its unique technological features. This early model is shown in Exhibit 20-1. It attracted hordes of innovators who wanted to be the first to own and demonstrate its captivating legerdemain. But it was also aided by the application of an important marketing technique—pricing. Its price was neither a skimming one that might restrict sales nor a penetration one that might cheapen its image; rather, the price was about halfway between the two. Then, whether by clever marketing design or by a series of technological innovations, new features were added, prices were reduced, and sales volumes increased over the ensuing 35 years. Exhibit 20-2 lists the major product improvements for the instant camera. By 1971, Polaroid had grown to a $500 billion firm, primarily due to its single product for which there had been no prior demand until its introduction.

## DECLINE OF THE INSTANT CAMERA

In 1985, the Polaroid Corporation was facing serious problems. For practically all of its corporate life, it had been a one-product company. Even after Kodak moved into the instant camera market in the late 1970s, Polaroid maintained its leadership, protected by a host of patents on instant photography technology. The market for instant cameras blossomed in the 1970s with the introduction of cheap color models and the popular Polaroid SX-70, with its Pronto counterpart a few years later. In the banner year of 1978, Polaroid sold 9.4 million instant cameras to Kodak's 4.5 million. Exhibit 20-3 shows sales of the two competitors from 1973 through estimates for 1985, and Exhibit 20-4 shows the decline in sales of Polaroid instant cameras and film.

The blossoming of the 1970s was short-lived. Polaroid's sales slipped 1.1 percent in 1979, and by 1984 they had dropped to 3.5 million cameras. During this period, Polaroid held on firmly to over two-thirds of the market—but this is two-thirds of only 45 percent of the 1978 sales.

Most analysts attribute the decline partly to market saturation, but mainly to changes in consumer preferences and needs. The most popular and fastest growing segment of the amateur photography market in the early 1980s was the 35mm single lens reflex camera, mainly the models selling for $100 to $200. These new models were more sophisticated, yet easy for amateurs to use, and the picture quality far outshown that of instant prints. Sales of these cameras in the United States nearly tripled, from about 1.2 million in 1976 to 3.5 million in 1980. Interestingly, however, many of the technological features of the new 35mms are the result of Edwin Land's extensive research in the Polaroid laboratories. Nonetheless, the 35mm models have had a direct appeal to the manipulative and practicality aspects of American culture. Although many processes of the photo-taking operation are automatic, there are still enough adjustments for the amateurs to make, so they feel more in control. As one industry analyst put it, "Instant photography for amateurs, at least, has become old hat."

## SOURCES OF PRESENT DIFFICULTIES

Today, the Polaroid Corp. is searching, more or less frantically, for new products or adaptations of present ones that can be sold in or out of the photography market. And this need was brought about by three elements, one inherent in the firm's long-term management and the others by an almost unforgivable failure to analyze the market.

The first involves the personality and business philosophy of Polaroid's president and founder, the late Edwin H. Land. His ideology is summed up in this quotation: "Our essential concept was—and mine still is—that the role of industry is to sense a deep human need, then bring science and technology to bear on filling that need. Any market already existing is inherently boring and dull." Because Land strongly opposed any moves into commercial photography or other areas of business, Polaroid's activities were restricted to the amateur market and tied to a single product line. So today, there are no other products to provide the income needed to pursue new interests, and what income there is is declining along with the demand for instant cameras. Even though Polaroid is aggressively trying to exploit its expertise in other markets, success seems to be several years away.

The second element was the judgment error Polaroid made when it failed to anticipate the peaking of demand in 1978 and its subsequent continuing decline. Instead, the company geared up to produce even larger quantities of instant cameras and saddled itself with unneeded capacity. This was certainly a major mistake for a firm that had created the product, marketed it for 40 years, and successfully held its own against Kodak's invasion into the instant camera market.

The third element was the Polavision fiasco, which all but dissolved the company's reputation as a technological leader in the amateur photography field and cost it millions in designing and marketing the product. Because of the importance of Polavision's failure, this source of the company's difficulties is described in more detail in the following sections.

## THE POLAVISION ADVENTURE

In the late 1960s, Polaroid initiated a research program under the code name "Project Sesame," which was concerned with experiments that are conducted with film especially designed for viewing by shining light through it. At the time, most conventional film produced printed photographs that are viewed the same as other objects, by light shining on them. It was the "shining light through" concept that helped produce Polavision, a new instant movie system that took nearly eight years to bring to market.

Historically, the Polaroid Corporation has excelled in both technology and marketing, but it failed in both when the new Polavision system was introduced in 1977. Under Land's direction, some $300 million was spent in research, development, and production to bring the system to market. Polavision was designed to take motion pictures with a special camera that developed them immediately for projection on a screen; it was a technological marvel that few consumers wanted.

The marvel had a few flaws. The camera was held by hand, and it used a very bright light that tended to frighten or annoy small children. Moreover, the movies were silent; there was no provision for sound, and the pictures themselves were quite grainy. When the instantly developed pictures were projected on the small 12-inch screen, they could only be seen clearly when the viewer was directly in front of the screen. Each instant movie film lasted only about two-and-a-half minutes, a short performance for the price. Although Polaroid was well aware of these flaws and imperfections, the company considered them to be trivial and introduced the system anyway.

There were other problems in addition to the design and technical deficiencies. Instead of trying to develop primary demand for the product through pioneering advertising where potential buyers are informed about the product and what it will do, Polaroid simply distributed it to the same channels that its SX-70 instant cameras used. Although consumers knew the Polaroid brand and its regular products, they were uncertain about what Polavision actually did and how it worked. There was no easy way to demonstrate the system in the regular distribution channels, so that its advantages would be highlighted. This was particularly true in discount and drug stores where a large share of Polaroid's instant cameras have traditionally been sold. When consumers buy a $500–$600 product, they want it demonstrated, and this was not possible in crowded camera departments, which are generally tended by part-time and often inexperienced salespeople. One Polaroid executive commented, "We learned we didn't know how to sell the system."

But Polaroid actually put out a considerable sales effort. A 1978 Christmas promotion promised a free personal delivery by Santa Claus to any purchaser of a Polavision system. About 3,000 buyers took advantage of the offer, and a battalion of Santa Clauses made the deliveries. If buyers did not want the personalized delivery, they could choose to take home their own Santa Claus suit along with the Polavision. And over 10,000 of them did. But the deficiencies in the system became all too apparent after it was used several times. Thus, the 13,000 innovators who took the risk of buying the product initially failed to become opinion leaders who should have been the information source that sparked the diffusion process. Consequently, the product gathered dust on retailers' shelves.

Not only were both technology and marketing faulty, but the company did not do its homework in researching the market itself or in forecasting demand. People had been shying away from home movies for many years. The photography trade's *Wolfman Report* indicated that 1.12 million 8mm movie cameras were sold in 1972, but that consumers bought only half that number, or 560,000 in 1978, so demand had been dropping for some time. Even if it missed this information, Polaroid should certainly have been able to predict the withering competition that was imminent from videotape cameras. The movies these cameras took could be viewed on a regular television screen, using a videocassette recorder, and the show they recorded lasted considerably longer than Polavision's two-and-a-half minutes. Polaroid's film could only be used one time; videotape could be used over and over. But the most attractive feature is that sound may be recorded at the same time that the pictures are taken. In 1984, however, only 2.8 percent of U.S.

households had a video camera, while 27.5 percent had a conventional home movie camera (Exhibit 20-5).

In 1979, Polaroid tried to correct some of the technological deficiencies in the Polavision system. It upgraded the film so that the pictures were not as grainy and added a slow-motion and stop feature. But it was too late. Early in 1980, Polaroid quietly withdrew Polavision from the market, taking a hefty $68 million writeoff in the 1979 fiscal year. As a result, total earnings for 1979 fell to $36 million from $118 million the previous year. And sales edged 1.1 percent lower, to $1.36 billion.

In mid-1981, the company introduced the Sun 600 series instant cameras that automatically combined ambient and electronic strobe light to eliminate shadows and harsh contrast. This was followed in 1983 by the 600 LMS with built-in flash and the SLR 680 with automatic focus. Several models in this series are shown in Exhibit 20-6. In late 1985, Polaroid announced the forthcoming introduction of the series 7000 camera, which would produce "vastly improved photographs."

Most experts in the photographic field concede that even though Polaroid's expertise and research improved the quality of both instant movie and camera prints and images, conventional prints are still much better. And the instant camera is old technology. Innovative research in photography, both amateur and commercial, appears to be concentrating on ways to store images electronically instead of on conventional film. Technology was on the threshold of this and other similar innovations when Polaroid introduced an outdated concept into a market geared for new innovative concepts.

## CASE ANALYSIS QUESTIONS

1. What consumer behavior cultural concepts were likely to be involved in the marked consumer switch to 35mm cameras from the improved, simple, one-process Polaroid cameras?

2. Why did Polaroid market Polavision with all of its obvious deficiencies?

3. How can you relate Polavision's failure to the concepts of consumers' changing needs and goals?

## REFERENCES

"Polaroid, What the Bears are Missing," *Business Week*, Nov. 5, 1990, p. 138; "What Will Polaroid Do With All That Moola?" *Business Week*, Oct. 29, 1990, p. 38; "Polaroid: Marking Time," *Business Week*, Apr. 30, 1990, p. 26; "Holidays Become War Days for Makers of Photo Film," *Wall Street Journal*, Dec. 13, 1989, p. B-1; "Why Polaroid Must Remake Itself—Instantly," *Business Week*, Sept. 19, 1988, p. 66; "Polaroid Hopes to Snap Out of a Sales Slump," *Wall Street Journal*, Nov. 11, 1985, p. 6; "Polaroid's Spectra May Be Losing Its Flash," *Business Week*, Jun. 29, 1987, p. 31; "Spectra's Instant Success Gives Polaroid a Shot in the Arm," *Business Week*, Nov. 3, 1986, p. 32; "Polaroid Stages Marketing Blitz," *Marketing News*, Jun. 6, 1968, p. 4; "Kodak to Drop Its Instant Camera Line if Ban on Sales After Jan. 9

Isn't Lifted," *Wall Street Journal,* Nov. 7, 1985, p. 18; Polaroid's Parts Look Healthier Than The Whole," *Business Week,* Jun. 24, 1985, p. 98; "New Line of Cameras Developed by Polaroid Could Brighten Concern's Financial Picture," *Wall Street Journal,* Jun. 4, 1985, p. B-1; "Polaroid's Ads Shift to Dependability," *Advertising Age,* Apr. 1, 1985, p. 18; "Polaroid Gropes for Another Winner," *New York Times,* Feb. 3, 1985, p. F-7; "How Polaroid and TWA Created a Monster," *Business Week,* Jan. 21, 1985, p. 39; "Polaroid Can't Get Its Future In Focus," *Business Week,* Apr. 4, 1983, p. 31; "Polaroid Explains Instant Color Slide System," *Chemical and Engineering News,* Nov. 8, 1982, p. 27; "Polaroid's New Focus on Computer Screens," *Business Week,* May 31, 1982, p. 29; "No Instant Success, But New Focus Brightens the Picture at Polaroid," *Barrons,* Jul. 5, 1982, p. 15; "Fast Film, Powerful Battery Improve Polaroids," *Chemical and Engineering News,* Jun. 22, 1981, p. 52; "Polaroid Struggles to Get Back Into Focus," *Fortune,* Apr. 7, 1980, p. 66; "The Chores Facing Polaroid's New CEO," *Business Week,* Mar. 24, 1980, p. 52.

**POLAROID CORPORATION**
**EXHIBIT 20-1**

*Source*: Courtesy of Polaroid Corporation

## POLAROID CORPORATION

### EXHIBIT 20-2

**Introduction and Major Improvements for the Polaroid Instant Camera**

|  | |
|---|---|
| 1948 | First instant camera sold |
| 1960 | 15-second picture and automatic exposure camera |
| 1963 | Color film and film cartridge |
| 1965 | Low-priced swinger camera |
| 1969 | Cheap color camera |
| 1971 | Improved cheap color camera |
| 1972 | SX-70 pocket-sized color camera, film out in 1.2 seconds and 4 minute developing |
| 1972 | No litter, no-peel-apart film |
| 1976 | Pronto, low-priced SX-70 model |
| 1977 | Polavision instant movie system |
| 1979 | Time Zero supercolor film for SX-70 models |
| 1981 | 600 Series, auto-Strobe light and ultrasonic range system |
| 1986 | (Planned) Series 7000, vastly improved photos |

## POLAROID CORPORATION

### EXHIBIT 20-3

**Instant Camera Sales, Polaroid and Kodak, 1979-85**

| | SALES IN MILLIONS OF UNITS | | |
|---|---|---|---|
| Year | Polaroid | Kodak | Total |
| 1973 | 5.6 | | 5.6 |
| 1974 | 5.6 | | 5.6 |
| 1975 | 5.8 | | 5.8 |
| 1976 | 6.1 | | 6.1 |
| 1977 | 6.9 | 3.4 | 10.3 |
| 1978 | 9.3 | 4.5 | 13.8 |
| 1979 | 6.7 | 4.6 | 11.3 |
| 1980 | 6.4 | 3.7 | 10.1 |
| 1981 | 5.5 | 4.2 | 9.7 |
| 1982 | 4.0 | 3.2 | 7.2 |
| 1983 | 3.7 | 2.5 | 6.2 |
| 1984 | 3.5 | 1.1 | 4.6 |
| 1985 | 3.7 | .9 | 4.6 |

**POLAROID CORPORATION**

**EXHIBIT 20-4**

**Sales of Instant Cameras and Film**

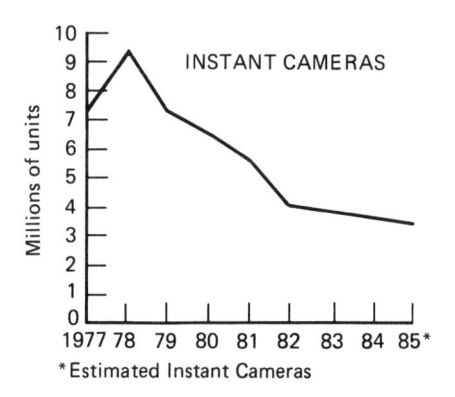

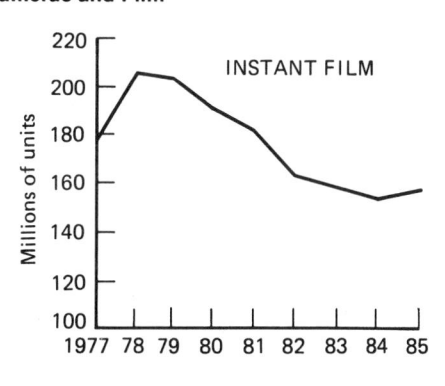

*Estimated Instant Cameras

**POLAROID CORPORATION**

**EXHIBIT 20-5**

**Camera Types Owned by U.S. Households, 1984**

| Type | Percent Owning |
| --- | --- |
| Traditional still camera | 93.2 |
| Instant print camera | 36.3 |
| Home movie camera | 27.5 |
| Video camera | 2.8 |

**POLAROID CORPORATION**
**EXHIBIT 20-6**
**1983 Model 600 Instant Camera**

# CASE TWENTY-ONE

# RADLEY DEVELOPMENT CO., INC.

John H. (Bud) Radley had just finished dictating the following memorandum to the divisional vice president for residential development of the Radley Development Co., Inc.:

---

**MEMORANDUM**

August 2

To: Charlie Shoburn
From: Bud Radley
Subject: Sales Strategy for Colonial Lakes

I have just looked over the sales report for Colonial Lakes and I am disappointed in what it shows, to say the least. Since we opened the development in May, we have sold only 14 units, and half of those are Lynwoods, the lowest-priced, half-acre models. Even the heavy promotion on TV and in the *Evening Times* hasn't helped.

I know the competition is heavy from Suncrest and Wood Trails and there will be even more when Larchmont starts construction this month. The four or five other developments we have built in the area are much lower priced and appeal to lower-middle and upper lower social classes, so I don't consider them as competition. But Colonial Lakes is the prestige property of the three now selling, yet we don't seem to be attracting prestige buyers and I wonder why. This may be our first high-priced development, but neither of us is an amateur in this business. You

> will remember how fast Oak Hills sold out, even though it had a lot fewer amenities than Colonial Lakes has.
>
> The builders are getting impatient with the delay and are calling me, complaining they can't get the revised plan from you for lot locations on the four house models. With sales as they are, I can understand why you want to wait. That's why I think we ought to do a little research to see if we can get a better handle on the problem here, and maybe change our sales promotion tactics. Please get our market research outfit to find out what our close competition is doing, who is buying from them, why the buyers bought from them, and if they looked at Colonial, why they didn't buy from us. We can also get some information on the 14 who already bought in Colonial and why they did. Maybe all this will tell us something new.
>
> When you get the information, please set up a meeting with me to go over it.

## BACKGROUND

The Radley Development Co. is a major developer of shopping centers, office complexes, and residential areas, with headquarters in a large midwestern metropolitan area. It is organized into three divisions: (1) retail development and shopping centers, (2) office and commercial development, and (3) residential development. Each of these is headed by a vice-president and Charles Shoburn heads division 3.

Over the past 20 years, the firm has developed some 32 residential tracts, the largest has 1,500 homes and the smallest has 32. As indicated in Mr. Radley's memo, all these projects were targeted to blue- and white-collar families who worked in skilled factory jobs as service technicians, in clerical jobs, and as working owners of small businesses. Generally, these developments offer two basic home models with some variations, on one-eighth to one-quarter acre lots. Colonial Lakes is the most recent project and is the firm's first venture into prestige residential properties.

## CHARLES SHOBURN

When he received Mr. Radley's memo, Charles Shoburn was somewhat concerned with its tone and the clear implication that he needed some help. This was his first major development project since his appointment to head the residential development division a year ago, and he was anxious to make it a success. But he was forced to admit that Mr. Radley was right and that he, Shoburn, should have been first to suggest the need for market research. Colonial's sales had been far below expectations, and to make matters worse, he heard that sales of the two closest competitors, Suncrest and Wood Trails, had been more than double those of Colonial Lakes in the past two months.

Mr. Shoburn had been in the real estate business for 15 years, ever since he graduated from the University of Illinois business school. He knew that both the business and its clients were changing. Prices of all types of homes were constantly climbing upward. Yet, many two-earner families were looking for homes in the $100,000–$150,000 range as symbols of their success. These were upwardly mobile families who were anxious to move in social circles that would help them advance in their careers. They hoped that living in a high-status suburban development would provide these circles. Shoburn and his division designed Colonial Lakes to appeal to this market, but so far the market had all but ignored it.

## DESCRIPTION OF THE DEVELOPMENTS

The three present developments, and the forthcoming Larchmont, were all located about 12 to 18 miles from the midwestern city of Occomac. It was a large industrial manufacturing city of 1.5 million and had recently been successful in attracting several large producers of electronic components for computer and national defense applications. The resulting influx of high-salaried engineers and executives created a market for new, larger suburban homes away from the older, smoke-stack atmosphere of Occomac itself. The relative location of the developments is shown on the map in Exhibit 21–1. The pertinent data and major features of each one are shown in Exhibit 21–2. Exhibit 21–2 lists several models of homes and an encompassing price range. Generally, models in similar price ranges are built in specific sections. In Colonial Lakes, for example, two basic models are available in the $185,000 to $210,000 range, on one-half acre lots in areas furthest from the lake. Similarly, $200,000 to $260,000 homes are nearer the lake, and the highest priced ones, up to $315,000, are lakeside. Options and extras can add considerably to the basic prices.

*Colonial Lakes* is situated in rolling hill country on former farm land. Young trees are planted along all streets and there is an impressive stone structure at the entrance. Many of the homes are set well back from the road, and a number of the higher-priced models have pillared fronts. About half of the homes have lake frontage or direct lake view and individual access. There are several sand beaches for use by nonfrontage property owners.

*Wood Trails* is a more rustic type of development with wooded lots and emphasis on contemporary styles. Colonial and split-level models are also available, however. The roads are high-grade gravel, which residents feel is in keeping with the rustic atmosphere and discouraging to sightseers and speeding teenagers. It targets younger, and health- and exercise-oriented families with its bicycle trails, pool, and racquetball courts. Its lake is artificially made and swimming is not permitted, although boating and fishing are. About one-third of the lots have lake frontage.

*Suncrest* is a traditionally styled development similar to Colonial Lakes. It is situated on the east bank of the Feather River. Swimming is not permitted at the present time, but the State Department of Environment expects that it will be in three to four years when pollution sources are cleaned up. Riverside land has been reserved for beaches when the ban is lifted. About 45 of the 122 lots have some river frontage, and many lots are wooded. Near the entrance is a clubhouse with a large restaurant, open to the public. Other club facilities, including boat docks, are reserved for Suncrest residents.

*Larchmont* will be the most prestigious and highest priced of the four developments. It is built on flat or gently rolling land, with many trees. A wide stream bisects the area and 200 feet of parkland have been reserved on either side. There are two vehicle and four foot or bicycle bridges over the stream. House styles include mainly colonial and Georgian, with some contemporary. It is targeted mainly to professionals (physicians, attorneys, etc.) and mid- to upper-range business executives and officers.

**RESEARCH**

Mr. Shoburn reviewed this information on the competition. He then checked with several of the largest real estate agencies, banks, savings and loan associations, and other sources to get an estimate of sales for these competitive developments. The estimate he prepared from these sources is shown in Exhibit 21–3 and includes the number of homes sold by model and price range. Keep in mind that the same model may be sold for several prices, depending on the extras and options the buyer selects. Apparently Mr. Radley had similar information, and that was what prompted his memorandum.

There was little doubt in Mr. Shoburn's mind that something about Colonial Lakes or its promotion either failed to attract prospective buyers or inhibited them from buying once they visited the site and the models. To get things started, he set up a meeting with Leslie Bensen, vice-president of Occomac Market Facts, a firm Radley had used in the past. During the meeting, he explained his problem and they went over the information Mr. Shoburn had collected about the competitive developments. He also explained why the research information was urgently needed, and she agreed to get a proposal to him in two or three days.

Two days later he received the following (abstracted) proposal from her.

**PROPOSAL TO RESIDENTIAL DEVELOPMENT DIVISION, RADLEY INC.**

We will conduct personal interviews with as many purchasers of homes in the three competitive developments as we can. We say "as many as we can" because there are relatively few of them and, in our experience, some of the buyers may not wish to cooperate. Word will also get back to the other developers, who may try to discourage their residents from participating. We try to work with community associations, and we have techniques that should provide an adequate sample for your needs.

> From today on, we ask you to try to get names and addresses of people who visit Colonial Lakes. You may want to assure them that no *salespeople* will call on them. We would also like to have similar information on any visitors in the past, if you can identify them. We will interview as many of them as possible, using the unstructured-direct technique.
>
> We will obtain demographic data on all buyers we interview and will provide a summary of the salient factors that emerge from the qualitative interviews. We will also summarize these factors from interviews with Colonial Lakes visitors who have not yet bought. We do not believe that demographics from this group will be particularly useful to you, so we will not collect them. Since this will be exploratory research (to determine what the problem is), we will not make recommendations as to what you should do.
>
> Since we understand the urgency involved, the study will be completed in 30 days from the date you give us formal acceptance. The cost to accomplish what is described above will be $5,500.
>
> Please notify us in writing of your acceptance and please include a retainer of 25 percent of the total fee.
>
> Presented by:
>
> LESLIE BENSEN

Mr. Shoburn quickly accepted the proposal and sent a copy to Mr. Radley, letting him know that his instructions were being carried out, and how soon to expect an answer.

In a little over three weeks, Ms. Bensen made an appointment to discuss the research report with Mr. Shoburn, and a summary of the findings in her report is in Exhibits 21-4 and 21-5. Two days later, they met with Mr. Radley and spent most of the afternoon discussing the implications of the data in the report. Shortly after five o'clock, Mr. Radley got up, stretched, and said, "I think it's quite clear what we have to do. Let's have dinner and see if we can put the details together."

## CASE ANALYSIS QUESTIONS

1. What factors seem to be influencing sales in Suncrest in recent months? What do Exhibits 21-1 and 21-4 suggest?

2. Is Mr. Shoburn correct in his assessments of what prospective buyers are looking for in a home and the area in which it is located? What is Mr. Shoburn promoting in Colonial Lakes?

3. What major changes should Mr. Shoburn make in his overall approach

to the market in relation to (a) advertising and promotion, (b) types of homes being offered in Colonial Lakes, (c) sizes of lots in Colonial Lakes, and (d) schools in Colonial Lakes district?

## REFERENCE

This case is based upon original research by the author. Data and developer name are disguised.

# RADLEY DEVELOPMENT CO., INC.
## EXHIBIT 21-1
### City of Occomac and Surrounding Territory

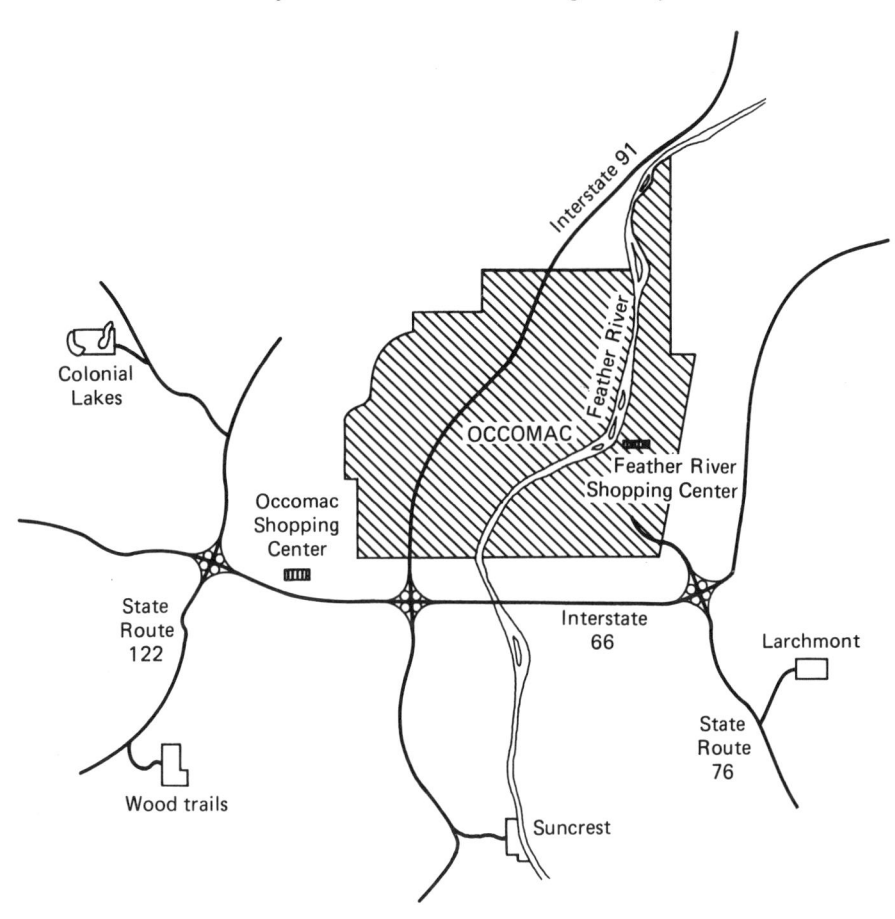

## RADLEY DEVELOPMENT CO., INC.

### EXHIBIT 21-2

### Characteristics of the Four Developments

| Development | # Home Models | Price Range | Sq. Ft. Range | Lot Sizes | Distance to City |
|---|---|---|---|---|---|
| Colonial Lakes (177 units) Expandable to 235 lots | 4 | $185,000– $315,000 | 1910– 3150 | 1/2, 1, & 2 acres | 25 min. rush hour |
| Wood Trails (92 units) | 3 | $135,000– $188,000 | 1830– 2300 | 1, 2, & 4 acres | 30–40 min. rush hour |
| Suncrest (122 units) | 3 | $150,000– $220,000 | 2250– 2850 | 2, 3 acres | 15–20 min. rush hour |
| Larchmont (109 units) Expandable to 127 lots | 4 | $190,000– $285,000 | 2540– 3200 | 2, 3, & 4 acres | 35–40 min. rush hour |

| Development | Major Features | Distance to Schools | Distance to Shopping | Utilities |
|---|---|---|---|---|
| Colonial Lakes | Natural lake w/beaches<br>Golf course<br>Park<br>Paved roads<br>Tennis courts<br>Swimming pool | 1.7 mi. to grade<br>5.2 mi. to high | Conv. store 1.5 mi.<br>Occomac Major Ctr. 6.7 mi. | City water sewers<br>Underground utilities<br>Cable TV |
| Wood Trails | Lake<br>Swimming pool<br>Large park<br>Bike trails<br>Tennis courts<br>Racquetball<br>Gravel roads | 0.5 mi. to grade<br>8.4 mi. to high | Strip stores 2.4 mi.<br>Occomac Major Ctr. 8.1 mi. | Well water<br>Septic field<br>Underground utilities |
| Suncrest | River location<br>Swimming pool<br>Clubhouse<br>Restaurant<br>Tennis courts<br>Paved roads | 4.0 mi. to grade<br>7.4 mi. to high | Local stores 1.7 mi.<br>Feather Major Ctr. 12.0 mi. | City water sewers<br>Gas<br>Cable TV |
| Larchmont | Golf course<br>2 pools<br>Security guards<br>Tennis courts<br>Park<br>Paved main roads | 3.4 mi. to grade<br>6.1 mi. to high | General store 2.0 mi.<br>Feather Major Ctr. 7.9 mi. | Well water<br>Septic field<br>Underground utilities |

## RADLEY DEVELOPMENT CO., INC.
### EXHIBIT 21-3
### Sales of Homes and Approximate Prices, March Through July

| Development | March | April | May | June | July |
|---|---|---|---|---|---|
| Colonial Lakes<br>n = 14 | — | — | 1–185,500<br>1–192,000<br>1–187,750 | 3–189,900<br>2–198,000<br>1–210,000<br>1–137,000 | 1–185,750<br>2–199,900<br>1–255,000 |
| Wood Trails<br>n = 41 | 1–136,000 | 1–138,750<br>2–135,500<br>2–142,500 | 3–142,500<br>3–145,000<br>2–137,300<br>2–139,900 | 3–147,300<br>4–139,900<br>3–154,500<br>1–158,500<br>2– 92,000 | 4–156,000<br>4–136,500<br>2–141,600<br>2–152,000<br>1–132,200 |
| Suncrest<br>n = 36 | — | 2–154,000<br>1–159,750<br>1–166,250 | 3–159,750<br>2–166,250<br>4–175,000 | 4–154,000<br>3–183,250<br>3–155,000<br>1–172,500 | 3–158,250<br>2–155,100<br>4–155,750<br>1–162,000<br>1–167,250<br>1–140,100 |
| Larchmont[a]<br>n = 3 | | | | | 1–245,000<br>1–220,500<br>1–262,750 |

[a] Preopening sales

## RADLEY DEVELOPMENT CO., INC.
## EXHIBIT 21-4
### Selected Demographic Characteristics of Buyers of Homes in the Three Existing Developments

1. Colonial Lakes:
   Total buyers 14
   Interviewed 9 (64%)

| | | |
|---|---|---|
| Age of adult buyers listed on deed | 25–34 | 4 |
| | 35–44 | 12 |
| | 45–54 | 2 |
| Occupations of buyers listed on deed: | Government | 6 |
| | Self-employed: | |
| |   Retail | 5 |
| |   Service | 2 |
| |   Other | 1 |
| | Professional | 1 |
| | Work in home | 2 |
| Education | High school | 17.6% |
| | Some college | 29.4 |
| | College degree | 29.4 |
| | Graduate degree | 17.6 |
| | Other | 6.0 |
| Number of children: | Zero | 28.0% |
| | One | 41.4 |
| | Two | 22.6 |
| | Three or more | 8.0 |

2. Wood Trails
   Total buyers 41
   Interviewed 30 (73%)

| | | |
|---|---|---|
| Age of adult buyers listed on deed: | 20–24 | 1 |
| | 25–34 | 36 |
| | 35–44 | 16 |
| | 45–54 | 4 |
| Occupations of buyers listed on deed: | Teacher | 5 |
| | Government | 10 |
| | Self-employed: | |
| |   Retail | 4 |
| |   Service | 5 |
| |   Manufacturing | 1 |
| | Professional | 2 |
| | Work in home | 11 |
| | Military | 2 |
| | Clerical | 7 |
| | Technical | 7 |
| | Other | 3 |

| | | |
|---|---|---|
| Education: | High school | 16.2% |
| | Some college | 26.8 |
| | College degree | 36.6 |
| | Graduate degree | 18.3 |
| Number of children | Zero | 45.0% |
| | One | 36.7 |
| | Two | 15.0 |
| | Three or more | 3.3 |

3. Suncrest

   Total buyers 36

   Interviewed  19 (53%)

| | | |
|---|---|---|
| Age of adult buyers listed on deed: | 25–34 | 9 |
| | 35–44 | 25 |
| | 45–54 | 2 |
| | 55+ | 2 |
| Occupations of buyers listed on deed: | Teacher | 2 |
| | Government | 3 |
| | Self-employed: | |
| |   Retail | 2 |
| |   Service | 1 |
| |   Manufacturing | 3 |
| | Professional | 9 |
| | Religious | 1 |
| | Clerical | 3 |
| | Technical | 4 |
| | Political | 2 |
| | Retired | 2 |
| | Other | 1 |
| Education: | High school | 10.9% |
| | Some college | 18.9 |
| | College degree | 45.9 |
| | Graduate degree | 24.3 |
| Number of children: | Zero | 19.0% |
| | One | 42.0 |
| | Two | 29.0 |
| | Three or more | 10.0 |

## RADLEY DEVELOPMENT CO.

### EXHIBIT 21-5

### Abstracts of Major Points from Personal Interviews with Buyers and with Those Who Visited Developments but Did Not Buy

I. Of the 110 names given to us by Mr. Shoburn, we obtained information from 82. These potential buyers fall into the following categories (those who bought in Colonial Lakes are not included):

1. Have already bought in:

   | | |
   |---|---|
   | Wood Trails | 21 |
   | Suncrest | 13 |
   | Larchmont | 1 |
   | Other develop | 25 |
   | Still looking | 22 |

2. Those still looking say they will probably buy in:

   | | |
   |---|---|
   | Colonial Lakes | 3 |
   | Suncrest | 6 |
   | Wood Trails | 5 |
   | Larchmont | 4 |
   | Other develop. | 4 |

II. From our interviews with those who bought in each development, comments on why they bought or expect to buy, are summarized here:

1. *Colonial Lakes*: Liked the lake, particularly the beaches—can swim in natural water. City water and sewer. People already there seemed pleasant; like people we already know. Very pretty setting. Easy trip to city. Close to schools. Well-planned homes.
2. *Wood Trails*: Liked large lots and contemporary home styles. Not a "trimmed-up" development. Reasonably priced for what you get. Have friends and business associates living there. Lots of exercise facilities. Great bike trails for kids. Area school system has good reputation.
3. *Suncrest*: City services. Nice location by river; cool in hot weather. Some well-known people in city, and executives in my firm live there or are thinking about it. High school has highest SAT scores in metro area. Quick access to Occomac downtown. Clubhouse is good place to meet people. Like the wooded lots. Activities for children.

III. Why those who chose or are considering Wood Trails, Suncrest, or Larchmont did not choose Colonial Lakes:

Homes there now seemed to be smaller and on small lots. The people we talked to who live there were nice but they had pick-ups and campers in their driveway. Salespeople did not have information on the school system. Seems as though the leading people in Occomac are moving to Suncrest or Larchmont. There do not seem to be many houses going up in Colonial Lakes.

# CASE TWENTY-TWO

# FROM INNOVATIVE TO TRADITIONAL: CAMPBELL'S SOUP

The Campbell Kids Are Back! A bit spruced up for the 1990s, they cavort about with their black and Asian friends. They even sing a little. This revival is part of Campbell Soup's new strategy—a "return to the traditional" after almost a decade of relentless diversification for the giant prepared-food company. Exhibit 22–1 shows an early ad featuring the "Kids."

## THE STRATEGY OF THE EIGHTIES

"The Swanson TV dinner is junk food. It was great in the 1950s, but in today's world it doesn't go into the microwave, it doesn't represent variety or good eating experience to my palate." These remarks in the early 1980s didn't come from a competitor in the frozen dinner business or from a food critic, but from R. Gordon McGovern, the 58-year-old, brand new president and chief executive of the Campbell Soup Co. And Swanson is one of Campbell's brands.

Until Mr. McGovern took over, Campbell was a stuffy, production-oriented company that produced what it could make easily. It depended upon the Campbell name and its other well-known brands, together with a standard quality, to satisfy present customers and, hopefully, to attract new ones. It didn't venture into much market research to find out what other similar products people wanted to buy. This rather narrow outlook may have been because Campbell is a family-owned company, with nearly 60 percent of the stock owned by the Dorrance family. Mr. McGovern replaced John T. Dorrance, Jr., who effectively controlled 31 percent of the stock, as president and chief operating officer in 1980. He soon recognized the near-insatiable demand of U.S. consumers for innovative convenience products, packaging, and preparation techniques, and he forced the company to heed the needs and desires of consumers in designing new products.

## COMPANY HISTORY

It is sometimes difficult to understand why large and successful firms often fail to anticipate consumer demand. To do so, we need to look briefly at Campbell's product history and how decades of producing basic staple goods have inhibited the firm's ability to innovate.

The brand and the product have melted together and achieved the status of a single word, "Campbellsoup," in the language, with virtual brand insistence in the marketplace. The company has monopolized the soup market in the United States for years and holds a firm two-thirds of the $2.5 billion market, selling over two billion cans a year. Exhibit 22-2, however, shows continuing increases in dollar sales, but decreases in market share. Campbell's early strategy was to keep expanding the kinds of soup it offered. Thus, grocers had to either expand total shelf space to accommodate the new soups or drop other brands. Since Campbell was the favorite, and adding more kinds didn't increase total soup consumption, they simply dropped competing lines.

### Campbell Symbols

The red-and-white can with a gold medallion has identified the company since its founding in 1897. It was the subject of a famous Andy Warhol pop-art production in the 1960s, which provided free brand reenforcement for the soup. Campbell's advertising, too, has been consistently clever and popular over the years. The cherubic "Campbell Kids" of the 1930s and 1940s were household figures, but they were dropped in the late 1970s, resurrected for a brief period in 1984, and revived again recently. The famous singing slogan "M'm!-m'm!-good" was hummed by more than one generation, and its replacement, which emphasizes the soup's nutritional attributes, "Soup is good food," is equally well known. This strategy, too, has been replaced as we shall see shortly

### Product Acquisitions

But the company was not very innovative. Even its early acquisitions, Swanson TV dinners, Pepperidge Farm bakery products, Franco-American canned foods and Godiva chocolates, were just extensions of the soup line, with nothing in them to appeal to a different target market. The same policies continued into 1978 when Harold A. Shaub was president and chief executive officer. Faced with a continuing lawsuit begun by H. J. Heinz in 1976 which charged Campbell with monopolizing the canned soup industry, Campbell countercharged that Heinz attempted to monopolize the industrial ketchup market. Shortly thereafter, Shaub announced that his firm was testing ketchup in the midwest. In May 1978, Campbell also acquired Vlasic Foods, Inc., with its lion's share of the pickle industry, and Robert J. Vlasic is now chairman of Campbell's board of directors. But these products, too, were merely extensions of the old line, selling to the firm's existing markets. Nonetheless, the company was rock-solid financially with cash and short-term investments of $159 million and only $17 million of long-term debt.

## A SHIFT TO MARKETING

In 1980, however, major earthquakes were rumbling below the Gibraltarian financial base. Gordon McGovern took the company helm and began changing its emphasis from production to marketing and developing a new mission: "to be positioned with consumers as somebody who is looking after their well-being." He also split the traditional four Campbell production divisions into 50 "business groups" and delegated both responsibility and authority to the group managers for manufacturing and profits. "These moves are designed to bring the managers closer to the market," he announced.

Following up on his previously quoted comments, McGovern introduced the high-priced LeMenu entrees in 1982, offering such upscale fare as sirloin tips with mushroom gravy, broccoli with cheddar cheese sauce, and O'Brien potatoes. Campbell also tested other exotic menus such as lobster thermidor and chicken cordon bleu. It promoted this line with commercials calling it "LeMenu's carefully orchestrated foods" while a string quartet played and a hand poured a glass of vintage wine. "You don't dare eat LeMenu without a vintage wine," intoned an aristocratic voice.

This is quite a change from 30 years ago when Clarke and Gilbert Swanson developed their TV dinner. It was designed so Mom, Dad, and the kids could sit in front of the television and munch fried chicken or spaghetti (the favorites) from tin trays. The dinners were filling but not very appetizing. But as consumers became wealthier, they wanted something lighter, more nutritious, and tastier. From 1979 to 1981, Swanson's sales dropped 16 percent, although the overall frozen dinner market was growing. More women were going to work and many of those in the burgeoning singles group didn't want to cook for one, and they soon tired of the meat loaf–fried chicken Swanson fare.

## NEW AND MORE INTERESTING PRODUCTS

As a result, sales of quality frozen dinners are increasing about 5 to 7 percent a year. The "TV dinner" tin tray has largely been replaced by plastic plates that look good enough to put on the table and can be used in microwave ovens. Campbell is also segmenting geographically by producing a salmon-based dinner for the northwest and a barbecue dish for Texas. To provide a fish alternative for both the LeMenu and the Swanson lines, Campbell acquired Mrs. Paul's Kitchens, Inc. Under McGovern, Mrs. Paul's market share rose from 24 to 27 percent in just one year.

Prego spaghetti sauce was brought out regionally in 1981, with a $15 million advertising campaign. It was not introduced nationally until 1982, with a $25 million advertising budget. It turned out to be one of the company's biggest winners. Even though it was not in full distribution, its sales approached the $100 million mark in its first year, and by 1983, it was second in market share after Ragu. But Ragu didn't take the challenge lying down. Initially, Ragu offered coupons good for 75 cents off the regular Ragu; then it brought out a new Homestyle spaghetti sauce, supported by a $20 million advertising campaign. Homestyle was followed in 1983 by Ragu Chunky Garden-Style sauce and a $22 million campaign. Prego is still the number two seller. Actually, Prego almost never made it to the market. In 1978, Campbell policy provided that any new product had to show a profit in its first year, but Prego wasn't projected to be profitable until the third year. Harold Shaub, then president, changed the policy and launched the product in 1980. "In the ten years before Prego, Campbell had only two major new product successes—Chunky Soups and Hungry Man dinners, and both were nothing more than glorified extensions to the product line," said Marketing Vice-President Herbert M. Baum. But by 1985, LeMenu and Prego together accounted for over $450 million of Campbell's $4 billion sales.

## WINNERS AND FLOPS

During the 1980s, Campbell rushed over 700 new items onto the market, in an all-out effort to meet the changing needs of U.S. consumers. The strategy was growth rather than profits. Exhibit 22-3 shows the number of new products introduced, and the marketing and sales expenses as a percentage of total sales, from 1980 to 1986.

LeMenu, the biggest star, was launched in 1982 and commands a whopping 35 percent of the $700 million upscale frozen dinner market. Lesser stars are Great Starts breakfast ($100 million) and Souper Combos, a soup-and-sandwich microwave package. Failures include Pepperidge Farm Star Wars cookies. "Pepperidge Farm Star Wars cookies are a travesty. They do not fit the brand's high-quality, upscale adult image. And, at $1.39 a bag, it's a lousy value." Again, not a comment from a competitor or a cookie specialist but from R. Gordon McGovern who ran Pepperidge Farm for 12 years before taking Campbell's top job. "But," he added, "I could be wrong." He wasn't. Another extraterrestrial flop were the UFO pasta Flying Saucers. Recently, two other losers, Soup for One and the premium Gold Label soup line were discontinued.

Pepperidge Farm also pushed "Juice Works" into the market in 1983. It was a 100 percent fruit juice product for children. But the quality image of the other bread-related products failed to rub off on either the cookies or juices, and Pepperidge eventually took them off the market. Another new product, a line of meat and cheese sandwiches baked in a crust called Deli's, was phased out in late 1985. Initial sales were high, but customers didn't rebuy. In a 1985 product review, Richard A. Shea, the Farm's new president, dropped 275 Pepperidge Farm products that weren't doing well. He hoped to return the firm to its basic attributes: "premium quality," "natural ingredients," "a bakery heritage," and "meeting consumer need."

There were indications in the market that consumers were "moving fresh." Business was booming at both fresh and service delis, and there were few indications that this market was price sensitive. Customers seemed to be buying "fresh" for current consumption, and nonfresh (frozen, canned, etc.) to be stored for "emergencies." Responding to this shift in demand, Campbell test marketed a new type of "refrigerated" prepared food in 1985.

## THE CATERING KIOSK—TODAY'S TASTE

The test products were as different from conventional product preparation and retailing as mom's homemade bread is from Wonder bread. First, the line was positioned to upscale even the upscale frozen "gourmet" entrees sold in stores at that time. Designed especially for the working couple or single professional, the line included 22 soups, salads, entrees, and desserts, such as Veal Medallions with Baked Tomato and Kiwi, or Filet of Salmon with Basil Sauce. And none of them contained preservatives and additives, such as monosodium glutamate, that are found in traditional frozen dinners. All could be reheated in a microwave or a conventional oven (20 minutes) and most of them contained fewer than 500 calories.

To retail these products, Campbell had to come up with a unique sales gimmick. They needed to be sure "Today's Taste" products were not confused with frozen entrees, since they could not be taken home and popped in the freezer. They had to be heated up and eaten right away if customers were to get the advantage of fresh preparation. But since the entrees were already cooked, consumers could also eat such things as salmon filet cold.

Catching the customer's eye was also important for this innovative product line, so Campbell designed a "Catering Kiosk" which was a free-standing refrigerated structure that housed the products. Photographs of the items were on the front side of the kiosk and the single-serving entrees, soups, and salads were stored on the other. Each item in the line came in a plastic throw-away dish covered by a transparent plastic top, inside an attractive cardboard sleeve. Prices varied from $4.25 to $7.95 for the entrees, somewhat high at that time. Exhibit 22-4 is a representation of the test market kiosk.

The single-serving packages were prepared daily at a catering facility just a short distance from the stores where the test was conducted. All the ingredients were purchased locally, and the dinners were cooked and assembled under the supervision of trained chefs. The packages were delivered as soon as they were put together and marked with a use-by date, four days later. Today's Taste representatives personally examined and accepted all shipments of food used in the soups, salads, and entrees to assure quality and freshness. In the test, however, unsold items were pulled in two days and given bacteriological tests for freshness.

**THE TEST MARKET**

Oddly enough, Today's Taste was test marketed in Washington, DC, a metropolitan area that is almost never used for that purpose since its upscale demographics exclude it from the "typical American city" category. But upscale singles and working families are exactly what Campbell was looking for and it found plenty of them there. Also, the suburban counties of Montgomery, Maryland, and Fairfax, Virginia, are at the top of the list of those with the highest per capita incomes in the United States, and other pricey prepared foods have sold well there.

Campbell asked consumers about the design of the product packages and the kiosk itself. A number of people thought the burgundy sleeve with its white lettering "didn't look like a food package." But it was used anyway because the producer wanted something different from normal supermarket packaging that would set Today's Taste apart from other frozen dinners.

During the test, one woman shopper remarked, "The prices are a little high. I wouldn't mind paying a dollar more than Lean Cuisine if it's good." Her remark suggested that the concept of Today's Taste might not be well understood and that the line was perceived as just another high-priced assortment of frozen dinners. At one supermarket, "waiters" in tuxedos gave out free samples of the soups, salads, and entrees while explaining the concept of "fresh preparation." After the explanation, one consumer wasn't impressed. "It seems to me you're talking about heating up a dinner that may have been prepared yesterday. It sounds a bit like leftovers." In late 1985, after the test was completed, the manager of another Washington suburban chain store that participated said, "The products didn't move too well, and I don't believe it was price. The customers here are not price conscious at all. There was some other problem with Today's Taste. People just didn't seem to understand what it was."

Clearly, the concept needed more work and it went back to the lab until late 1986 when it was tried again as "Fresh Chef." The challenge in distribution is coping with the product's short shelf life, but even the second time around, Campbell failed to deal with this problem. Fresh Chef products were sent through supermarket warehouses, the traditional channels. By the time the "fresh" items reached the stores, they were already a week old. Consumers turned away from them and retail returns were as high as 30 percent. In May 1987, the line was withdrawn from national distribution.

Sara Lee and others are also trying to enter the "fresh" market since deli-type foods are the fastest growing sector today. Even though supermarkets are able to handle in-store fresh-food preparation, the movement and control of fresh items from preparer to consumer is a problem yet to be fully resolved.

## THE MOVE BACK TO BASICS

The decade of new and innovative products stretched Campbell's resources and pummeled its net profits. In 1989, the firm was close to last among food producers in both profitability and return on equity, although sales were at a record level of over $6 billion. With a complaining group of Dorrance family stockholders nipping at his heels because of low earnings, Mr. McGovern quit abruptly in late 1989. He was succeeded by David Johnson, who had just revived Gerber Products, the baby-food producer, with a several-fold earnings increase and an accompanying surge in the price of the common stock. Johnson seemed to be just what the Campbell heirs were looking for.

But the cost of the many failed innovations was substantial, and recovery may be slow. Although sales of the soup products have increased steadily, their share of the market has declined. Changing the purchasing behavior of soup consumers may not be easy, since per capita consumption of soup has been flat for several years at about 44 bowls per person annually.

Mr. McGovern had approached the profit problem mainly by corner-cutting. In one such move, soup recipes using as many as 28 ingredients were cut to as few as 11. Consumers who tested the new mixtures, however, liked them as well or better than the originals. Another problem was the introduction of the oriental ramen noodle soups from Japan and Korea. Sold in dry blocks or in styrofoam cups at low prices, consumers merely add hot water and eat. Campbell was not only slow in recognizing and producing the product itself, but also tardy in exploiting an entirely different way of eating soup out of the package, like corn flakes. The company now has a ramen product, but not before competitors cornered a sizable 9 percent of the market.

## FOLDING THE UMBRELLA STRATEGY

CEO Johnson's strategy is to extract more growth from the company's traditional moneymakers, the standard, well-known brands. Best-known, of course, is the flagship Campbell brand. For well over ten years, however, soups have been advertised collectively rather than individually. The "Kids" pushed the full line, as did the "M'm! M'm! Good!" and "Soup is Good Food" themes. But none of these approaches whets a consumer's appetite for a steaming hot bowl of, say, chicken noodle or tomato soup. Now, this umbrella strategy has been replaced by product-specific ads for Campbell's tomato, showing different ideas for toppings, including popcorn. Other ads suggest how mushroom soup may be used as a base for different dishes. The Kids feature the new Teddy Bear and other children's soups. Exhibit 22-5 is an example of a product-specific ad.

Not only will soups be advertised separately, but they will be tailored to ethnic and regional markets. A red-bean soup for Hispanics, a nacho-cheese in California, and a Creole in the South are being tried thus far, with more to come.

Promotional strategy, too, is being redesigned to increase soup consumption. Previously, cents-off coupons were good for purchasing single cans, but now they apply only to two or more. Or consumers can get a free can by buying three others. The company also plans to use the beer industry strategy by introducing six-packs of soup—all the same or assorted. In addition, the number of different kinds of Campbell's soup has been reduced from 91 to 70, dropping the least popular ones.

## A NEW KIND OF CAN?

Campbell is also looking carefully at its traditional soup container. "The can isn't as user friendly as it used to be. It is being battered and beaten in consumer surveys," Anthony Adams, the company's research director is quoted as saying. But others are concerned about the risk of using a new container that might cause problems.

There are a lot of consumers who avoid using canned soup, particularly convenience-oriented singles. They don't like to use a can opener; mix the (sometimes gummy) soup with water; heat it for a while; then wash the pot, dish and, utensils. And on top of all that, the metal can't be heated in a microwave oven, now used by an estimated one-third of U.S. households. Strangely, some younger consumers associate cans with old-fashioned preservatives and artificial ingredients. They also believe that cans don't keep the nutrients in. So Campbell is testing several alternative containers. One is a plastic microwavable bowl, with an easy-opening top, which is the basis of the successful Souper Combo. Another more conventional one is a plastic container shaped like a metal can and covered with the red-and-white label. In early 1991, Campbell finally developed a bowl-shaped container for microwave soup. Bearing the traditional Campbell label, the product was introduced in five of the standard varieties.

Campbell's present management expected the winter of 1990-91—the "soup season"—to be the test of whether additional sales and profits can be squeezed out of soup and other traditional brands. By the spring of 1991, thanks to the new microwave line, it appeared the squeeze was successful.

## CASE ANALYSIS QUESTIONS

1. Did Campbell really have a choice in the 1980s in terms of developing new consumer products? What seems to be the reason that so many of these products failed? Give example(s).

**2.** Consumers have "learned" the Campbell Soup brand and logo over a period of many years, and there is no indication consumers perceive the product quality to be deteriorating. Why, then, is the company losing soup market share?

**3.** What type of innovation are the Today's Taste and Fresh Chef lines? Do you think this type of product will eventually be accepted by consumers?

**4.** Was Campbell wise in abandoning the "umbrella" advertising for the product-specific strategy in today's market?

## REFERENCES

"From Soup to Nuts and Back to Soup," *Business Week,* Nov. 5, 1990, p. 114; "Can Campbell's New Chef Stand This Much Heat?" *Business Week,* Jan. 15, 1990, p. 22: "Family Group to Sell Stake in Campbell Soup Co." *Washington Post,* Dec. 29, 1989, p. F-1; "Campbell Seeks to Boost Global Presence," *Wall St. Journal,* Sept. 26, 1989, p. A-10; "M'm! M'm! Bad! Trouble at Campbell Soup," *Business Week,* Sept. 25, 1989, p. 68; "The Campbell Kids Fight For the Middle of the Store," *Wall Street Journal,* Mar. 28, 1989, p. B-3; "FTC Attacks Campbell Health Claim," *Advertising Age,* Jan. 30, 1989, p. 89; "Stirring Up Profits at Campbell," *New York Times,* Nov. 20, 1988, p. 3-1; "Campbell Soup is Seeking to Be Numero Uno Where Goya Reigns," *Wall Street Journal,* Mar. 28, 1988, p. B-3; "Campbell's Taste of the Japanese Market is MM-MM Good," *Business Week,* Mar. 28, 1988, p. 42.; "Just How Healthy Are Campbell Soups," *Wall Street Journal,* Mar. 1, 1988, p. B-1; "Goya: A Lot More Than Black Beans and Sofrito," *Business Week,* Dec. 7, 1987, p. 137; "Food Firms Fresh Approach: Elegant Refrigerated Entrees," *Wall Street Journal,* June 18, 1987, p. 33; "Marketing's New Look," *Business Week,* Jan. 26, 1987, p. 64; "Now Starring at a Grocer Near You," *Washington Post,* Oct. 10, 1985 p. 28; "Burned by Mistakes, Campbell Soup Co. Is In Throes of Change," *Wall Street Journal,* Aug. 14, 1985, p. 1; "Today's Taste: Washington Gambles That Washington Will Flock To Fresh Entrees," *Washington Post,* Feb. 17, 1985, p. K-1; "Cashing in On Fitness Foods," *New York Times,* Nov. 4, 1984, p. 3-1; "General Host Makes Its Mark in Gourmet Frozen Entrees," *Wall St. Journal,* Oct. 18, 1984, p. 33; "Entering Middle Age," *American Demographics,* Feb., 1984, p. 4.; "Campbell Kids Back–At Age 80." *Advertising Age,* Jan. 16, 1984, p. 67., "Campbell Soup: Cooking Up a Separate Dish for Each Consumer Group," *Business Week,* Nov. 21, 1983, p. 96.; "Swanson Spices Its Menu," *Business Week,* Apr. 10, 1983, p. 41.

## CAMPBELL'S SOUP
### EXHIBIT 22-1
### Early Campbell "Kids" Ad

*We blend the best with careful pains*
*In skillful combination,*
*And every single can contains*
*Our business reputation!*

## CAMPBELL'S SOUP
### EXHIBIT 22-2
### Campbell vs. U.S. Soup Sales
### 1985-1990

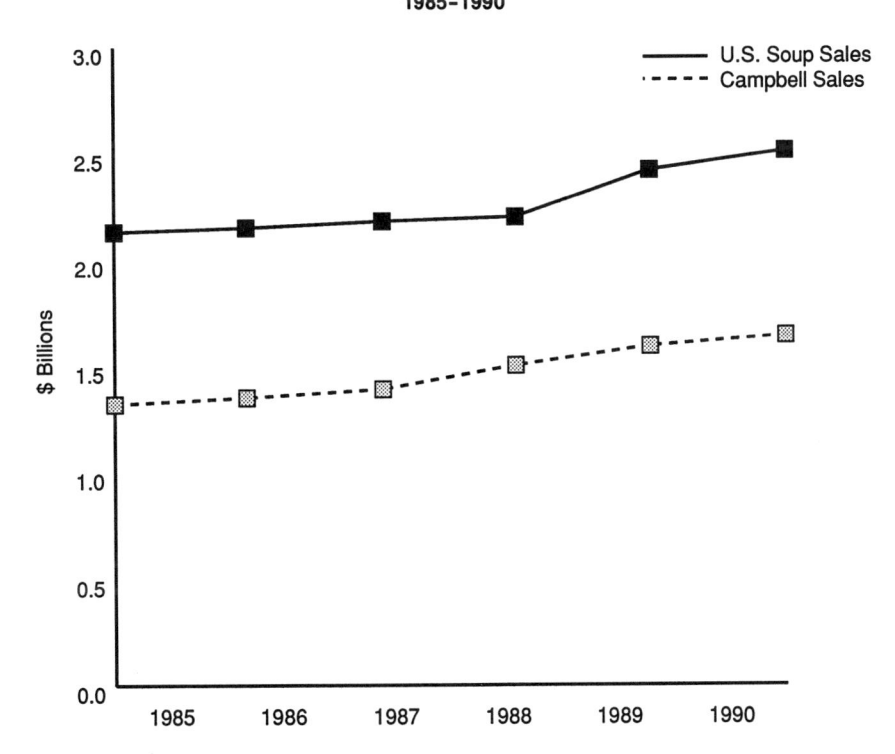

## CAMPBELL'S SOUP

### EXHIBIT 22-3

**New Product Introductions and Percentage of Marketing/Sales Expense to Total Sales**

| Year | Number of New Products | Mkts/Sales Expense as Percent of Sales |
|---|---|---|
| 1980 |  | 8.3% |
| 1981 | 22 | 9.2 |
| 1982 | 77 | 10.3 |
| 1983 | 90 | 11.1 |
| 1984 | 91 | 11.7 |
| 1985 | 118 | 12.0 |
| 1986 | 102 | 12.4 |

**CAMPBELL'S SOUP**
**EXHIBIT 22–4**
**Representation of Today's Taste Kiosk**

**CAMPBELL'S SOUP**
**EXHIBIT 22–5**
**Example of a Product-Specific Ad**

# CASE TWENTY-THREE

# THE DISTILLED LIQUOR INDUSTRY

John McGowan, president and CEO of the Merriwether Distillery, took his place at the head of the table. He glanced at the somber faces of the board of directors and wondered what the outcome of this year's meeting would be. Other company executives sat apprehensively on the opposite side of the room, ready to make their respective reports.

## BACKGROUND

The Merriwether Distilleries is an old-line firm that had produced its own brand, Old Merriwether bourbon whiskey, for many years. In the early 1970s, sales flattened out, and a spurt in 1977 appeared to have lost steam by 1978. Beer consumption was rising steadily, and wine sales were erratic, although they reached an all-time high in 1977. Most disturbing of all was the slight sales decline of the long-time leader in liquor brands, Seagram's 7 Crown Blended whiskey. Although the brand was still in first place in 1976, it showed signs of being edged out by Smirnoff Vodka. Moreover, other vodkas, Bacardi Rum, gin, and Canadian Mist, a light Canadian whiskey, showed the highest percentage gains. The trend certainly appeared to favor the lighter liquors, but it remained to be seen whether the rise in popularity would be sustained over the next few years. Consumption of lighter scotch whiskies increased in the trendy northeast and on the West Coast, and one producer, Brown and Forman Distilleries, produced a clear bourbon called Frost

80/80, which it hoped would attract those who followed this trend. This product was not what customers wanted, however, and it was dropped soon after its introduction.

**What Is Bourbon Whiskey?**

Kentucky bourbon, as differentiated from other bourbon whiskies, is distilled from a mash composed of at least 51 percent corn grain, with malt and rye added. It was named for Bourbon County, Kentucky, where it originated in the eighteenth century, and is considered to be the most distinctive American whiskey. The alcoholic strength of whiskey is known as its *proof,* which is double the percentage of alcohol. Pure, or absolute, alcohol is 200 proof. Most whiskey produced in the United States is 86 proof, which means it contains 43 percent pure alcohol by volume. It may be called *straight* whiskey if it is distilled at 160 proof, then reduced to no more than 125 proof by adding water when it is placed in barrels for aging. U.S. regulations require that bourbon (and other whiskies) must not be distilled at more than 190 proof and must not be less than 80 proof when bottled. Thus, whiskey of less than 80 proof must be labeled *diluted.* Most whiskey sold in the United States is 80 or 86 proof.

**Regulatory Restrictions**

One major problem facing distilled liquor producers was an array of state government restrictions on advertising. Their products could be advertised in newspapers, magazines, billboards, and other media, but they could not use national television. Beer and wine producers could, but they were not allowed to show anyone actually consuming the beverage in an ad. Even with this restriction, being able to advertise on television at all was a distinct advantage. Another difficulty facing liquor producers was the wide variation in state laws controlling liquor advertising. At one time, six states did not permit price to be shown in an ad. Holiday packages could not be used in two states, and a woman could not be depicted in a liquor ad in two states. Exhibit 23–1 lists these and some of the other advertising constraints that were placed upon distilled liquor ads.

## JOHN MCGOWAN

As the grandson of the previous president, Seth Merriwether, Jr., John McGowan had shown an avid interest in the business, and in its technical aspects, since he first toured the distillery at the age of eight. Earning his MBA from a large eastern business school in 1968, he came to Merriwether after two years with a building materials conglomerate. After short periods in the production, aging, and accounting departments, he moved into marketing in 1976, where he became part of the three-person sales force. There, John was a little disappointed because the job did not seem to have much challenge. The wholesalers he called on were more interested in hunting and fishing stories, or telling ribald jokes than they were in the product. Mostly, they gave him the same orders each time he called, with quantities building up only slightly over the years. They were not particularly concerned about promoting Old Merriwether because that would simply reduce sales of the other brands they carried and bring some retaliation. He did notice, however, a quiet but persistent note in conversations with wholesalers that some changes seemed to be brewing in the liquor business.

In 1976, John became vice-president for marketing, when the then V-P retired. Shrewdly, John believed that the undercurrents he felt in contacts with the wholesalers might be the rustlings of something more serious, so he began to look at consumption information for the various distilled liquor products on the market. His marketing people watched bourbon sales closely, and they had seen its share of the whiskey market rise slightly from 14.2 percent in 1960 to a peak of 18.5 percent in 1973, then drop slightly to 18 percent in 1976.

## A NEW PRESIDENT

In 1978, John McGowan was elected president, although he was only in his middle thirties. But his fast rise through the ranks was due more to his ability to look ahead, anticipate problems, and take action to avert them than to family connections. He was respected by all levels in the company, and by his relatives who held controlling interest.

He uneasily followed the trend in distilled liquor consumption which continued to fall for "brown" products such as bourbon, scotch, and other whiskies, but increased for "white" ones like vodka, rum, and gin. In the event this trend continued, he started production of a premium brand of both gin and vodka, as well as an 80 proof bourbon, which was only slightly lighter in color, but lighter in alcohol content. The new bourbon sold at about 15 percent less than the regular version. Despite a substantial advertising budget, only the vodka attracted attention in the market and was able to woo customers from other national brands. In 1981, the gin and light bourbon labels were discontinued.

## THE BOARD OF DIRECTORS' MEETING

Mr. McGowan called the meeting to order and asked the vice-president, Seth Merriwether, III, for the latest information on the distilled liquor industry. Seth showed the 1989 data on whiskey sales, together with those of directly competing distilled products. These are shown in Exhibit 23-2. He noted that Seagram's 7 Crown Blend was still the highest rated whiskey among the top 50 distilled brands in the United States, in terms of sales. It remained number three, overall, a position it had held for the past ten years. Indeed, the first place Bacardi Rum, and second place Smirnoff vodka had not changed their positions for ten years, either. Canadian Mist, very popular as a lighter whiskey in the early 1980s, had sky-rocketed from eighth place in 1981 to fourth in 1987. Its popularity was short-lived, however, and it was in seventh place. Jim Beam, a brand that has hovered between fifth and sixth place for many years was now back as the best-selling bourbon. Jack Daniel's, a Tennessee bourbon was in eighth place, down from fourth in 1982 (see Case 6, Jack Daniel's). So there are four whiskies in the top eight distilled products sales, and two of them are bourbons. A list of the top ten brands of the Top 50 Distilled Liquor brands in terms of sales in shown in Exhibit 23-3. "We need to keep in mind," Seth cautioned, "that even though Jim Beam and Jack Daniel's have had small sales increases since 1987, all four whiskies in the top 8 had negative growth in the past five years." He concluded by pointing out that about 20 percent of U.S. households today consume 90 percent of the bourbon, a much smaller proportion of consumers than in past years.

## COMPETITION, DEMOGRAPHICS, AND PSYCHOGRAPHICS

"Not to make the situation any bleaker than it is," said Janice Olsen, vice-president for marketing, "but the total whiskey share in a declining market has dropped 10.3 percent since 1979, and of that, bourbon's share fell 4.1 percent. The nonwhiskey group of distilled products has picked up the ten percentage points we lost, and even rose 0.3 percent in the past year alone." She referred to a chart shown as Exhibit 23-4, which also indicated that 435 million gallons of spirits were consumed in 1979, sliding to 374 in 1988 and 368 in 1989.

"Another strong competitor that all of us in the distilled spirits market tend to overlook has been Perrier," she continued. "It seems as though the Yuppies moved first to light liquors, then they went even further to completely nonalcoholic beverages. A few years ago anyone ordering soda water in a bar might have been laughed out of the place, or at least a few eyebrows would be raised. Today an order of Perrier with a twist, or, more recently, Evian, is commonplace." (See Case 4, Source Perrier II).

Ms. Olsen then discussed demographics, noting that singles, as a group, exert considerable influence in the distilled liquor market, accounting for one out of every five dollars spent on those products. But their life-styles change as they grow older and get married. Their household consumption of distilled products drops sharply, and they tend to drink wine, beer, or no alcohol at all. The downscale age group is even more health- and weight-conscious. They believe that alcohol is not only fattening but detrimental to health. Also, they perceive lighter-colored liquors to be lighter in caloric content as well and that wine and beer contain less alcohol per drink. One distiller, Seagram's, ran a series of ads in the early 1980s that compared the amount of alcohol in similar portions of the three beverages. One such ad is shown in Exhibit 28-5.

## OTHER COMPETITIVE THREATS

"Another disquieting change in the liquor market," she observed, "is the appearance of more specialty products in the upper ranks of the Top 50 sellers." Kahlua, a coffee-flavored liqueur, languished in forty-fifth place for some time, then moved rapidly to twentieth, a place it has held, more or less, since 1982. Cordials such as Peach, Apricot, and Creme de Menthe have also soared in recent years. De Kuyper cordials, not on the list at all in 1984, and twenty-third in 1985, were in tenth place in the latest ratings. And Hiram Walker cordials, twenty-sixth in 1984, jumped to eighteenth in 1989. She pointed to Exhibit 23-6 which indicates the rise in specialty product consumption since 1980.

## THE ADVERTISING AND PROMOTION DILEMMA

Bob Randall, the advertising and sales manager, was next. "The most serious problem we have," he began, "is how we can get positive exposure for our brands in the media." Under the 1988 law, all alcoholic beverages sold after November 1989 had to carry a label "in a conspicuous and prominent place" saying:

> According to the Surgeon General, women should not drink alcoholic beverages during pregnancy because of the risk of birth defects. Consumption of alcoholic beverages impairs your ability to drive a car or operate machinery, and may cause health problems.

In addition, a new bill was introduced in the U.S. House and Senate in June 1990. It proposed an additional label saying "Drinking alcohol may be Addictive" for all alcoholic beverages. Although it did not pass, similar bills are expected in future sessions.

As if that weren't enough, the new federal tax on alcoholic beverages will raise prices substantially. And the individual states didn't miss the implications of a poll conducted just before the 1989 elections. In it, more than 80 percent of U.S. adults favored higher taxes on liquor, beer, and wine. New York and Virginia jumped the gun by raising alcohol taxes in early 1990, and other states are likely to follow suit, expecting no repercussions from voters.

"I am going to propose that we follow the lead of our competitors and get exposure wherever we can," Mr. Randall said. He outlined a plan to run regular commercials wherever closed circuit entertainment channels are available—on some airlines, cruise ships, and in hotels. (Some airlines accept such ads, but others do not.) Other ads appear on local Spanish-language television stations. However, Univision, a Spanish-language network, recently discontinued liquor ads, while another, Telemundo, runs them after 9 P.M., when few children are watching, according to a network spokesperson. Such ads may be legally shown on local stations, but because of pressure from temperance groups, most channels don't accept them.

Another method of getting exposure is the "news video." One report described a special video that was run in some 40 cities as an item on the local news. It was about the use of Canadian rather than American grain to produce bourbon whiskey, and it urged consumers to buy only U.S. brands of bourbon—any U.S. brand. The report included an interview with a master distiller that "happened" to be at the Jim Beam distillery. Also, in the background, the product was being packaged with the Jim Beam name prominently displayed on each carton. Of course, Beam produced the video, but many local stations are usually glad to have "fillers" such as this to use during periods when news is scarce. And the brands benefit by getting exposure without violating the law. Some producers think it is more effective than a regular ad.

## COMPETITION OUTSIDE THE "FAMILY"

Mr. McGowan continued the presentation. "The figures you have just seen and the analysis along with them are vitally important to us. But they don't really tell all of the story." He went on to observe that a few years ago Merriwether's competition was entirely from other bourbons and whiskies in the market. "Then, as Seth pointed out, we lost share to the 'white' products, and to specialties as Janice just said." He continued to describe market conditions. "Today, we are besieged on all sides. Many consumers see scotch as a status, prestige product, and blends as bar whiskies. But bourbon is perceived as more of a mixing drink for the middle class. Unfortunately, that is where most of the taste changes are occurring. Our Old Merriwether is a mid-range, quality brand, but with no other unique attributes. So it is difficult for us to promote new uses for it or a different position in the market."

## WINE IS MORE THAN JUST A DRINK

"There seem to be both tangible and intangible deterrents to expanding our sales," Mr. McGowan continued. Wine, for example, is not only a cocktail drink, but it is served with meals as well. It is also a highly versatile beverage in other ways. It comes in three basic types—red, white and rose—while bourbon comes in only one. There are also sweet wines, appetizer and dessert wines, still and sparkling wines. Sangria, or wine diluted with fruit juices, was popular in the early and mid-1980s, but it has been largely replaced by wine coolers. These are wines with some fruit juices and carbonated water to give them more zing than Sangria has. And for the younger married market, the one we seem to be losing, wine also has a lore. Knowledge of it bestows a certain status on the holder. It can be the attraction at wine-testing parties, and wines can be discussed, compared, or laid down in the cellar as an investment.

Unfortunately, with the possible exception of scotch, most distilled liquors have little, if any, conversational value. One research group predicted the shift away from scotch to vodka, rum, and gin because younger consumers were seeking instant gratification. It took too much time to "learn" to enjoy the heavier brown liquors. Also, bourbon and scotch were what Dad and Mom drank. The younger group is less concerned with drinking the conventional thing.

Nevertheless, wine sales seem to be flattening, and the trend seems to be toward consumption of less alcohol, or none at all. Some analysts have suggested that social drugs of various kinds are substitutes for alcoholic drinks, but there does not appear to be widespread acceptance of their use for social occasions.

## ARE FAD BRANDS FADING?

Mr. McGowan also pointed out that some alcoholic beverage brands whose sales rose rapidly in the 1980s, and who picked up substantial market shares, are winding down. Absolut Swedish vodka, with heavy growth every year since 1981, and with 57 percent of the imported vodka market, expects only about a 10 percent growth in 1990. Also, stiffer drunk driving laws may influence consumption since nearly 70 percent of sales are made for on-premise consumption.

Sales of Corona Mexican beer, with its lime slice, soared to over 22 million cases in 1987. But 1990 sales are expected to be somewhat lower than the 16 million in 1989. However, it still ranks as the number two imported beer. To bolster sales, Corona Light was introduced in 1989, and both it and Corona Extra are available in 12-packs.

If the declines continue and other fads fade away, the market share may move back to conventional products. Or, it may simply be transferred to new fads. Brands such as Absolut and Corona also face the problem of holding onto the trend setters who first "discovered" them, as they gradually move into the mass market.

## FORECASTING THE FUTURE

As the meeting drew to a close, Charles Bostwick, an influential director, said, "Mr. McGowan and the others have given us a very complete picture of the changes in our culture that influence consumption of many foods and beverages. They have noted that not only are health and weight major factors, but social concerns are also extremely important. The ravages of drunk drivers have brought about more stringent laws and penalties. These, in turn, have caused many people to drink less, or change what they drink. We need to consider these factors in our advertising and promotion. Mr. McGowan also urged his market research people to go beyond the facts and figures to see what kinds of changes are occurring in the population. Are there impending changes in our social structure that will continue to influence liquor consumption? Can we project behavioral and social trends for aging baby boomers, for example? Will they continue their emphasis on health and physical fitness? Some physicians urge older people to drink moderately. Can we weave that into our advertising? What the researchers discover about these and other influences on consumption of our product will help us to chart the course of the Merriwether Distillery for the next decade."

## CASE ANALYSIS QUESTIONS

1. Data in the case show what is happening in the distilled liquor market, but not why. Which of the several possible factors in the case (e.g. social, personal, legal, or political) would you say has the greatest effect on the sales decline?

2. Mr. McGowan talks about the versatility of wine. How might consumer perception be involved in switching from distilled liquor to wine? Consider Exhibit 23-5.

3. How do you explain the marked increase in consumption of "special liquors" over the past few years?

4. What, if anything, can the distilled liquor industry do to stabilize or to increase sales?

## REFERENCES

"Reality of the '90s Hits Yuppie Brands," *Wall Street Journal,* Dec. 20, 1990 p. B-1; "Down the Hatch Lightly: A Hard Sell for Low-Cal Spirits," *Newsweek,* Dec. 17, 1990, p. 48; "With Yuppies Fading, Absolut May Too," *Wall Street Journal,* Oct. 17, 1990, p. B-1; "It's Enough To Drive Distillers to Drink," *Business Week,* Jun. 25, 1990, p. 98; "Seagram Taking 'Light' Whiskey to All of U.S.," *Wall Street Journal,* Apr. 23, 1990, p. B-1; "Yo, Ho, Ho, and a Battle for Bacardi," *Business Week,* Apr. 16, 1990, p. 47; "Amended Warning Labels Due for Liquor Bottles," *New York Times,* Feb. 11, 1990, p. 18; "The Maverick Boss At Seagram," *Business Week,* Dec. 18, 1989, p. 90; "Vodka—With a Few Tasty Twists," *Business Week,* Jul. 25, 1988, p. 81; "Media and Marketing: Market Watch, Liquor," *Wall Street Journal,* Apr. 7, 1988. p. 34; "Despite Ban, Liquor Marketers Finding New Ways to Get Products on Television," *Wall Street Journal,* Mar. 11, 1988, p. 29; "In Sales, Liquor Isn't Quicker," *Business Week,* Jun. 27, 1987, p. 120; "Glenmore Retires Mr. Boston," *Wall Street Journal,* Apr. 9, 1987, p. 35; "The Ferment in California Winemaking, *Business Week,* Feb. 27, 1987 p.27; "Alcohol, Tobacco Marketers Battle New Ad Restraints," *Marketing News,* Jan. 30, 1987, p. 1; "New Entries Sweeten Wine Cooler Market," *Marketing News,* June 20, 1986, p. 8; "What Slump? It's a Vintage Year for Premium California Wines," *Business Week,* May 19, 1986, p. 98; "What's New in the Liquor Business," *New York Times,* Dec. 29, 1985, p. 34; "Will Real Men Ever Drink Low Alcohol Beer?" *Business Week,* Oct. 21, 1985, p. 42; "To Stir Up J&B Scotch Sales, Ads Hype Its British Heritage," *Wall Street Journal,* Oct. 17, 1985, p. 31; "Liquor Firms Ply Consumers With Gifts and Hefty Refunds," *Wall Street Journal,* Sept. 12, 1985, p. 35; "Liquor Ads Look Less Macho as Female Drinking Increases," *Wall Street Journal,* Jun. 6, 1985, p. 31; "Beverage Makers Are Thirsting to Claim Booze is Healthy; Critics Won't Swallow It," *Wall Street Journal,* May 9, 1985. p. 31; "When Tastes Change . . . How Can a Host Know What Guests Will Drink?" "Home Entertaining," *New York Times,* May 5, 1985, p. 42; "Sober Prospects for Distillers," *Business Week,* Mar. 22, 1985, p. 229; "The Sobering of America: A Push to Put Drinking in Its Place," *Business Week,* Feb. 25, 1985; *Impact* magazine, various issues.

## DISTILLED LIQUOR INDUSTRY
### EXHIBIT 23-1
#### State Laws on Liquor Ads

| Restriction | State |
|---|---|
| No local liquor advertising | Mississippi<br>Oklahoma |
| Price may not be shown in advertisements | Arkansas<br>Georgia<br>Wyoming<br>Minnesota<br>Maine<br>Iowa |
| Only specified sizes of bottles may be shown in ads | Florida<br>Kentucky |
| Cannot refer to price savings or use the word "sale" | Michigan<br>Montana<br>Virginia<br>Washington<br>N. Carolina<br>Ohio<br>Oregon<br>Pennsylvania<br>West Virginia |
| Holiday packaging not permitted | Alabama<br>Utah |
| Cannot say "No extra cost" | Massachusetts<br>South Dakota |

## DISTILLED LIQUOR INDUSTRY

### EXHIBIT 23-2

### 1989 and Estimated 1990 Sales of Top Ten Distilled Liquor Brands, Cases (000)

| Rank | Brand | Type | 1989 | 1990 est. |
|---|---|---|---|---|
| 1 | Bacardi | Rum | 8,000 | 7,990 |
| 2 | Smirnoff | Vodka | 6,905 | 6,910 |
| 3 | Seagram's 7 Crown | Blended | 4,145 | 4,030 |
| 4 | Popov | Vodka | 3,825 | 3,840 |
| 5 | Seagram's Gin | Gin | 3,745 | 3,800 |
| 6 | Jim Beam | Bourbon | 3,715 | 3,700 |
| 7 | Canadian Mist | Canadian | 3,650 | 3,605 |
| 8 | Jack Daniel's | Tennessee | 3,545 | 3,520 |
| 9 | Seagrams V-O | Canadian | 2,555 | 2,495 |
| 10 | De Kuyper | Cordials | 2,415 | 2,480 |

## DISTILLED LIQUOR INDUSTRY

### EXHIBIT 23-3

### Top Ten of Top 50 Liquor Brands in Terms of Sales

| Brand | 1982 | 1984 | 1986 | 1988 | 1989 |
|---|---|---|---|---|---|
| Bacardi Rum | 1 | 1 | 1 | 1 | 1 |
| Smirnoff Vodka | 2 | 2 | 2 | 2 | 2 |
| Seagram's 7 Crown Blended Whiskey | 3 | 3 | 3 | 3 | 3 |
| Jack Daniel's Tennessee Bourbon | 4 | 6 | 7 | 8 | 8 |
| Seagrams V.O. Canadian Whiskey | 5 | 7 | 11 | 10 | 9 |
| Canadian Mist Canadian | 6 | 4 | 4 | 5 | 7 |
| Jim Beam Bourbon | 7 | 5 | 6 | 6 | 6 |
| Canadian Club Canadian | 8 | 9 | 14 | 12 | 11 |
| Windsor Supreme Canadian | 9 | 9 | 10 | 13 | 15 |
| Seagram's Gin | 10 | 11 | 8 | 7 | 5 |
| Popov Vodka | | 8 | 5 | 4 | 4 |
| De Kuyper Cordials | | | 9 | 9 | 10 |

*RANK BY YEAR*

## DISTILLED LIQUOR INDUSTRY
## EXHIBIT 23-4
### Market Share, Brown and White Liquors, 1979-90

|  | 1979 | 1986 | 1988 | 1989 | 1990 |
|---|---|---|---|---|---|
| Whiskey |  |  |  |  |  |
| Bourbon | 14.1% | 11.2% | 10.9% | 11.0% | 10.9% |
| Scotch | 13.9 | 9.9 | 9.3 | 9.0 | 8.8 |
| Canadian | 12.1 | 12.6 | 13.0 | 13.1 | 13.2 |
| Blend | 9.5 | 7.0 | 6.4 | 6.2 | 6.0 |
| Other | 0.2 | 0.2 | 0.2 | 0.2 | 0.2 |
|  | 49.8% | 40.9% | 39.8% | 39.5% | 39.1% |
| Nonwhiskey |  |  |  |  |  |
| Vodka | 18.5% | 20.6% | 21.9% | 22.2% | 22.5% |
| Gin | 9.3 | 8.7 | 8.6 | 8.5 | 8.4 |
| Cordials | 7.7 | 12.0 | 11.2 | 11.1 | 11.2 |
| Rum | 7.0 | 7.7 | 8.3 | 8.5 | 8.5 |
| Brandy | 3.9 | 4.8 | 4.7 | 4.8 | 4.7 |
| Other | 3.8 | 4.5 | 5.7 | 5.4 | 5.5 |
|  | 50.2% | 58.3% | 60.4% | 60.5% | 60.8% |
| Total Gallons Distilled Liquor Consumed (Gallons-Millions) | 435 | 304 | 374 | 368 | 361 |

## DISTILLED LIQUOR INDUSTRY
### EXHIBIT 23-5
#### Alcohol Content Comparison: Beer, Wine, and Liquor

# IT'S TIME AMERICA KNEW THE FACTS ABOUT DRINKING.

12 oz. of beer, 5 oz. of wine and 1¼ oz. of liquor all have the same alcohol content.

## It's time ABC, CBS and NBC let the facts be heard.

We submitted TV commercials to the networks which simply stated the facts of alcohol equivalency, and they have refused to put them on the air. Network policy bars advertising for distilled spirits. But these announcements are not commercials for products...ours or anyone else's. The message here is the fact of equivalence. A fact people have a right to know. A fact we want to tell.

### It's Time All Of Us Were Heard.

We share the concern of other public spirited groups who believe that the popular misconceptions about beverage alcohol can be dangerous. The National Institute on Alcohol Abuse and Alcoholism urges every American to know the facts of equivalency.

The American Automobile Association incorporates the facts of equivalence in its driver safety and alcohol education programs.

The Motor Vehicle Departments of California and New Jersey explain the facts of equivalence in their drivers' manuals. And the National Football League, the Insurance Information Institute and Citizens for Highway Safety, to name a few others, are also publicizing the facts.

This message is *that* important.

The facts are, there is the same amount of alcohol in a 12 ounce can of beer, a 5 ounce glass of wine, and a 1¼ ounce serving of 80 proof whiskey, vodka, gin or rum. To be exact, the typical serving of beer contains 0.54 ounces of alcohol. The typical serving of wine contains 0.55 ounces of alcohol. The typical serving of spirits contains 0.50 ounces of alcohol.

### THE HOUSE OF SEAGRAM
© 1985 THE HOUSE OF SEAGRAM, N.Y.

*Source*: Courtesy of Jos. E. Seagram & Sons

## DISTILLED LIQUOR INDUSTRY
## EXHIBIT 23-6
### Top 60 Specialty Liqueurs Rank, 1978-89

| Year | Rank | Product | Sales (Cases, 000) |
|---|---|---|---|
| 1982 | 21 | Kahlua | 1,500 |
|  | 30 | Southern Comfort | 1,125 |
|  | 41 | Bailey's Irish Cream | 850 |
|  | 51 | Amaretto | 675 |
| 1984 | 19 | Kahlua | 1,650 |
|  | 32 | Southern Comfort | 1,075 |
|  | 36 | Bailey's | 925 |
|  | 48 | Amaretto | 650 |
| 1986 | 9 | De Kuyper Cordials | 2,900 |
|  | 20 | Kahlua | 1,500 |
|  | 27 | Southern Comfort | 1,100 |
|  | 37 | Bailey's | 800 |
| 1988 | 9 | De Kuyper Cordials | 2.930 |
|  | 19 | Hiram Walker Cordials | 1,800 |
|  | 21 | Kahlua | 1,705 |
|  | 29 | Southern Comfort | 1,305 |
|  | 43 | Arrow Cordials | 880 |
| 1989 | 10 | De Kuyper Cordials | 2,415 |
|  | 18 | Hiram Walker Cordials | 1,850 |
|  | 20 | Kahlua | 1,730 |
|  | 26 | Southern Comfort | 1,360 |